TRIBUTES TO MICHAEL KIRBY

It seems almost impossible to think of Ballinskelligs Bay without Michael Kirby in the middle of it, observing everything, then writing his poems, his stories or making one of his wonderful paintings ... The way he lived his life affirmed something I have always known about creative expression: that it comes from the heart as well as the mind, and it comes from living a full life in a much loved place in the company of a much loved family.

Jane Urquhart

There is a beautiful ease, a joyous relaxation in his style, no matter what he's writing about, that suggests a mind and an imagination completely at home in the world they are confronting and creating in a spirit of wonder. I think this is due, in some degree at least, to the fact that his English is enriched by his Irish and his Irish makes space for his Skelligs' English. Equally important is the fact that he is a born storyteller, a seanchaidhe, and a contemplative, lucid, musical poet, for the most part, who draws his images from the world about him. Reading and re-reading *Skelligs Sunset*, I kept on thinking of Wordsworth and Thomas Hardy, two writers at home in their worlds of nature. Michael Kirby's love of nature is passionate and convincing ... Kirby doesn't judge, he presents his own vision, a vision that is both limited and enhancing ... What comes across is a humane blend of wisdom and humour, perplexity and determination to learn, trouble and the quest for tranquility, the words of a man who lived long enough to witness and chronicle old Ireland and modern Ireland in two languages happily dancing with each other in his own mind, his own place. Also, the oral tradition of storytelling joins hands with the literary tradition in a way that gives Kirby's stories a unique tonality, as if Eamon Kelly and Frank O'Connor were somehow both telling the same story in their individual ways. Kirby brings the past with him and introduces it to the present as if to say, 'Please get to know each other. You need each other. If you look and listen patiently, you will educate each other.' That is a crucial aspect of the book's humane intelligence. Those who read it will remain surprised and happily haunted.

Brendan Kennelly, *The Irish Times*

Anybody who ever read, viewed, heard or met Michael Kirby was invariably moved. Writer, poet, artist, storyteller, folklorist, fisherman and family man and lover of life – Michael Kirby left a trail of treasures in his wake.

Aidan O'Connor, *The Kerryman*

Michael Kirby ... wrote beautifully, both in his native tongue and in English. He had a deep appreciation and understanding of his surroundings, the power and beauty of nature, and the energy held within an ancient folk tradition, which defined the people he belonged to. His descriptions of the sea and marine life are particularly special. His pages come alive with the sounds, smells and sights he knew so intimately ... I once asked him why he left it so late to start writing. He responded with a wink of wisdom, '*Is mar a chéile an scríbhneoireacht agus an sméar ar sceach, má phriocann tú ró-luath é ní bhlaisfidh tú an mhílseacht*' [The gift of writing is like a blackberry – if you pick it too soon its sweetness will elude you].

Seán Mac an tSíthigh (@Buailtín)

His writings are artless and full of wonder, acclaimed as among the last authentic expressions of the Gaelic tradition.

Justine McCarthy, *Irish Independent*

He felt himself to be 'part of nature's picture'. He was. His writing is nature observed. Nature is the basis of his spirituality and the frame of reference of his belief system ... Here is a storyteller at ease, threading the ordinary life of an extraordinary man, building a patchwork quilt of philosophy, spirituality, tradition and legends.

Joe O'Toole, *Irish Independent*

A generous glimpse it is of people who plied lost trades: basket-weaver, cobbler, journeyman tailor, cooper, of fishing, turf-cutting, flax-growing, of customs, beliefs, wakes, folk tales, cures – all presented with the touch of a poet and a free-and-easy style.

Des Rushe, *Irish Independent*

The gift of being a wordsmith is a true virtue. Having the choice of fashioning images in two rich languages makes that virtue even more rare. Michael Kirby had that virtue, which made him a performer rather than a writer ... [He wrote] perfectly formed tales featuring colourful characters, fellow storytellers, local superstitions, games, pastimes, and gipsy magic. All are spun in a charming, unselfconscious way; effortless and organic.

Mark Evans, *Irish Examiner*

Kirby's voice is akin to that of the Blasket writers, and is one of the last authentic expressions of the Gaelic tradition, artlessly using the worlds of flesh and spirit ... it resonates in the mind like the purest music.

Aodhan Madden, *Sunday Press*

Kirby claims he was born with the sea in his blood. That may well be, but he was also born with words already formed in his head. He writes charmingly with colour, fun, and a flair few others have ever bettered ... That a man of such an age could summon up the energy and motivation to write with such committed endeavor, care and beauty is a magnificent triumph of giving us everything he has to offer ... Michael Kirby claims he once heard a razorbill singing in Irish, and who am I to argue? For, make no mistake, this is a book set apart, a classic of its kind by a man set apart who describes a place set apart in a charmingly set apart way.

Tom Widget, *Sunday Tribune*

In the tradition of the great Kerry autobiographers, Michael Kirby writes of his life and the people and landscape of Ballinskelligs. No less than Ursula Wyndham, he loves the lore and the traditions of his people, which he expresses with passion and conviction.

Ronan Sheehan, *Irish Press*

Michael Kirby's ability to draw a perfect picture with a few words transports the reader to the headlands; you can almost find yourself leaning into the wind as the monks did centuries ago.

Bill Cullen, *Ireland on Sunday*

Skelligs Haul

Michael Kirby

Edited by Mary Shine Thompson
Introduced by Paddy Bushe

THE LILLIPUT PRESS
DUBLIN

First published 2019 by
THE LILLIPUT PRESS
62–63 Sitric Road, Arbour Hill
Dublin 7, Ireland
www.lilliputpress.ie

Copyright © 2019 Literary estate of Michael Kirby
Preface © 2019 Mary Shine Thompson
Introduction © 2019 Paddy Bushe
Images © 2019 Literary estate of Michael Kirby

Paperback ISBN 9781843517672

All rights reserved. No part of this publication may be reproduced in any form or by any means without the prior permission of the publisher.

A CIP record for this title is available from The British Library.

10 9 8 7 6 5 4 3 2 1

The Lilliput Press gratefully acknowledges the financial support of the Arts Council / An Chomhairle Ealaíon

Set in 11.5 pt on 14.2 pt Sabon by Compuscript
Printed in Spain by GraphyCems

CONTENTS

Illustrations	xi
Preface by Mary Shine Thompson	xii
Introduction: Messages from an Astral Traveller by Paddy Bushe	xvi

SKELLIGSIDE: 'A GREAT PLACE TO WAKE IN THE MORNING'

The Skelligs	2
Skellig Michael in the Lobster Season	13
The Soft South Winds of Skelligs	18
Placenames of the Skelligs Shore	20
The Red-Haired Friar of Scariff	30
Coastguards and Shipwreck	32
Floating Mines	41
Ballinskelligs Cable Station	46

BOY AND MAN

An Early Schooling	57
Tug of War in the Classroom	61
Penance and Grace	73
Games and Pastimes of My Boyhood	79
Heart Attack and the Drunken Ballet Dancers	83
A Painting is Born	88
My Garden	93
A Garden: In the Waning Light of My Years	99

FAMILY AND LOCAL FOLK

Our House	103
Haste to the Wedding	106
The Lady of Horse Island	115
A Family Wake	119

Contents

The Journeyworkers	122
Beachcombers	125
Silence! Silence in the Court!	133

GRAFT AND CRAFT
The Giant's Grave at Coom	139
Kelp and Potatoes	141
Growing Flax	145
Cutting the Turf	147
Oats and Hay	150
The Gentleman at Home	153
Building and Thatching	157
The Basket-Weaver	161
The Cooper	163
The Blacksmith	164
Tailors	168
The Village Cobbler	172

AMERICA CALLING
Famine and America	175
Voyage to America	179

THE RUNNING TIDE
Early Sea Memories	196
The Sea in His Blood	198
A Fisherman Loves His Boat	202
The Wreck of *The Hercules*	209
The Night Haul at Bolus	213
The Riches of the Sea	217
Sea Kelp, Rock Pools, Beaches and Strands	237
Rock Clams at *Tráigh Fraisce*	242
Digging Sand Sprat	244
Sea Grass	245

FIN AND FEATHER
Sharks and Other Species	248
Squid, Cuttlefish and Octopus	256
The Gannet	257
The Puffin	261

Contents

The Rock Pipit	263
The Storm Petrel	265
The Manx Shearwater	268
The Herring Gull	269
The Great Black-Backed Gull	271
The Skua	273
The Kittiwake	274

SPINNING YARNS

Seán Ó Conaill: King of the Storytellers	278
Some Poets and a Storyteller	283
The Tale of the Haunted Piper	294

A NET OF VERSE

Turas na Sceilge	300
A Fisherman's First Visit to Skellig Michael	301
Sean-Sceilg Mhichíl	302
My Lovely Skellig's Shore	303
Mo Bháidín	305
My Boat	305
Dán dom' Athair	306
To My Father	307
Miangas	308
Yearning	309
Coinne	310
Tryst	313
Deireadh na Buana	316
The Harvest Moon	316
The Road to Bolus	317
Caiple Bána	319
Am	319
Storm Petrel	320
Who Scattered the Stars?	321
An Bleachtán Órga	323
Cranna	324
Duan-Phaidir	325

Contents

Faire go Deo	326
Gairdín Gréine	328
Ollscoil Scairte	329
Litir do Dháithí	330
Editorial Note	333

INDEXES

General	339
Local Placenames	343
Personal Names	349

ILLUSTRATIONS
Paintings by Michael Kirby

Illustrations between pages 170 and 171.

Puffin Island, early 1990s

Iveragh Hills, 2005

Horse Island and The Priory (Ballinskelligs Abbey), 1995

Horse Island and The Priory (Ballinskelligs Abbey), 2003

Horse Island and The Priory (Ballinskelligs Abbey), 2003

Horse Island and The Priory (Ballinskelligs Abbey), 2004

Sceilg Mhichíl in sunlight, 2003

The Skelligs and Bolus Head, 2000

The Skelligs and Bolus Head, 2002

Ballinskelligs Castle by moonlight, 2003

Moonlight on Glen Strand, 1989

Sceilg Mhichíl from Saint Finan's Bay, 2004

Sea Pinks, 1992

Endpapers by Tim O'Neill show a map of the Ballinskelligs Bay, South Iveragh peninsula, County Kerry.

PREFACE

I was not fortunate to meet that extraordinary ordinary man, Micheál Ua Ciarmhaic, Michael Kirby, or Maidhcí (1906–2005), as his friends knew him. However, by the time he died, aged ninety-nine, I was well aware – like numerous others – that he had earned a distinguished reputation as a folklorist, storyteller, artist and poet synonymous with South Kerry. I knew that he was cast in the mould of that other great chronicler of Uíbh Ráthach, Seán Ó Conaill, whose tales folklorist Seamus Ó Duilearga collected and published in book form in 1948. Like Ó Conaill, Michael Kirby was a storyteller and an observer and recorder of nature, and he was also a poet. I knew that his work had attracted the attention of Dáithí Ó hÓgáin, Associate Professor of Irish Folklore at University College Dublin, and of the discerning Ollamh Liam Mac Mathúna, also of University College Dublin, and formerly registrar at Saint Patrick's College in Drumcondra; and I was aware that Liam had recorded Michael reading. It comes as no surprise that in 2017 University College Cork added his extensive archive of manuscripts to its collection, thereby underlining the importance the University attaches to his work.

I was honoured, therefore, when his daughter, Anne Coffey, and her husband Pat Coffey, invited me to prepare a selection of his writings for posthumous publication by The Lilliput Press in 2006. That selection became *Skelligs Sunset*, Michael's thirteenth publication, if a Romanian translation of his 1994 collection of prose and poetry, *Chuireas mo Líonta,* by Christian Tamas, entitled *Riul năvalnic* (2004), is counted.

Preface

Uppermost in my mind when I was sifting through the many works that might be included in *Skelligs Haul*, this latest selection of Michael's writing, was that I wanted a new generation of readers to hear his lucid, poetic voice. I wanted them to glimpse the once simple life of Uíbh Ráthach (or Iveragh), in that most beautiful part of South Kerry, which he captured in clear, unsentimental language, and also in his charming landscape paintings.

Michael had spent his days almost entirely in Ballinskelligs (apart from a brief sojourn in the United States), under the shadow of the World Heritage site of Skellig Michael, eking out a living fishing and farming. He knew intimately every inch of its land- and seascapes, and he was on intimate terms with its inhabitants, human, animal and maritime. To survive in such a rocky outpost demanded persistence, passion, civility and good humour: and no one had more than Michael. He realized too well the vicissitudes of life lived at the whim of the elements, with hunger and emigration around every fuchsia bush. For decades he battled the pounding Atlantic surge on flimsy fishing vessels; little wonder he was alive to the plight of the medieval monks who clung to life on the bare rocks of Skellig Michael. He needed no one to explain to him the modern concept of sustainability, the balance between the human claim on natural resources and the need to avoid depleting them.

One remarkable aspect of his dual-language writing career is that it only began in his eighth decade, while he was recovering from a heart attack: the first book he published was *Cliathán na Sceilge*, in 1984, when he was seventy-eight. Pat Coffey knew that the confinement which Michael's illness imposed on an unfettered soul would take its toll, and, to occupy the long hours of recovery, he supplied copybooks and the suggestion that the patient fill them. Michael took to the pen as he had taken to fishing as a lad: with determination, alacrity and innate skill. He wrote elegantly and economically about what he knew and felt, knitting the fresh, passionate insight of an artist with the dispassionate slant of a scientist. His knowledge of local birds and fish was as encyclopaedic and forensic as his grasp of place names and local lore. In *Skelligs Haul*, for example, he names at least twenty-four caves as well as numerous rocks, cliffs, headlands and sea-routes. He was also a mystic who found his god in every living thing, and solace and serenity in elemental Iveragh. That inward eye led him to write verse both in the romantic vein and in the fine tradition of Irish-language religious verse.

Yet he kowtowed to no priest or scholar, and had no truck with pietistic reverence. His description of the skua – *Tomáisín chac na bhFaoileán*, or 'Little Tommy Gull-shit' – is brief and forthright. Kirby balances the evidence of sensory data with an imagination alive with pirates and Bluebeard's Castle. He describes tinted sea anemones that he observed as a boy on the seashore as 'things like cows' teats growing on rounded boulders beneath the sea'. His father responds by tossing out their Latin term: 'Nothing new, my boy! Nothing new ... Scientists call them *metredium dianthus*. Take to the books, boy, take to the books.' The exchange offers the young Kirby the opportunity to undercut his father's casual erudition with a succinct dismissal: 'Ah! but Dad was droll.' No one, not even his father, is safe from his uncompromising sound sense. It comes as no surprise to find him capable also of verse in a satirical vein.

I have organized the contents of *Skelligs Haul* around eight themes that reflect Michael's deep rootedness in his own place. Given the importance to him of Skellig Michael, the island site of a medieval Christian settlement, and of the identity of South Kerry, pride of place is given to his writings on the Skellig. Next comes an autobiographical section, ranging over the tug of war of the classroom through

Preface

the declining days spent in the garden. The reader is then introduced to the lives of members of his family and local folk. We glimpse farmers, thatchers and numerous tradespeople at work, and follow the young emigrant Kirby to the United States. Predictably, the hazards of life at sea and the secret skills of fishermen engrossed him, as did the fish and fowl that he observed minutely. Iveragh has a vigorous storytelling tradition, and the penultimate section of this book revives it in Kirby's distinctive tones. A small haul of verse that includes nature poetry, satires and some of the poet's own free translations, completes the text, but I have also included a selection of Michael's paintings. The writing presents certain editorial challenges, not least because of the plentiful sprinkling of Irish-language names and terms; I have briefly addressed my approach to these issues in the 'Editorial Note' at the end of the book.

It is fitting that Paddy Bushe, a dual-language poet and member of Aosdána who has spent much of his adult life in Waterville, down the road from Ballinskelligs, should write an introduction to this haul of Kirby's work. Bushe edited a collection of poems, *Duanaire Mhaidhcí*, in homage to the elder writer, and his insights are those of a fellow astral traveller, poet and lover of the locality and of Kirby. Bushe notes his spirituality, his humour as well as his roguery, the centrality of poetry within his legacy, and his significant contribution to local history. Paddy's special contribution to this book is a translation of his favourite poem by Michael, 'Dán dom' Athair' / 'Poem for my Father'.

Mary Shine Thompson, Editor

INTRODUCTION: MESSAGES FROM AN ASTRAL TRAVELLER

I first met Michael Kirby in 1984, at the launch of his first book, *Cliathán na Sceilge*, in Listowel. I was attending a workshop, and it was to be another five years before I, a late starter myself, would publish a book of my own. But here was a man of seventy-eight years launching his first book. That in itself was impressive, inspiring even. But none of us then present could have guessed that it was to be the first of almost a dozen books to literally flow from the pen of a man whom Michael Davitt shrewdly invoked as '*a astraishiúlaigh*' – astral traveller – an invocation which I have come to see as less and less an exaggeration as time goes by. I knew his reputation as a custodian of the indigenous culture of Iveragh, especially of Ballinskelligs, and he knew of me as a teacher in nearby Waterville, a blow-in from Dublin. He dedicated the book '*don mháistir léannta*'. Although the dedication pleased me, I knew enough even then not to let it go to my head. A mischievous sense of fun was always integral to Maidhcí's personality, and notions of rank or status were there to be punctured. If you want an example, just go to 'Giant's Grave at Coom' on pages 139–40. And, of course, the dedication was also a reference to 'Amhrán na Leabhar', the masterpiece of Iveragh's master poet, Tomás Rua Ó Súilleabháin. The dedication I now read as both a test and an invitation. In the following years, as I got to know Maidhcí, I accepted that invitation and I hope I passed the test.

Introduction: Messages from an Astral Traveller

Recently, Maidhcí's daughter Anne Coffey and her husband Pat Coffey invited Fíona and myself to have a look at the archive of Maidhcí's work prior to it being lodged in the library of University College Cork. It was both a privilege and a revelation to do so. To see the series of old-fashioned 'copy books' and the meticulous handwriting that filled page after page was to be struck again by the level of sheer achievement involved. It was also to realize the debt owed to those who nurtured the talent of this almost octogenarian fledgling writer, and to pay particular tribute to Pádraig Ó Snodaigh of Coiscéim, who was his original publisher and long-term friend. And of course a similar debt is owed to Anne and Pat, keepers of the flame.

Micheál Ua Ciarmhaic was a tradition-bearer, an inheritor of a rich oral culture that he had, sadly but perhaps inevitably, seen die around him. In his youth he knew Seán Ó Conaill, the great *seanchaí* from a tradition that was preliterate and monoglot, and also Ó Conaill's academic amanuensis, Professor Séamus Ó Duillearga. He then experienced, and rejected, the world of the emigrant in the United States. Maidhcí therefore came to maturity in a culturally liminal world, a world of enormous cultural, linguistic and demographic changes and contrasts that gave him footholds in very different parts of that world. Hence, I think, the unique perspective that Michael Davitt so memorably characterized.

It is a multifaceted perspective that is enhanced by Maidhcí's deep sense of spirituality. He was a religious man, steeped in the piety that seems to have haemorrhaged from Ireland in recent times. It is a piety that can be seen in his poetry and perhaps most intensely in his paintings. But his piety could never be equated with the narrow Puritanism which was so dominant in Ireland throughout much of Maidhcí's life. I remember him laughing at some prelate or other who had inveighed against the evils of contraception when condoms went on legal sale. What was bothering him, Maidhcí wondered, wasn't a condom just something like a raincoat? This humorous approach to the world of religious belief served him well in his last days. Several times – and I knew him only as an old man – I heard him make light of death. I have been told that during his final decline, which coincided with that of Pope John Paul II, he regularly asked how the pope was getting on, joking that it was a contest between them to see who would first approach the gates of heaven. Michael Kirby, I might add, was rightfully never in any doubt about his own status, despite a wonderful line in self-deprecation. But whatever the reader's own belief, or lack of it, Michael's ability to enter imaginatively into other worlds of time, space, language, or whatever, is testament to the only spirituality that I believe matters. It is an ability that offers riches to us as readers. That it is here primarily embodied in the land-and-seascape where I live, especially that of Skellig Michael, makes it very precious to me. Here is a writer listening to the place he physically inhabits, listening to what it says now and listening to what it has said in the past; listening in two languages. And as well as being immersed in what the landscape says, he is immersed in its physical presence, its flora and its fauna. It is a relationship which, societally, both globally and locally, we need urgently to rediscover if our planet is to survive.

Taken on the level of social history, this book is a rich hoard. Abstract issues such as economic and demographic decline, emigration, the change from subsistence and labour-intensive farming to commercial and mechanized farming (with the consequent marginalization of agriculture in marginal land), small scale fishing and its decline, language loss and the consequent demoralization, emigration – all of these and indeed much more are here given an imaginative but down-to-earth narrative that illuminates the statistics

Introduction: Messages from an Astral Traveller

and humanizes the abstractions behind the social changes in an area which is now almost completely dependent on seasonal tourism, with all the economic, social and cultural challenges thrown up by that dependency. In the works selected here, we can imagine ourselves back into a different world, a world which, though it cannot be recreated again, can still offer us very valuable guidance in how to deal with our contemporary world.

So many of these extracts from Michael Kirby's work recreate the omnivorously receptive way he lived. A favourite of mine is his description of a trip to Little Skellig with an eminent English ornithologist to record and photograph the 20,000 pairs of gannets on Little Skellig. He describes the ornithologist, as 'the bird woman six foot three inches tall, and broad in the beam as well, God bless her' who, when he was helping her down the cliffs of Little Skellig, sat on 'both my palms under the cheeks of her buttocks, just as she would sit on a chair'. And, he continues, 'I glanced fearfully upwards, to see the whole weight of the ornithological department (in the broadest posterior sense), appearing to descend on me like a great parachutist clad in black knickers.' Even in these days of ultra-correctness, it is a hilarious picture, and the twinkling mischievous eyes of Kirby invite you to admire it. But the humour is only one aspect of this episode on Little Skellig. We also share the young Kirby's wonder: the ornithologist was 'a fluent speaker, and easily understood', and 'that day among the birds was an education in Nature's own university . . . She awakened in me such a great interest in bird life that I later bought some books on the subject and studied them.' When we put that in the context of the young man getting paid two pounds for being her guide, and two pounds being 'hard to come by in those days', we realize that we are getting an insight into the creation of a mind and sensitivity that has so much to offer us, and that the fortuitous flowering of that sensitivity into publication in old age was, and remains, a reason for rejoicing.

This selection from Micheál's work includes, I am delighted to note, a generous sampling of his poetry, in both languages. It may be a case of *I would, wouldn't I*, but I think poetry is central to his literary *oeuvre*, and perhaps even antecedent to all of his creative work. Poetry, his own and that of others, is constantly quoted to illustrate the prose, and the prose itself is never very far from the poetic, almost as if its author were trimming his linguistic sails, restraining himself lest he outrun his medium. It reminds me a little of the monastic scribes taking time off from their heavy scriptorial duties to write some verse in the margins or as interpolations in a weighty text.

I am delighted also that it is a bilingual poetry selection, because the Irish language is also antecedent to all of his work. Michael Kirby's English is no hesitant or broken Hiberno-English; indeed it is rich and fluent. But it looks over its shoulder at centuries of Irish, and seems to seek the approval of those centuries. And yet, in some ways, the poet / translator in English also seems to revel in a new freedom, a freedom from tradition that can be enabling. I think particularly of 'Miangas' and its translation 'Yearning', which are both included here. The Irish version is a polished rhyming and rhythmic poem, well written and lively. But the constraints of its form, to my mind, have inhibited it more than its translation, which ends

> All I ask,
> That time be measured
> By the looping wing
> Of that homeward heron.

The Zen-like intensity of these lines, the exactness of the observation of a heron's 'looping wing' and the lovely

Introduction: Messages from an Astral Traveller

chiming of 'measured' with 'heron' have always intrigued me. These lines – and I recognize that I contradict what I said about Irish being antecedent – seem to me to be far better than the original Irish. But they are perhaps the exception that proves the rule. And indeed the 'lowing kine' that 'wend homeward' earlier in the poem are more hidebound than the language of the original poem in Irish, although at the same time they remind us that this bilingual writer, lacking education in the formal sense, was born in one of the most remote parts of Ireland in the year 1906, when, even in literary metropolises, the nineteenth century was alive and well. But really, the twists and turns of language and languages are all secondary to the primary poetic instinct and insights which infuse the work of Micheál Ua Ciarmhaic. He was not one of those – all too common on both sides of Ireland's linguistic divide – who choose to close their ears and hearts to one of the country's two languages.

For me the apex of Micheál's poetry – it is no accident that I use different forms of the name of this shape-shifting man – is his wonderful poem for his father, 'Dán dom' Athair'. The poem, which is definitely and immeasurably better in Irish, is made up of just two nine-line stanzas. It is a poem where tradition and intensity of emotion combine with a vividly realized physical world to embody filial love with a love of place. It is a work of richness and simplicity, the most fertile poetic soil which this poet tilled. It is I know, impertinent, not to say downright cheeky, for me to offer my own translation of my favourite poem by Micheál Ua Ciarmhaic as part of this introduction. Cheek, or maybe what he would have called *rógaireacht*, however, was something that appealed to him, and somehow I feel sure that if he disapproves, Kirby will let me know. *Seo chugaibh é, mar thabhartas cuimneacháin ar Mhaidhcí*:

Skelligs Haul

Poem for my Father

There you go, Dad,
Let's raise our shadowy sails
And leave this haven astern.
Swing her around windward.
Haul in on the jib sheet
So that she heels over
To shoulder off easily
Those soft foamy buffetings
Across the waves.

Yourself and myself, Dad,
With God the extra man,
The Pole star of knowledge
Dancing above our mast,
Every tuneful little gust
In our lines a harp being played,
As we coast on in for home
Snug and shipshape
Across the waves.

Is pribhléid agus ábhar mórtais agam gur iarradh orm an rogha seo as saothar Mhichíl Uí Chiarmhaic a chur i láthair an phobail. Tá moladh ag dul do Mary Shine Thompson as an dua a chaith sí leis an obair eagarthóireachta, agus an rogha a dhein sí. Seo chugaibh mar sin an saothar, ag scaoileadh seoil an athuair, agus tá súil agam go mbeidh cóir gaoithe leis, agus ancaireacht fáiltiúil ar fud na cruinne.

Paddy Bushe, Uíbh Ráthach, Lúnasa 2018

Skelligside: 'A great place to wake in the morning'

THE SKELLIGS

Skelligside

The Great Skellig, *Sceilg Mhichíl*, is situated nine miles west of Bolus Head. The rock is a mile in circumference, and more than seven hundred feet high. It consists mostly of grey-black slate, with mixtures of other rock; traces of white and red marble, brownstone, rock crystals, quartz and copper. Beautiful spires and turrets of rock, made by Nature's hand across aeons of time, give Skellig Michael an outline as majestic as a great cathedral. Sea pinks grow thick and heavy on the south-western side of the rock and offer shelter for nesting to the different species of seabirds. Petrels, shearwaters and puffins burrow beneath the deep accumulation of turf-like soil, created by the centuries-long growth and decay of sea pinks and campion. These birds must go underground to avoid that most murderous predator, the great black-headed gull, whose own nest hangs precariously on a few inches of space, wedged in between hundreds of other nests. Arctic terns and kittiwakes scream plaintively, crying 'kittiwake, kittiwake', while the little auks stand like statues of graven stone, forever staring out to sea, seemingly oblivious to human presence.

A partly submerged reef runs south-westward from the Great Skellig, and shows in two jagged sections above the high-water line. The rocks are called The Women or *Na Mná* in Irish. This was a rich crayfish ground until teams of divers began to come with sophisticated equipment and put an end to shellfishing. The sea around the Skelligs was alive

The Skelligs

with different species of fish in my young days. May God be good to Paud Jack O'Sullivan, that king of fishermen: I wish him a little boat in some lovely harbour among the Isles of Heaven. I still seem to hear him say to me, 'A great place to wake in the morning, Michael, west of the Great Skellig.' Many a moonlit night we spent at anchor with our captain, Jim Fitzgerald, sleeping peacefully, our lobster trap ready for hauling at the dawning of a new day.

It was there, in the bosom of the ocean, that a community of anchorite monks settled some time before the sixth century. They raised stout, strong, sheltering walls of grey slatestone. Within those thick walls, seven hundred feet above sea level, they built a monastery of beehive stone cells culminating in a capstone with an aperture for smoke. The entire fabric was of dry stone without bonding mortar, yet the squared interiors were dry, airy and comfortable. The monastery today is as sound as when it was first built. Every priest or monk must have been an expert in building with stone: the labour and effort that went into the construction of the settlement can only be imagined. Within the enclosure are two springs of clear fresh water. Engineers say it is the pressure of the ocean that forces seawater upwards through porous rock which filters out the salt. The monks are buried within a small mound. Over the grave of the abbot stands a great stone hewn to represent a cowled monk in his Mass vesture. Seven hundred steps of heavy footworn slabs lead up to the entrance in the monastery wall. Near the top, suspended between the northern and southern spires, is a bare valley-like gap called Christ's Saddle. According to local tradition, the hermits named it thus. The Blind Man's Cave is on the south side. Legend has it that a blind man from Ballinskelligs asked to be landed there, then crawled on his knees up the entire pathway until he reached the monastery, where the light was miraculously restored to his eyes.

Skelligs Haul

The great spire of Skellig is on the western shoulder of the rock. The monks chiselled crude footholds into the cliff which leans out over the sea. Dangerous steps and rock barriers lead up to an opening in the cliff face called the Needle's Eye. After you pass through the Eye, you go to the highest point, called the Stone of Penance, which leans out 718 feet over the depths below. The stone itself is shaped like a horse's back, and ten feet out a cross is carved at the end. Fearless pilgrims scramble out and kiss the cross, with nothing below them but the blue ocean. This is not for the squeamish. Yet it is said only one person ever fell to his death – one who had mocked at the idea of a spiritual pilgrimage.

Tradition locates the grave of Irr, son of Milesius, on the Great Skellig, where he received Christian baptism when his ship was wrecked on the rock. Skellig Michael was dedicated to the Archangel Michael. Saint Finan is said to have established canons of Saint Augustine on the rock. *The Annals of Loch Léin* [recte *The Annals of Inisfallen*] record the 'repose' of Flann Macallach, Abbot of Great Skellig, in the year 885, and [*The Annals of the Four Masters* record the death] of Blathmac Sgellice in 950. A third abbot, Aed, 'chief of the Gael in piety', died in 1044.

The monks used boats of frame and leather. Great oxskins were tanned with the juice of the oak bark, then sewn on to the light frames of oak and ash. When the boat was finished, the leather was smeared with mutton fat.

A treacherous reef called the Monks' Rock lies under water on the south side of Skellig Michael. It is said that the monks' *naomhóg* was wrecked there one day with the loss of some lives, and the monks carved a Christian cross on the reef. A strange formation of rock stands overlooking the reef. This is called *Bean an Uaill* or The Wailing Woman. On the western side the monks carved two heads, one male, one female, representing Adam and Eve, gazing forward towards the far horizon.

The Skelligs

Tourists come from many parts of the world to visit Skellig Michael. Some have a special interest in Celtic culture, and in the archaeology of the period of early monasticism. It is also a delightful place for the student of bird life.

One day during the 1930s Jim Fitzgerald and I took two ladies to the Skellig. They had hired the boat for an agreed sum. Mother and daughter of a distinguished family, they were intensely interested in archaeology, and had done a world tour to look at antiquities. They had come from Istanbul to Ireland to see the Great Skellig, on their way back to America. The mother told me how she had listened to the late Professor James Delargy deliver a lecture in Chicago about ancient Irish culture. In his lecture he spoke of the Great Skellig – its monastic life, its beehive colony of stone cells, its beauty and its bird life. On hearing the lecture she decided she must see it at some future date.

On arriving at the rock, Jim Fitzgerald stayed with the boat while I accompanied the women as their guide. It was a warm summer evening – a perfect setting to reward the tourists for their long journey. The sky was a hazy blue and the ocean beneath a mirror of tinted blue glass with the various seabirds floating in space. We had arrived near Christ's Saddle, not far from the entrance to the monastery, when the mother stopped suddenly, telling me that she could not go on. I saw that she was frightened, though I assured her there was no danger. She told her daughter to go on alone and see the monastery. I got her seated on a great smooth slab of slate, and stayed with her. I talked to her about the folklore of the Skelligs and I noticed she became more comfortable and relaxed. She then told me the cause of her anxiety. Some years previously she and her husband had been in Mexico climbing up the steps of an Aztec sun temple, when her husband suddenly collapsed and died of a heart attack. Both places seemed so strikingly similar in structure that she imagined she saw for a fleeting

Skelligs Haul

moment the entire sad scene of her husband's death. Mother and daughter assured us they enjoyed the trip, despite the emotional setback.

Another lady visited Ballinskelligs in the year 1938. She had a doctorate from a university in Germany and had permission to travel among the Irish people collecting folklore and taking photographs. She wanted to visit the Great Skellig and include it in her writings, although she made no secret of her revulsion for Christianity and constantly mocked the idea of a Supreme Being. Her argument was that all was chance, but she took umbrage when I remarked that if this were so we were all included in the word chance, which reduced us to being born chancers. The astonishing thing was that she always kept in her pocket a brass talisman like a little monkey, and although she dismissed the idea of God, she believed her talisman had mysterious powers. She kept repeating, 'My talisman will keep me from harm.'

The weather was broken and unsettled. A great heavy sea and severe surf prevented us from making the trip for two weeks, and in the meantime she took photographs of pilgrims at Saint Michael's Shrine on Pattern day saying the Rosary around the well. She thought these people were deranged. In the end the weather cleared and we made the trip to the Great Skellig the next Sunday. She was anxious to see the monastic settlement and to write about it.

We had several tourists with us on the same trip. Jack Fitzgerald was our skipper and Miss Fenton, the Ballinskelligs national schoolteacher, and myself were with the German lady. We started to climb the flagged pathway up to the monastery, and it wasn't long before we noticed our German doctor sinking slowly to the ground, complaining of feeling faint. Jack Fitzgerald and myself seated her at the point we had started out from, and gave her some refreshments. She quickly recovered

The Skelligs

and expressed her desire to attempt the journey upwards once again. After a short rest to restore her energy – in Irish, 'the rest of the blacksmith's boy: from the anvil to the bellows' – we continued once more, and everything went fine until we reached the place where she had fallen before. It was fortunate that we were walking by her side, for this time she asked to be taken down again, saying that both her legs were paralysed. It was true for her: they seemed to have no feeling or movement. With the assistance of the other boatmen we took her bodily to the roadway where she immediately walked. That ended her chance of ever seeing the monastery. She told us that her experience was most strange, in so far as she was not afraid of heights. One old fisherman's verdict on what had happened made us all laugh: 'Don't you know the holy monks in heaven wouldn't let that bitch into the monastery!'

We came home that evening. The learned doctor had nothing to relate about her trip to the Great Skellig: no photographs, no notes – perhaps the little brass monkey had taken the day off. She told me she was not going back to Germany because she said a world war was imminent. She left Ballinskelligs the next day.

Some months afterwards Miss Fenton got a letter from a friend living in Toronto, enclosing a copy of a supplement from a Canadian newspaper. Under the name of the learned German doctor the newspaper carried a headline in large print: 'The land of Saint Patrick as it is today, a land of devilry and laughter.' A photograph of the schoolteacher's aged mother, Nora Roche, saying her Rosary in the garden, was accompanied by the words: 'This old woman carries a Rosary beads but utters the words of a spell.' Another picture of praying at Saint Michael's Shrine carried the caption: 'They still worship water in a so-called Christian land.' Under a picture of children was written: 'Barefoot Irish maidens laugh easily.' I don't want to splash more water on drowned mice. I'll reveal nothing more about the learned doctor who was granted licence by the authorities to walk among my people and who wrote scurrilously about them. May her spirit climb the stairway to Paradise without fear or emotion, and the holy anchorites welcome her to the eternal city. And on her way up may she cast from her that little idol of a brass monkey!

* * *

Little Skellig, situated half-way between the Great Skellig and *Lomán* Rock, is a wild, spiky, splintered rock formation, hard to climb because of the huge slabs of rotting slate that slip down on the sloping cliff face. Many days and nights I spent fishing the reefs and caves for great blue lobster and crayfish with the Fitzgeralds, Jack and Jim. You need a fine day for lobster fishing around this rock. To the northwest the ground is rough and uneven, with several sunken reefs which are dangerous in rough weather. Strong ocean currents run on high tides, making it difficult to haul lobster gear. Herds of grey Atlantic seals can be seen on the rocks as the tide goes out, including great bulls whose weight must be close to half a ton. They especially like the heat of a midsummer's day.

But it was not fishing I intend to write about now, but how I became interested in seabirds. It happened that a woman ornithologist was commissioned by the British government to carry out a count of the seabirds around the coast of the British Isles. She was equipped with all kinds of cameras for both prints and slides. After completing a survey of the Faroe Islands she was now to survey the Little Skellig and had asked to be put ashore on the rock when the weather was suitable. The rock itself is not easy to step ashore on, with no steps or jetty but the slippery deceiving cliff face. On that particular day, Jim Fitzgerald,

The Skelligs

John Peter O'Shea, myself and the bird woman set out, towing astern a twenty-foot rowing boat attached to a stout cable. By the time we reached the rock the weather was rapidly deteriorating: sheep's fleece in the sky, the breeze quickening from the south-west, and a look of rain in the eye of the morning sun. The captain told me I was to accompany the lady up among the birds. I can truthfully say that I was not eager to face up that frowning cliff. I was burdened with a haversack sixty pounds in weight, and got strict orders not to fall, because the gear was worth a small fortune. The lady then instructed me how I should conduct myself among the birds, and she herself put on a pair of special climbing shoes. We boarded our craft to approach the surf-bound cliff and chose a suitable landing place after anchoring the big boat in deep water away from the rock. Then Jim Fitzgerald and John O'Shea rowed us towards the landing point. An old Irish saying could well be applied here. 'Study the river, lest you enter the whirlpool.'

After searching for some time we found a place with deep water and a broad sloping slab of flat rock. The bird woman was six foot three inches tall and broad in the beam as well, God bless her – a miniature Amazon. She had boasted to me that if she were young again she could run up the face of that rock. We were both standing on the stern sheeting, waiting for Jim Fitzgerald's order: he had told us that when he said the word 'Go!' we were to obey his command at once because of the great rise and fall of the breaking surf. He held the boat steady for seconds with the oar blades thrust deep in the churning sea. After hearing the signal we found ourselves standing safely on the rock.

Losing no time, we climbed outward to the level of the bird colony, but the terrain became more difficult, until at last it was clear that we were already trapped. I took off the cumbersome haversack and wellingtons and searched for a way forward, in my stockinged feet. The slippery rock where we stood did not afford very safe ground, for it slanted abruptly at about fifty degrees towards the sea. The only escape route which presented itself was a narrow fissure, not much wider than a toe-hold, which led to a larger platform of rock above our heads. To reach the gap in the cliff face we would have to crawl across a narrow ledge of rock, there to stand upright to pull and squeeze through the gap. I went first, pushing the haversack ahead, and succeeded in getting through safely. She came next, not running but crawling carefully, and when she stood upright I grasped her right hand and hauled her up into the narrow gap to safety. One time when I had exerted more pressure than she could bear, she entreated me not to break her arm. She was getting on in years, and not so nimble any more.

The climb became less difficult from then on, and in a short while we were surrounded by birds, thousands of great gannets on their nests all around us. We sat on a rock without stirring or speaking. It was wonderful to watch these ferocious creatures only inches away, showing no fear, no interest in our presence. Her instructions were to ignore the birds and move very slowly. We chose a vantage point for the camera and during the next hour she took photographs of the different areas. She also had a map of the rock. For me, that day among the birds was an education in Nature's own university.

She spoke about the habits of the different species of seabirds on the coast of Ireland, explaining and teaching as she continued to work. She was a fluent talker, and easily understood. She spoke about gulls, large, medium and small, the great diving birds, the gannets or Solan geese, crossbills, razorbills, guillemots, auks, terns, Arctic terns, puffins, petrels, black sea witch and fulmar petrels, Manx shearwater petrels, the great Northern diver which in Irish is called the *lóma*, rock pipits, blue rock pigeons, choughs, cormorants, and the green shag. She awakened in me such a great interest in bird life that later I bought some books on the subject and studied them. There was a rich smell of guano: every nook and cranny was overflowing with rank manure, dead remains of fish, chicks and eggshells. Neighbouring mothers could be seen stealing pieces of precious nesting material from one another. The clamour of the different tones blending with the raucous 'craak, craak' of thousands of gannets, together with the booming of surf in the caves and the rising wind, gave us the signal that it was time to depart. We packed all the gear into the haversack, which was once more strapped on my back. We proceeded downwards until we came to the difficult part we had met on our way up. I eased myself down carefully until I found with my feet the narrow ledge beneath, where I stood upright and told her to face in and lower her body very carefully down.

I stretched my arms above me until I got both my palms under the cheeks of her buttocks, just as she would sit on a chair. I helped her slowly downwards. Once I glanced fearfully upwards, to see for a fleeting moment the whole weight of the ornithological department (in the broadest posterior sense), appearing to descend upon me like a great parachutist clad in black knickers. It was a miracle that the weighty Saxon female and myself came safely off the dangerous cliff face. At one point one of her shoes became wedged in the rock: I might not have lived to tell the tale had she not torn her foot from it. The shoe detached itself and sailed over our heads down into the sea below. I pulled on my Wellingtons and we both made for the boat. The men guided it gently into a perfect position, and on Jim's order, we were aboard in a flash. Experience is the best teacher. If you ever go climbing, take a rope along.

The bird woman estimated that more than twenty thousand gannets were on the Skellig that year, among several other species. We were happy that the trip was over, as the weather got steadily worse, with white surf like a collar of lace around the Little Skellig. I got two pounds extra for being her guide. Two pounds was hard to come by in those days. [...]

My native village is forever linked with Skellig of the Shadows: it is called Ballinskelligs and our parish of Prior derives its name from the priory of Saint Michael's Abbey, once renowned as a seat of learning. A saying is still heard which is as old as the abbey itself: 'Better a week in the priory than a year at school.' Canons Regular of Saint Augustine were the last to occupy the abbey. The last abbot was called Blowick, a name not common in the locality.

The late Professor Delargy searched universities on the continent for information about the abbey and the castle by the sea. He discovered very little, so we have to fall back on local lore handed down for generations. All we have otherwise are the broken walls, and a silent chasm in so far as written history is concerned. There is not a whisper of information about when the monks were forced from Skellig Michael – it is thought that the Church reformer Saint Malachy of Bangor visited during his exile in 'Ibraceuse' in the 1120s and that the Augustinians took over from the Anchorites – or how many years it took to build the once great monastery at Ballinskelligs. The priory had many rooms and chapels, even streets and houses whose foundations can still be seen. As many buildings again vanished through sea erosion. Many questions can't be answered. Why were there no monks' graves in the monastery garden here, but only on Skellig itself? Where did the monks go? What happened to the books they wrote? What became of their sacred vessels that not a single artefact from that time was ever found? Some say that the religious community survived into the 1630s, but I fear this breach in our history will stay forever covered by the cold grave-slab.

At a point between the castle and the monastery, which was once a green field near the shore, there showed a long narrow hollow. One morning after a great storm the sea exposed the front of the field, and it was full of skeletons and skulls, each cut in front as if by axe or sword. I heard my father say there were scores of skulls in a common grave. Were those the remains of the monks who once occupied the Priory of Ballinskelligs?

SKELLIG MICHAEL IN THE LOBSTER SEASON
Skelligs Calling

I always enjoyed lobster fishing in summer and early autumn, by the side of the great Skellig Michael. For me personally it had an emotive influence. I felt the power and natural beauty of the place, so complete in colour and formation. Wild, savage beauty on the one hand, blending harmoniously with great beds of near-crimson sea pinks and cliff-dwelling clumps of brittle little white, yellow and blue flowers, filling the hollows and rock crannies between the stately spires of weather-worn multicoloured rock of slate blue and grey, including a mixture of brownstone and marble veins, iron and geodic rock crystals. The brittle flowers I have referred to, a lightkeeper told me that climbers called them 'dead men's flowers'.

The approach to the rock on a sunny day presents a picture of colour only to be found in the secluded bowers of isolated nature, exuding tranquillity and sheer beauty. The various sea-fowl flitting lightly among the rocky peaks or nesting in the caves, give evidence of a constant sustenance of life and order, combined with an aura of peace, unbroken by the intrusion of man.

Skelligs Haul

Remembering a day in my youthful thirties, while ashore on the Skelligs, I rested on a lofty rock ledge overlooking the Blue Man's Cave where I could gaze down into the clear green depths, to where the water was calm and lightly ruffled. I noticed a school of mackerel circling and also hundreds of glossan pollack moving very slowly, while in another cave near at hand, a school of porpoise seemed to be either hunting or playfully cavorting, puffing and diving, never leaving a seemingly chosen area. Several great black-backed gulls stood on points overlooking the marine display, as if in total indifference. I suddenly became aware of a puffin flying in from sea and heading straight toward me, only to land on the ledge just an arm's length away.

Now, I had read about Saint Francis and his way with birds and wild animals, but other than that, the good saint and I had nothing in common. For a while I was afraid to move or breathe lest I disturb my feathered companion. At the same time I couldn't help admiring the perfect colour scheme nature had arranged for its plumage. The creature seemed to accept me as another wild species, an appraisal I would be happy to get away with. The bird completely ignored my intrusion into its domain. I thought – was this the land of ultimate bliss where the lion shall lay down with the lamb? Strive as I may to become a lamb, the transition would only be miraculous.

But what has all this got to do with lobster fishing? Where you have sea and rocks you are sure to find seabirds, but as the wise old fisherman said, '*Ní fios cá bhfaighfeá gliomach*,' 'You can never be sure where you'd find a lobster.' It was during the lobster season that I was able to observe more closely the great rock in all its aspects, and above all, its crowning glory – the old-world monastery, a masterpiece of its time and an inspiration of wonder. Every quarried stone, from the heavy slab to the rough splinter spoil, found a place in the scheme. Hundreds of tons of stone

Skellig Michael in the Lobster Season

were quarried, lifted and carried and set by skillful artisans who must have worked like Trojans. They built walls of dry stone on the edge of overhanging cliff-face, which have stood the test of centuries. Theirs was undoubtedly a labour of love. They were craftsmen whose ancestors had emerged from the Stone Age. They evidently wanted to get away from the hurly-burly of the world, seeking the peace which the risen Christ had promised when he said, 'The peace I leave you is not of this world.'

Alas, their dream of seclusion and peace was rudely shattered in the ninth century by the plundering greed of the Northmen.

The beehive, dome-shaped cells, completely habitable, leave a legacy to be marvelled at. The completed settlement, surrounded by an outer rampart of solid stone wall protecting and enclosing the entire structure, was at the time a massive undertaking. The evidence is to be found in the amount of work left behind by those early Christian monks, suggesting that occupation and construction on Skellig Michael started at a very early date and spread over many centuries – therefore, perhaps it is safe to assume that Rome wasn't built in a day.

Another distinctive feature of the rock is its two lighthouses, one now electronically controlled from the mainland. The earlier lighthouse, built up high on the north-west corner, was abandoned. It is suggested that early mariners complained of the lamp being often obscured by low cloud.

Now I must return to the realm of a lobsterman, and to the reality of hard work, and as this document relates to fin, fur and feather, give variety to the menu by adding plenty of shellfish. Lobster traps must be baited and set in the most likely ground, usually by the side of the reef which extends westwards from Skellig Michael called 'The Washerwoman', or *Na Mná* in Irish. In the twenties and thirties the reef teemed with red crayfish. Now, as a result of over-fishing, illegal diving and nets, crayfish will soon become an endangered species.

In those days we carried eighty large unwieldy barrel-traps that today would be considered old-fashioned in comparison with modern equipment. Our ropes were fibre grass, which chafed and raised blisters on our hands. Mechanical winches were unheard of in our neck of the trade. When hauling by hand in deep water, all that was required was a strong back and a weak mind. We overcame the chafing somewhat by improvisation, using old part-worn woollen socks as mittens, cutting a hole for the thumb.

Now, what would a fisherman wish to find in a trap? Lobsters and crayfish, of course, but if wishes were lobsters, a fisherman could become a wealthy merchant perhaps. But woe betide, this is not always the case. The worst and most unwelcome freeloader of all is the conger eel, a dangerous powerful marauder causing havoc and disruption to the fishing gear. In those days we didn't have a market for red edible crab, which were most numerous, and are up to the present plentiful.

All the species I have found in tidal rock pools and have already mentioned come as unwelcome guests to dine at the lobsterman's expense. Tonight I will overhaul my lobsterpots, evict unwanted tenants, and replace torn or missing baits. I must use a number of different fish pieces to attract lobster. Salted mackerel is my first choice, but alas, congers love salt mackerel and so I must use other fresh bait like pieces of fat bollan wrasse, which we get in our trammel net; fresh gurnard we get from the trawlers. Small flatfish, any kind of bait, scraps of fish not used for sale; I have tried pieces of meat, and portions of conger eel, and parts of drowned seafowl. Meat seemed to be rejected by the most voracious freeloaders who frequented our lobster table. Now, having prepared our traps, let us set them in the most likely places for the evening, to dusk haul. The lobster is a hermit, but will sally forth if attracted by the smell of bait in twilight.

It was an evening to remember, sixty-five years ago. Jim brought the Island Rover to a gentle stop in shelter of the 'Blue Man', telling me to cast the mooring stone, the great ocean like a millpond. It seemed so unreal, as if all nature was resting. The boat swung gently to the mooring, the only sound the gurgling ebb and flow of the darkening water between the rock fissures in the cave.

We put the kettle on and made ourselves mugs of nice hot tea, with delicious crab claws and slices of boiled crayfish tail, not forgetting homemade bread and butter. It was our usual cheap fare, but this evening, somehow, it seemed special. Then Jim said suddenly, 'We'll lay our head, before we make the last haul.' Ah, but Jim was like Napoleon, who had only to hit the pillow and was gone. The last rays of a declining sun filtered like threads of gold, as if sewn specially, through the Needle's Eye and into the valley of Christ's Saddle, lighting up the ramparts of the old monastery, casting a last soft glow of lingering light along the south face of the rock. I couldn't sleep – perhaps not tired enough to relax – looking up at the old settlement walls and listening to the plaintive calling of roosting kittiwakes, mixed with the lone-call of passing gulls. I could not help thinking of how many beautiful evenings such as this, centuries ago, did the monks of Skellig Michael chant their evensong of prayer in praise of the risen Christ. [...]

Skellig Michael was plundered three times by the Vikings in the ninth century, eventually forcing the decimated order to abandon the rock and build the Priory called Saint Michael's near Horse Island. It is ironic, and interesting also, to note that what the Danes failed to achieve in the ninth century, Elizabeth I and Cromwell carried out on a more grandiose scale of total suppression and annihilation.

Skelligs Haul

The last Franciscan monk was captured and beheaded on Scariff Island in Ballinskelligs Bay by Cromwellian forces, bringing monastic Christianity in Ireland to face a grim future. The Ireland of saints and scholars became engulfed in the funeral pyre of Saint Oliver's fire-branding yeomanry. The Priory at Ballinskelligs, known to us today as the Abbey, was razed to the ground and its monks exterminated.

THE SOFT SOUTH WINDS OF SKELLIGS

Skelligs Calling

Never was a day more to my liking than when soft zephyrs sang from the south, blowing gently across the bay of Skelligs whose waters reflected an azure sky adorned with the fluttering white of the gull's wing. It was the threshold of a new summer, a time to be glad. I could feel the life-giving energy of the great ocean, which seemed to enter my very being, calling nostalgically, 'come away ... come away ...'

Glittering rays of morning sun sparkled, spilled and splashed from wavelet to wavelet and onto the back of a slow heaving billow that arose lazily from the depths of a mighty bosom. Lesser gulls wearing white aprons and little black caps, were scattered like 'sea daisies' across the blue-green fields of the bay. Some birds seemed to hang suspended above the waters, their wings a special whiteness unlike the whiteness of snow – a colour which stood out to me and could be seen flashing against a background of blue. Even away in the distance their wings seemed like a glint of white lightning in the sky. Black guillemots and razorbills called in shrill voice, singing or composing poems, diving and reappearing from the spume white froth, their bills laden with silver sprat.

The Soft South Winds of Skelligs

On a day such as this could be heard the music of the ocean, the deep throated, husky laugh of that fickle monarch of the deep, the sea god Poseidon, who might fume and fluster into a raging tempest or wear the smile of an infant in the cradle of a May morning.

As the sail filled with a belly full of freshful fragrance, I could feel the tautening of the canvas when the little boat comes alive, leaning her shoulder against the sudden rush of water from her bow wave, leaving a furrow in her streaming wake like a ploughshare in the blue field of the bay.

Congregations of screaming Arctic terns with scissor-pointed wings swooped, plunged and dived for their share in the fruits of the kingdom, where myriads of silver sprat had surfaced, much to their excited delight.

Puffins with their multi-coloured beaks, like circus clowns breaking the water, and little auks and crossbills all feasted at nature's free table, provided for their survival.

Little white clouds like puffballs of thistledown danced ballet across the blue ceiling of the sky. All things alive, and life in all things: praise the Lord for the resurgence of life I felt around me and in my very soul that morning when the soft south winds sang across the bay of Skelligs.

The molten mirror of the sun trundled its fiery wheel across the southern sky, climbing the ladder of infinity and marking the milestone of yet another day. The grey-blue rock of the holy hermits, Skellig Michael, standing sentinel by the Kerry headlands came into view, as we swept by the wild head of Bolus out into open sea, where the south wind took on a more lively singing note, causing the boat to dance and increase in speed, tossing her bow over little hummocks of water which laughed and sparkled in her sea way, throwing white blossoms of spray aboard as if to bless her.

Out here all things lived. Ronan the seal played and revelled in the churning surf. An ugly, hook-beaked cormorant pointed its tail feathers heavenwards disappearing beneath the green waters. Manx shearwaters skimmed the surface. Together with the swallow-like flight of the grey fulmar, the great solan goose, mighty bird of the Atlantic, flew towards Little Skellig, bearing a long streamer of bladder wrack in its great beak, the building material of a new nest, in expectation of this year's offspring. Little dolphins puffed and played, racing alongside, looping, bending and curving their sleek forms, perhaps in wonderment of man and his little boat.

On a morning such as this what would I wish for? Swallow wings! Yes, swallow wings, wished for by a mere mortal who would fain divest himself of all earthly inhibitions.

I have looked upon the great water asleep like a smiling infant in a cradle, only to awaken to a rosy dawn to watch white horses charging across the bay. I have witnessed sunsets leaving a golden staircase painted on the wave, leading to a flaming crown of molten gold hanging momentarily on the horizon. I can only say – who is the artist? If it be you, oh God, then thank you!

PLACENAMES OF THE SKELLIGS SHORE

Skelligs Calling

Placenames, like old family heirlooms, should be treasured and stored in the archives of our educational institutions, and revealed to our students from time to time. Placenames are not new: most of our names go back to before the advent of Christianity. Some names have deep roots in history, telling of battles, heroic deeds, mythical warriors, invasions, pagan ritual, etc.

Placenames of the Skelligs Shore

The placenames I wish to present to the reader belong to the rock-bound coast of South Iveragh. Names of caves, reefs and cliffs which I took from my father and mother, I now take to be part of my heritage. Perhaps they were unaware of the legacy they were handing down, and I'm afraid a wealth of information is covered by the grave slab.

On the headland of Scariff Island, a reef comes up out of the deep to a height of sixty feet above sea level. Because of their natural formation, they appeared like a group of wooden wedges driven into the sea. The Irish name for the reef is *Na Deanncacha* – the Scariff Wedges. Scariff Island takes its name from the Irish word *garbh*, meaning 'rough or wet territory'.

The first cave on the face of Scariff headland is called *Cuas na nDrisleoga*, 'The Cave of the Briars'. Why briars should grow on the barren exposed windswept cliff is beyond me.

The next cave, *Cuas an Chopair*, takes its name from a blue-green vein of copper ore evident on the rock face from the top of the cliff to under the sea. The copper cave lends its name to the geology of the island. The next point is an overhanging cliff called in Irish *An Cromán* – 'The Hip'; in human terms it could mean the quarter. The next cave is called *Cuas an tSolais* – 'The Cave of Light'. The rock formation is like a one-arch bridge built against the cliff; the light tends to shine through the eye of the arch, hence its name. The exact same rock formation happens on the north-west side of the Small Skellig, with the very same bridge structure, and light. Although twelve miles apart, the Great Artist, it is apparent, worked on both projects simultaneously, using time, erosion, wind and water as the tools of His trade.

On the north side, near the middle of the island, the rock face slopes gently down to the water's edge, making it easy to go ashore. This hollow is called *Clais na nÉamh*, and would mean 'The Hollow of the Groans', or it may refer to the word *naomh*, and mean 'The Hollow of the Saints'. Perhaps it has something to do with a giant's grave on the cliff top. The next cave is *Cuas an Bháid* – 'The Boat Cave'. Then we have *Bealach Scarbh*, the gap between Deenish Island and Scariff Island; 'Deenish' comes from the Irish words *dubh*, 'black', and *inis*, 'island', hence Black or Brown Island.

The island itself has a large area of barren rock, only a few acres of grazing land, and a small pebble beach. A family lived there until the Great War in 1914. A reef on the eastern tip of Deenish has a strange name – *Na Glaibhinní*. Some say the word has a connection to the French *'glaive'* for 'broadsword'.

Coming across to the headland on the southern side of Ballinskelligs Bay, there stands *Ceann Muice*, 'Hog's Head'. The reef, a few cable lengths outside the nose of the Hog, is called *Magairle na Muice*, or 'The Pig's Testicles'. Two other rocks near the cliff face are known as *An Seanduine* and *An tSeanbhean*, 'The Old Man' and 'The Old Woman'. A cave on the south side is *Cuas an Ghabhair*, 'The Goat's Cave'. Two other caves are *Cuas Mór*, 'The Large Cave', and *Cuas Beag na Muice*, 'The Little Pig's Cave'. It is interesting to see evidence of the Ice Age on the headland. Large square blocks of stone weighing several tons sit precariously on the bare green fields on the edge of the cliff as if dropped from the sky.

The word 'Reen' is from the Irish word *rinn*, denoting a reef, and is used in general, being applied to townlands such as Reenard, Reenroe, Rinneen, etc. The next point east of Hog's Head is called Rinneen Point, and the curve of the shoreline is named *Lúb an Rinnín*, 'The Loop of Rinneen'. 'The Point of the Reeds' stands out on the eastern corner of the loop – *Pointe na mBiorraí*, meaning 'thatching reeds or bulrushes'.

Next comes Rinneen Strand. Under the townland of Rinneen is *Trá na Spáinneach*, 'The Spanish Strand', and the rock in front is named *Carraig Oisín*, 'Oisín's Rock' of Celtic mythology. Oisín was spirited to the Land of Youth by Niamh Chinn Óir on her fairy steed. A nice name for a rock, but I was disappointed to learn that more than one Oisín's Rock can be found on the southern coast of Ireland.

Next in line is 'The Red Cliff', *An Fhaill Dhearg*, and the rock that stands in front of Waterville village is *Carraig Éanna*, which is linked in history with the coming of the Milesians, where it is said Ír and Éanna, both sons of Milesius, came ashore. Waterville is a name given to the village by the Normans, and later by the Palatine planters. The original name, *An Coireán*, 'the whirlpool', or 'weir', from which it is derived, is the correct old placename.

Continuing north along 'Inny Strand', *Tráigh na hAoine*, there is a submerged reef called 'The Blue Boys'. The old place name is *Na Fir Ghorma* [The Blue Men]. Then we have the townland of *Muiríoch*, meaning 'land near a beach or a strand'. It has a long stretch of sand dunes; with the placename *Corcacha an Mhuirígh* – 'Sand Dunes or Marshes'. Next is *Béal Átha an Inne*, 'The Mouth of the River Inny Ford'. On the north bank of the ford we have a two-mile stretch of beach running parallel to the Emlagh townlands. The word in Irish is *Imleach*, meaning 'on the rim, edge, margin or border'; in this case the townlands bordered the sea: *Imleach na Muc* ('of the pigs'), *Imleach Draighneach* ('of the sloe tree / blackthorn'), *Imleach Mór* ('the big emlagh').

Part of the beach is *Tráigh na Sasanach*, referred to in history as 'The Englishmen's Garden', where an armed force was repulsed and defeated by the Irish peasantry when Sir Richard Denny failed to seize by force the local herds of cattle at the order of Queen Elizabeth I.

Skelligs Haul

The townland of Rinn Rua, meaning 'the red reef', is adjacent to *Abha an Churraigh*, 'The River of the Wet Bog Land', which enters the sea at the eastern end of *Mill a' Ghóilín* strand, *mill* or *meall* meaning 'a little hill or knoll', and *góilín*, a neck or inlet by the sea. On the west we have *Cloch an Chófra*, meaning 'the rock resembling a trunk or a box'. Then we come to the first of the caves on the *Dún Géagáin* side of Ballinskelligs Bay, *dún* meaning 'a fort or fortress', but there remains a void in folklore as to who Géagán was or represented. Perhaps *géagán* here simply indicates an arm of the sea, referring to no one in particular.

The first cliff-face with a little boat cove is called *Faill an Rois*, which got its name from the wild flax – *an líon bréagach*; *bréagach* means 'not true flax'; *ros* means 'fairy flax'. Next is 'Hector's Point', *Pointe Hector*, which got its name from a Scottish family who settled there in the seventeenth century. Then comes *Cuas an Airgid*, where the pirate ship *Hercules* was wrecked with its 'silver' cargo.

Farther west is 'The Otter's Cave', *Cuas an Mhadra Uisce*, and 'The Cave of the Brown Sea Algae', *Cuas an tSleabháin*. (*Sleabhán* is a brown, edible seaweed.) Around the corner is 'The Cave of the Chough', which is related to the crow family, hence the name in Irish – *Cuas na Cáige*.

Now we arrive at Ballinskelligs Strand, which in olden times carried the name of *Tráigh an Ghleanntáin*. At its eastern end is the *Bearna Dhearg*, which had a place in folklore, telling of a nocturnal ghostly equestrian who galloped furiously along the hard, sandy beach on moonlit nights, the beating of hooves echoing in the night air. The old tale referred to him as *Marcach na Bearna Deirge*, 'The Rider of the Red Gap'. Part of the mossy green beach running westward bore a very ancient placename, *Cnocán na mBuachaillí*, 'The Knoll of the Boys', where the clash of the ash and the laughter and support for the invisible sporting boys, called the *slua sí* or 'fairy host', were heard.

Cnocán na mBuachaillí – what a pity we do not hear them play anymore.

Near the ruins of the old monastic abbey, the Priory, from which the parish takes its name, *An Phriaracht*, otherwise known as Ballinskelligs Abbey (*Mainistir Mhichíl*), was occupied by monks of Skellig Michael as early as the eighth century. Owing to severe coastal erosion at this point, many old placenames have vanished and are now no longer to be seen as points of identification. Gone is the pebble strand we called the *Bréitse* – 'The Pebble Foreshore'; gone is the *Coinigéar-Conneigire* – 'Rush-grown Beach'; gone is the *Cusbae / Cusbao* – 'Calm Tidal Lagoon'; gone is *Bearna na gCorp* – entrance to the Abbey graveyard where the dead were left to be buried in 1847. Gone too is the *Seanphóna*, 'The Old Pound', a place for keeping trespassing cattle or cattle whose owners refused to pay their dues to the monastery, and *Púicín na gCeann*, 'The Place of the Skulls'.

Several acres of land with these placenames have disappeared from the local scene during my lifetime because of constant erosion by the sea. This is why I wish to place on record many old placenames that have been lost or forgotten in the passage of time.

We will now go across Ballinskelligs Harbour to 'Horse Island', *Oileán na gCapall*. Why it was called Horse Island I do not know, except that we have other islands on the coast of Ireland which carry the same name. Two families, the Barrys and the Fitzgeralds, occupied the island until the late fifties. The land was poor and exposed to the harsh weather conditions, especially in wintertime. It was no longer possible to keep in step with modern amenities on the mainland.

The people have marched on into a new technological world, but the Irish placenames of centuries remain behind as a memorial to their Gaelic culture. We have *Cois an Oileáin* – 'The Foot of the Island'; *An Banc Bán* – 'The

Skelligs Haul

White Sandbank'; *An Drom* – 'The Back of a Place or a Knoll'; *Lochán na nDonnán* – 'Pool of the Rockling'; *Cuaisín an Ghrin* – 'Little Cave of the Gravel'; *Leac an tSaighne* – 'Flagstone of the Seine Net'.

On the south side of the island we find also a wealth of Irish names like *Leac na bhFachán* – 'Flagstone of the Periwinkles', *Cuas na Leacach* – 'Cave of the Flagstones', *Cuas an tSéideacháin*, an underwater cavern that ejects the seawater violently from its entrance. Next, we have *Pointe an Fhionnaidh*, 'Fur Point', perhaps because it is a favourite place for sea otters that come ashore to clean and dry their fur. *Clais an Locháin, Clais Rua, Pointe Buí* denote 'The Hollow of the Little Rock Pool', 'The Brown Hollow' and 'The Yellow Point'.

On the western head of Horse Island is a detached rock called *Na Fiacla*, 'The Teeth', and a cave called *An Cuas Mór*, 'The Big Cave', where the grey stork makes a nesting place. *Carraig an Phollóig*, 'Pollack Rock', and *Céim*, meaning 'a step', are nearby. Some of the island's fields also have names, such as *Páircín*, 'Little Park', *An Stráice Caol*, 'The Narrow Streak Field', and *Páirc an Tobair*, meaning 'The Field of the Well'.

The island sound is called *Bealach an Oileáin*. On the north side is the townland of Reen (*Rinn*), meaning 'a reef or stony ground'. The cliff-face extends westward to Bolus Headland, and around into Saint Finan's Bay to Valentia. The great cliffs stand in unbroken sequence, wild and imposing in splendour, on the other hand, awesome and formidable.

The cliffs I have become familiar with during my life as a fisherman were known to me only by Irish placenames, which go back to our Gaelic ancestors. Some placenames have baffled historians and experts as to their meaning. Perhaps rocks were named before books were written. One of the many caves on the Reen-side is *Cuas Elinore*. Who

Elinore was is not known, a lover of some poet, no doubt. Then we have the headland called *Cloigeann an Chrainn* – meaning 'Head or Skull of the Wild Cats'.

Several caves take names suggested by their shape or natural outline, others from bird life, or perhaps some event in history. We have 'The Cave of the Peat', *Cuas na Móna*, *Cuas na gColúr*, 'Cave of the Pigeons'; *Carraig an Staighre*, a cliff-face with a perfect stair formation, *Cuas an Iallait*, 'Cave of the Saddle', *Cuas na Gaoithe*, 'Cave of the Wind', *Creatlach*, 'Headland', *An Chráiteach*, meaning that a tormented choppy sea was usually experienced when passing by the head.

Two rocks face the entrance to Boolakeel Strand; one is the *Gamhnach*, meaning 'a milch cow', and the other is *An Mheadar*, meaning 'the churn'. *Cuas na Léime*, 'The Cave of the Leap' is so called in folklore as it is said a person escaped from his pursuers by leaping across the chasm. Several old names apply to rocks and reefs near the ancient townland of *Cill Rialaig*. The real meaning of the Irish name is only a matter of conjecture. The answer is blowing in the wind. It was home to Seán Ó Conaill, storyteller extraordinaire, who told stories to himself in the fields when his audience diminished.

Another name from the past is *Ceann an Aonaigh*, 'The Headland of the Fair', or *Aonach*, no doubt going back to the druids. Overlooking the headland is a *cathair* with ogham symbols. Another reef is named *Scoth na hEaglaise*, whose derivation or origin has faded from memory. Nearby is a rock called *An Scéalaí*, 'The Storyteller'. When certain signs of surf or currents were seen near the rock, it meant the rock was giving a weather forecast, telling a story of the weather.

Carraig na bhFiach, 'The Rock of the Raven'; *Leac na mBeathach*, 'The Flagstone of the Good Yield'. '*Beatha*' in this case meant that an angler fishing from *Leac na mBeathach* would be rewarded. *Cuas an Daimh*, 'The Cave of the Ox', *Cuas an tSeaga*, 'The Cave of the Cormorants', *Faill an Reithe*, 'The Cliff of the Ram', *Carraig Dhaingean na nGabhar*, 'The Rocky Fortress of the Goats': all these caves and many more are to be seen on the cliffs leading westward to Bolus Head. I mention only interesting features such as 'The Pedlar's Box', *Bosca an Pheidhléara*, a cube of polished rock tottering on the lip of a precipice; and 'Pipín's Cave', called *Poll Pipín*: Pipín in local folklore used the cave as a hideout to evade the authority of the law; *Boilg Thomáis*, The Reef of Thomas, and the great sunken reef on the head of Bolus – *An Charraig Shuncáilte*, *bólus* meaning 'a cowherb'.

The cliffs between Bolus and Duchealla headlands are steep and precipitous, wildly beautiful and still exuding a savage pristine picture of an era when both time and matter merged. Within this kingdom of surging mighty Atlantic sea is found a haven of refuge to many creatures – herds of grey Atlantic seals and seabirds – that survive and renew the order of their species, year after year, responding to some inborn power which I, myself, for want of a better explanation, call instinct. *Dúchealla*, means 'the black cells': the origin of what the black cells were is unknown.

Now I will pass by *Dúchealla* headland and enter Saint Finan's Bay. The first placenames on the starboard side are 'Cave of the Bald Knoll', *Cuas an Mhaoláin*, then the *Licín Rua* or the 'Brown Flat Rock'. Next is a rock feature called *Láimh Cláir*. I do not know the origin of this very old name meaning perhaps 'a wooden hand'.

Then we come to a series of teeth-like rocks barely showing above the surface of the sea, in off-circular formation, resembling rock pools. The apt Irish name given here is *Na hUmaracha*, meaning 'The Wells', a place to be given a wide berth by the night fisherman. Then we have the 'Devil's Cliff', or *Faill an Deamhain*, where it is said in folklore that a man from Ballinskelligs wrestled with the demon on the cliff top. There is also the 'Cave of the Descent', or [The Cave] 'Resembling a Slipway', *Cuas an Fháin*, and 'The Slender Reef', *An Rinn Chaol*. Next we have a nasty, sunken rock called *Builg an Phriósúin*, 'The Prison Rock'; then *Ceann Garbh*, meaning 'The Rough Point', and *Rinn an Chaisleáin* – *caisleán* meaning 'castle'. Perhaps the reef gets its name from a landlord's eighteenth-century house on the nearby townland, now a ruin.

Then we have *Leac na mBan*, the flat rock where it is said three women were drowned (the date is not known) while collecting limpets, hence, 'The Women's Flagstone'.

Under the townland of Tooreen, meaning *tuairín* or turret, we have 'The Cave of Paddy Bhuí', and *Cuas an tSrutháin*, 'Cave of the Stream', where the four-masted sailing ship, the *Nielsen Hauge*, was wrecked in the nineteenth century with a full cargo of pine wood. The ship was in perfect condition, all sails set, no living person on board except for a scrawny cat. Many such ships were abandoned in the Atlantic in mysterious circumstances. Under the townland of *Athghort*, meaning 'a garden being tilled continually', we have a little corner-strand of rounded stones called *Trá Leagaigh*. I do not know the meaning of the name, except at this point a cairn of stones is seen in memory of a priest who, according to folklore, was slain there. To the north of this is Keel Strand, *Trá na Cille*, also known as Saint Finan's Bay, a wild Atlantic beach with high-rolling breakers, suitable for surfboarding but dangerous for swimmers, owing to violent undertow.

The townland of Faha, *Faich* – denoting an even, grassy strip of ground without humps – was a playing pitch in early writing. Underneath Faha the cliff-face is much lower. Here we find lovely old Irish names like *Dúna* and *Púicín an Tobac* and *Caladh an Bháid*. Reaching westward are the pleasant slatey cliffs of Moyrisk, *Maothroisc*, until we come upon Puffin Island sound, immortalized in a poem by the Iveragh poet Tomás Rua Ó Súilleabháin. The sound is called *Bealach na nÉamh*, 'The Gap of Sighs'. *Oileán na gCánóg*, Puffin Island, is now a national bird sanctuary. *Ceann Dubh*, or 'Black Head', stands high and deep at its western end. Two and a half miles west is the bald, lone rock of *Lomán*, bastardized as Lemon Rock. *Lomán* comes from the word *lom* meaning 'bare'.

I owe a special debt of gratitude to my parents, who spoke the ancestral language to us when we were children. The music of the tongue mixed naturally with the growing pains of our adolescence, giving us the status of native Irish speakers.

I remember listening spellbound to my mother telling me the story about 'The Island of the Fairy Women', or 'The Foolish Wife and the Golden Shoe'. My father, on the other hand, bestowed on me the wealth of these resonant Irish placenames that are fast vanishing from the spoken language of a new generation.

THE RED-HAIRED FRIAR OF SCARIFF

Skelligside

The ancient Irish name of Saint Finan's Glen in the parish of Prior was *Gleann Orcáin*, the glen of the wild boars. Here was born Francis O'Sullivan, who later became a priest of the Order of Saint Francis. He and his brother Dónall, a layman, fought against Cromwell in Munster. The priest succeeded in collecting money and arms, including four cannons, where others had failed to obtain help. His brother Daniel was also famous throughout Iveragh. They belonged to the '*Ceann Eiche*' or 'Horse Head' Sullivans, a small clan which still survived in South Iveragh. Folklore tells that Father Francis was head of the Order of Saint Francis at the time he went to fight against Cromwell. He was known as *an Bráthair Rua*, the Red-Haired Friar of Scariff.

Scariff Island in Ballinskelligs Bay contains three hundred and sixty-five acres and once supported three families. It was good land for sheep-rearing and cattle, well sheltered on the south, and had plenty of fresh water and good fertile soil for cultivation. It had one terrible disadvantage: no beach or landing facilities, only the dangerous, slanting cliff face. Only in good weather could contact be made between island and mainland.

On this island fastness Father O'Sullivan sought refuge. The country and his beloved Iveragh was overrun by the Redcoats, with Cromwell loose upon the land. The spectre of his bloodstained sword seemed to hang over the people as a fearful symbol of his authority. An edict was issued to army officers that all Roman Catholic priests living in the area or anyone who gave them shelter were to be hunted down and put to the sword. Eventually the Red-Haired Friar was captured by a party of Redcoats searching the Island. He was decapitated on the spot with a sword-swipe across the mouth, delivered by an officer of the Cromwellian garrison billeted on Valentia Island. On Saint John's Eve, 1658, 'his lifeblood stained the heather'. (The patriot and Gaelic poet Piaras Feiritéir was hanged at Gallows Hill, Killarney, a few years earlier.)

The upper portion of Father O'Sullivan's skull remained in the possession of the O'Connell family of Derrynane, who kept it as a treasured relic until it disappeared from the house, which now belongs to the nation. It is said that the relic returned mysteriously by parcel post bearing a British postmark some years later.

Alas! Friar of Scariff, who is left to pray for you? Who will remember the part you played? Your dirge will be the pounding surge of the grey Atlantic billows, forever thundering a protest on the rocks beneath *Cuas an tSolais*, the Cave of Light, and the plaintive calling of the great gull wheeling the sky above *Clais na nÉamh*, the Hollow of the Groans.

COASTGUARDS AND SHIPWRECK
Skelligs Calling

The Coastguard Station was part of rural life along the entire coastline of Ireland. Built towards the end of the eighteenth century, the stations flourished during the nineteen hundreds and were manned by a reduced personnel until the end of the 1914 world conflict. Vitally important in the eyes of the British Empire and the sea lords of the Admiralty, they were closely linked on the Iveragh coast at Waterville, Ballinskelligs, Portmagee, Valentia, Cahersiveen and Kells.

The Ballinskelligs Station situated at Reen consisted of five residential buildings in a terrace, a boathouse with a slipway and longboat, together with a private residence for the head officer, Captain John McGready. John Harms, Harry Knox and Bob Twomey lived in the married quarters. Their children attended Ballinskelligs National School (opened 1867), where they learned English, in a townland where Irish was the spoken language of the entire peasant population.

According to stories relating to the period, it is evident that Captain McGready was not popular among the people or his men. His rigid observance of the law was known to one and all. Even the most barnacled and battered piece of driftwood was to be regarded as Crown property and therefore surrendered to the Revenue Commissioners. McGready was also known to inflict penalties on men for any laxity of rules.

The ruined monastery of Saint Michael's Abbey was once a seat of learning in the thirteenth century, under the Order of Augustinian Canons, until it was despoiled during the regimes of Elizabeth and Cromwell. This lonely, ruined, roofless sanctuary by the sea became the first Christian burial ground in Ballinskelligs, with its Romanesque, fire-blackened walls and its Gothic bell-tower, full of crude strange structural tombs, where an erring coastguard would be detailed to stand watch at the sudden whim of a strict captain.

A story was told of a young man who, having never endeared himself to Captain McGready, was ordered to stand guard within the ruins, one dark and stormy night, as a precaution against smuggling. The young coastguard standing beside a tomb during his lonely vigil observed what he thought was movement somewhere nearby. Getting down on all fours, the coastguard crawled around in a circle until, to his surprise, he saw a figure of a man in close proximity in front, standing still, whom he recognized as his Captain. Jumping forward, he thrust the barrel of his carbine between the kidneys of his superior officer, shouting, 'Don't move or you're dead.' John McGready didn't panic, saying, 'Don't shoot, Tommy. I only came to keep you company,' which of course wasn't true. This was the last time a man was detailed to stand watch in the ruined Abbey.

Coastguards were mostly naval reservists, or men approaching the end of their service, trained in the Nelsonian tradition in the use of firearms, swordplay with cutlass, how to engage in hand-to-hand combat and how to repel a boarding party.

Paddy Haren's tavern was one of the licensed premises in Ballinskelligs at the time. The other was Paddy Ó Céitinn's,

Skelligs Haul

'Keating's', in Dungegan. Paddy Haren was a Clare man, and a retired naval officer; hence the coastguards and the local fishermen frequented his bar. Paddy kept a plentiful supply of ship's rum, thick and dark. It was readily available in wooden casks, imported in its purest form. A thimbleful of undiluted black honey would sweep your throat free from all germs and was much sought after by men of the sea.

Old Donal McCarthy drank here also. The old man witnessed the Famine, its aftermath, the years of recovery and the shameful spectacle of faction fighting between cudgel-wielding clans. He too, among others, was expert in the use of the cudgel in self-defence. This art was the equivalent of the cut, thrust and parry of swordplay, as practised in the naval sailing fleet of the time. The faction-fighting clans called this form of self-defence *boiscín*, or 'boskeen'. The so-called shillelagh took the place of the sword. Irish shillelagh-wielders were known to have beaten some swordsmen.

Coastguard Tommy Adams suspected that old Donal was perhaps an expert in the use of the shillelagh as a weapon of self-defence and therefore wished to test the old man's skill. Then came the day when the old man grew tired of Adam's persistent challenging him to fight a duel with cudgels. At last, Donal accepted the challenge. The proprietor of the tavern, Paddy Haren, was appointed the referee. The winner was to be the contestant who first made bodily contact three times. He would receive a half bottle of ship's rum, the loser a quart of ale. Each man was to have the approved shillelagh of equal design. A day was appointed and the floor of the tavern cleared of furniture. The bout itself was to be kept secret, in case the law would frown on such an activity.

Old McCarthy, divested of his jacket and homespun gansey, rolled up his sleeves and carefully pulled his

Coastguards and Shipwreck

stockings over the hem of his frieze trousers, before taking off his heavy brogues and stepping nimbly on his vamps. With Donal's scant, grey locks and beady blue eyes, he performed a short ritual dance, twirling his shillelagh like some Zulu warrior. The coastguard explained very sincerely to the old man that he only wanted to ascertain the truth of whether the Irish stick-wielders were skilled in the art of fencing. McCarthy replied, '*B'fhearr dhuit ciall a bheith agat,*' meaning, 'Better for you to be sensible.'

Paddy Haren, who was also a swordsman, bringing the two unequal protagonists together, advised them to show their skill in imitating sword play and, drawing a line on the floor, he called the word, 'Advance!' following in raised voice, 'On guard,' then the final word, 'Go.'

Old Donal danced like a paper doll and it was soon evident that he was under pressure from a very skilled adversary, a product of naval training. As yet an opening for a touch had not presented itself. Old McCarthy was backed into a corner. Then it happened: the knob of Donal's shillelagh made contact over the coastguard's left ear. Tommy Adams winced under the sudden, stinging impact, only to receive two more resounding taps in quick succession, directly in line over the left ear.

Paddy Haren stepped in, declaring the contest over. Adams shook the old man's hand, who remarked, '*Ná dúirt mé leat ciall a bheith agat,*' meaning, 'I told you have sense.' Three lumps like thrushes' eggs began to grow over Tommy's ear, to which he applied cold water. This convinced him that cudgel fighting and fencing derived from the same art. The above account I heard from my cousin, old John Fitzgerald of Horse Island.

The coastguard's long boat was thirty-five feet overall by seven feet beam, propelled by oar and sail, built to endure and be seaworthy in severe conditions. The boat and gear were always tested during a regular monthly drill. During the last century of sail, many fine ships were abandoned at sea, several for unknown reasons, with full cargoes and sound rigging. Ships abandoned in the Atlantic drifted on to the south-west coast of Ireland, several foundering on rock-bound inlets of South Kerry.

One such ship was a four-masted barque, the *Nielsen Hauge*. With full rig, it was seen to sail slowly from the west into the outer reaches of Saint Finan's Bay. On the second day the wind dropped, leaving the ship becalmed, only to drift aimlessly, 'As idle as a painted ship / Upon a painted ocean'. It was not unusual to see a ship becalmed, especially when having plenty of sea room. Towards the evening of the third day, a wind came up from a south-westerly direction, filling the idle sails of the becalmed vessel. Suddenly the sails billowed with a strengthening breeze, driving the vessel on an erratic course towards the rock-bound Finan's Bay. People on the shore, becoming suspicious, prompted local fishermen to launch a boat. The fishermen rowed within hailing distance of the ship but no life was observed on deck. The westerly wind had grown to gale force, making it urgent that the fishermen return to shore. By this time the ship had drifted towards the high craggy cliffs of Tooreen, *Tuairín*.

The people of Saint Finan's Glen who watched from the cliff-side saw the stately barque drift towards her last resting place, the kelp floor of *Cuas an Tuairín*, in ten fathoms of clear Atlantic water. How often did she bring joy to a sailor's heart, running down her easterlies under full canvas, or bounding across the line with a bone in her teeth? It was a sad sight surely, without a master's confident, gentle touch on her helm. The hand to steer her safely through the perils of the mighty ocean had now forsaken her. *Bád gan stiúr nó cú gan eireaball*, meaning 'a ship without a rudder, or a hound without a tail'. No lively crew to trim her down or man the capstan. She was rocking and rolling, drifting helplessly, like a dead seabird, caught in the froth of an ocean current. A westerly, long, rolling swell developed, which increased with a flood tide.

Inch by inch, the once stately barque drifted, until at last the top rail of the *Nielsen Hauge* seemed to caress the toothed crag, her cross trees now and then touching the cliff-face. A long, rolling swell, carrying a white curl on its lip, caught her amidships, causing violent contact with the more shallow ledges. With each rise and fall, a grinding, creaking, sickening sound of wood cracking developed. The crashing of spars, the tearing of shrouds, as she listed, showing a gaping tear below and above her water line, refusing to founder, because of her cargo of pine. She continued to break up, spewing her great cargo, until the waters of the cove were covered with planks of all dimensions, great beams, trebles and scantlings. The tip of the main mast remained visible for some days. A sad reminder of how a ship can die.

As shades of evening darkened, the local folk tried to salvage some of the valuable planks by working constantly into the night, knowing that on the morrow their efforts would be restricted by servants of the Crown. It was, at most, a desperately hazardous task. Men could be seen standing on dangerous rock shelves with casting hooks, gaffs, and ropes, using any method to salvage a plank, risking their lives time and again, enveloped in the obscurity of a dashing drenching murky sea spray. Willing hands worked unceasingly, pulling on ropes attached to planks. They hid the wreckage among furze and rocks on the nearby hillside, away from the prying eyes of John McGready, who arrived on the scene the next day, when news of the shipwreck had reached him at *Rinn* Coastguard Station. He immediately placed the salvage operation under the watchful eyes of his men, armed with carbines, making it clear to the natives that anyone found guilty of concealing or taking planks for their own use would be prosecuted and suffer severe penalties. A local man called Murphy was appointed to keep record of the amount each person had salvaged. They would receive only a pittance for their labours.

The coastguards kept weary vigil during the wet foggy nights, which very much hampered the strict surveillance they were to observe. Often what was salvaged by day seemed to mysteriously disappear under cover of darkness. My father, helped by his cousins, the Fentons of Coom, together with other neighbours, concealed a goodly amount of the splendid pitch pine under the deep heather and bracken of the hillside. The work required Herculean effort on their part: such was the desire of the people to outwit the servants of the Crown!

To many people the windfall of the *Nielsen Hauge* became a godsend. The timber wrested from the sea and from the Realm, however illicit it might seem, helped to repair the roofs of the old thatched hovels of that period.

Some years previous another fine ship called the *Menthaur*, laden with a cargo of dried fruit from Greece, mostly raisins, packed in wooden boxes, was seen by the Coastguards, drifting dangerously close to the reef, called in Irish, *Dingeacha na Scairbhe*, 'the Scariff Island Wedges'. The reef resembles a set of large stone wedges, as if driven in by some giant hand. On perceiving the plight of the hitherto unknown vessel, John McGready and his 'Jolly Tars' wasted no time. Launching the long boat, they were soon seen pulling lustily across the bay, each man swinging to his oar with muscular precision, the Captain himself at the tiller exhorting his crew to put their backs into it, 'with a heave ho, my hearties'. On reaching the *Menthaur* and having hailed her, they decided to put a crew on board, finding no sign of human life, except a cat so scrawny and pitiful, perhaps using the last hours of its ninth life!

To John McGready and his crew the ship presented a valuable boon in prize money. Therefore, they set about sailing the ship across the bay. Helped by a southerly breeze, under the shelter of Horse Island, Captain John brought the vessel into safe anchorage in seven fathoms of water. It seemed so simple an operation to a trained crew, the task of dropping anchor, but some unknown fate decided otherwise. As the heavy chain started its run, a tangled loop of cable formed a knot, unyielding to any frantic effort of John McGready or his men. The hawse port remained totally obstructed, preventing the anchor from reaching the floor of the harbour. The *Menthaur* drifted astern, helped to what seemed her inescapable doom, by the same southerly breeze that seemed so favourable only moments before. In a very short time the ship grounded between the teeth of *Rinn Dubh* and *Boilg Anders*. As the tide ebbed, the *Menthaur* lay on her beam end across the reef, spiked to her last resting-place, thus depriving the coastguards of prize money.

The Revenue Commissioners took the cargo and all things moveable, leaving only the hull, which was covered with copper sheeting. The local peasantry, working under the cover of darkness, removed some of the valuable sheeting and sold it to scrap dealers which in turn infuriated Captain McGready who placed an immediate armed guard on the wreck when the tide was out. Despite his strict administration of the law, little pieces of the stranded hull kept on disappearing until large holes appeared and the copper was no longer visible. Helped by a winter storm, the hull of the *Menthaur* became a total wreck, in which the authorities held no further interest.

Some years prior to 1847, another crewless ship was driven ashore at a place called *Bun na Féithe*, 'Bottom of the Marsh', on Inny Strand. I heard local historians refer to it by its cargo as *Long an Ghráinne Bhuí*. The vessel carried in its hold a cargo of Indian corn from the Americas. The authorities were unable to remove the entire cargo, owing to the short time available to them, before the hull became completely engulfed by the bed of quicksand on which she had landed.

Some years later, when grim famine stalked the land, South Iveragh was no exception. A large peasant population struggled to survive starvation; hoards of emaciated people roamed the roads of Munster suffering the gnawing pains of hunger.

People were drawn to the foreshore, the strands and the beaches; a crude net, a little boat or even a fishing line would make the difference between survival and an early grave. Because of the edible shellfish, groups were seen to forage among the rock pools as the tide receded, even edible seaweeds were boiled and eaten, anything to allay and slake the terrible hunger. One day some local fishermen in the course of conversation mentioned how welcome a shipload of Indian corn would be, like *Long an Ghráinne Bhuí* that lay beneath the sand at *Bun na Féithe*, with most of its precious cargo still in its hold.

Someone suggested that a portion of the cargo might still be free from dampness. In this case, hunger became the mother of urgency. Without further ado, a group of local men armed with long iron rods converged on the sand at *Bun na Féithe*. They began probing the sand in the place where the vessel was supposed to lie.

A number of days elapsed before finding the wreck under six feet of sand. She was lying on her beam-ends, very near the high-water mark of a spring tide. This was favourable for the excavation of sand when the moon was on the wane with slack tides. A throng of near starving people commenced to shovel away the sand. The prospect of finding food uppermost in their minds, they worked feverishly, keeping the area clear of water, digging canals and bailing with buckets.

Floating Mines

At last, to the great excitement of the workers, the bulging planks of a wooden ship became exposed. It was then the local tradesmen took over; the blacksmith, the cooper and carpenter, using sharp tools cut a large hole into the hull of *Long an Ghráinne Bhuí*. A medical man gave advice about gas or contaminated grain. A large cheer went up when it was discovered that a goodly portion of the grain was still dry and free from damp. If boiled for gruel, it was found fit to eat; a people who were hungry were not choosy about the menu.

The coastguard barracks are now firmly entrenched in the past. Only roofless ruins to remind us, standing as visible evidence of an imperial colonization. *Nielsen Hauge*, the *Menthaur*, *Long an Ghráinne Bhuí* and many others become ghost ships of the past that keep on sailing, dipping and appearing on the horizon of my memory, helped by little wavelets from the storytellers of my youth.

FLOATING MINES

Skelligs Calling

Whatever knowledge I have in regard to floating mines comes from the fact of having examined the interior of a device, which the expert rendered harmless. He kindly explained to me its mechanics and how the explosion was triggered. I do not wish to pontificate or set myself up, other than to relate as best I can of my experience as a fisherman and the happenings in my own locality with regard to floating mines.

Floating explosives at sea were much more in evidence during the last war, than that of 1914. The floating mine became a lethal scientific instrument of death and destruction. Many and various were the designs created by the armament engineers of the warring nations, electronic science playing a more significant part in the latter years. Cunning devices such as the magnetic and later the acoustic mine were invented, manufactured and used with deadly accuracy. The magnetic device was sown in the narrow shipping lanes leading to harbours, and in the more important ports. Like mines of the magnetic device, the acoustic mine could be sown from the air in narrow estuaries. The magnetic device was triggered by proximity of the ship's hull, while the acoustic mine was triggered by the throbbing sound of an internal combustion engine or the whirring of an electric turbine.

The most common device was cone-shaped, like a child's spinning top or a giant hen egg. Some mines were five feet in height, weighed five hundred pounds, and had a diameter of fifty inches. The explosive substance, which looked like a type of grey butter, was contained in a separate cylinder of steel, within the interior of the mine and would weigh at least two hundred pounds. Heavy spiral coil steel springs were compressed with nuts and bolts on the explosive chamber to increase its power. The minor detonators, which protruded through the outer shell, called the horns of the mine, were each, in turn, wired to the main detonator and connected to a watertight system of electric spark.

I had occasion to witness a large mine being rendered harmless by an army officer who was qualified to deal with such an emergency. I remember while on our way to the fishing grounds, on the southern approach to Ballinskelligs Bay, we were about to cast our train of mackerel nets, when I was ordered by our captain, who was on the forepart of the boat, on the lookout for signs of mackerel schools, to change course because of some large, partly submerged object directly in front of our line of passage. It was our first sighting of a large mine of German – as we discovered

Floating Mines

at a later date – manufacture. It stood upright in the water, exactly like a spinning top, and kept continually rocking like a child's cradle. Even in the gentle swell it rocked and half spun, bobbing its horned head as if to mock us. A large lifting ring eyebolt topped its umbrella-like pot. It bristled with horns, each at least twelve inches in length.

As night was falling, we waited in the vicinity of the unwelcome infernal intruder, which had strayed and entered our peaceful waters, until we showed its position to Jim Fitzgerald's boat, which was travelling in our direction. Having decided to keep well windward of the troublesome wayfarer, we entered our bay by a different route. We expected to find the mine washed ashore onto one of the local beaches sometime the next day. The wind blew favourably for days on end. Every fisherman and even the Corvette scoured the area to no avail. The local coast watchers and police began to think it was a hoax and that we had invented a tall one. As time went by, we fishermen often discussed among ourselves the disappearance of the mine and came to the conclusion it had to drift ashore locally.

Several weeks passed before the mysterious mine made local news once more. Old men and younger women, the postman, the sergeant of the Garda, the parish priest and his housekeeper, the local butcher, the shopkeeper and the blacksmith who crowned it all with: 'Did you hear the latest? Wasn't he lucky! One belt of the sledge and his ghost would go to heaven so quickly he'd stretch Saint Peter in the door.'

The elusive mine went ashore at high tide on the tip of Bolus Head, where it sat perched on top of a flat rock in a precarious position, with the cliff-face towering above. It was not known for wreckage to be found in this most exposed headland, and how it managed to float into place without exploding baffled the experts. It seems that a local farmer had been searching for a missing sheep, and happening to notice the strange object, he climbed down the cliff-face to investigate. Having inspected the mine, he decided it wasn't a very useful contraption, except for the iron horns of course. Oh, the very thing, they'd make excellent bolts to replace the worn ones on his wooden-frame farm harrow. If only he had a hammer or a sledge. With the help of a piece of rock he managed to bend one bolt a little sideways but failed to dislodge it. He decided to call on his neighbour, Séamus Fada, for the loan of a heavy hammer, some other tools and perhaps a word of advice as well. Séamus Fada was known by one and all to be one of the most knowledgeable men in the locality. You could ask him any question from astronomy to a cure for smelly feet. As for guns and powder and bombs, wasn't he with the Munsters at Mons. Séamus declined point blank to loan his neighbour the hammer but decided instead to accompany him to the scene where the horned monster sat sedately on the only flat rock to be found from there to *Oileán na bhFaoileán*, 'the island of gulls'. Séamus Fada surveyed the mine and recognized immediately the danger of the situation.

'Somebody must have saved you from a sudden death, Seán,' he said. 'If you hit the tip of the bolt that you bent sideways, you'd have no need for the heavy hammer, you'd be judged, damned or sainted by now. I don't like the bristling hairpins on that *biorránach's* head. Come, let's go and report the matter to the coast watchers.'

Some hours later an army officer inspected the uninvited blow-in, which had taken up residence and was sitting smugly like a horned toad on the tip of Bolus Headland. The army officer ordered the area leading to the cliff to be sealed off from the general public, until the mine was examined in more detail. The usual type of mine was of British manufacture but this one was made in Germany.

Floating Mines

Several days elapsed before the experts decided that, owing to being tampered with by Seán, the damaged detonator was on a very delicate hair trigger and would warrant no rough handling. When all was ready, the army laid a wire connected to an explosive charge over the brow of the cliff, which they attached to the mine. Before they pressed the plunger they had ordered the natives to open all doors and windows. A terrible explosion rocked the evening air leaving a yellow white scar on the cliff-face that was visible for many a day.

Some mines broke loose from their moorings. One such mine drifted into our bay, trailing its mooring until finally getting held up on rough ground inshore. A naval corvette destroyed it by gunfire. Some smaller mines were tied in pairs with a spacing wire of many fathoms between them. The bow of the ship would connect with the spacing wire thereby causing a double explosion.

Irish mackerel fishermen were fearful of floating mines not so much of colliding with them in the hours of darkness but of coming into close contact when entangled in their nets. This usually meant cutting away valuable fishing gear and steering clear of any intimate relations with the unwelcome toad. One calm night while hauling mackerel nets near the Skellig Rock, a large mine appeared very close to the side of the mackerel-fishing trawl. A member of the crew delicately manoeuvred the mine clear of the boat's stern with the help of a long wooden handle of a boat hook, while another fisherman kept a light trained on it.

The rock-bound shore of the Iveragh peninsula served as protection against accident by helping to trigger mines that bumped against the cliff-face. It was not unusual to hear the rumble of a loud explosion disturb the peaceful air of the locality, followed by screaming of gulls on the headlands or the sudden stampeding of cattle. On one such occasion, a horse with a loaded creel of peat took fright on a local bogland, ending up in a capsized and wrecked position. The aggrieved farmer, knowing there would never be any form of redress or compensation from the warring empire builders, could only find consolation in consigning them all to hell.

BALLINSKELLIGS CABLE STATION
Skelligs Calling

The first submarine cable was laid from the United States to Ballinskelligs in 1875. The cable was called the D.U.S., an abbreviation for Direct Union States. The station buildings were constructed by a London-based company in about the year 1865. English and Scottish contractors were employed. The buildings were of mass concrete construction and consisted of the main offices, a clock tower and modern living quarters, in an enclosed compound comprising three or four acres. Gardens were attached to each dwelling. The whole area was enclosed by a well-built wall. Spring water was supplied by gravity flow from the base of a hill, about a mile distant. There were septic tanks and a complete sewer system for modern bathrooms, and also plumbing providing hot and cold water. The lighting was provided by a carbide gas plant built on the premises. A wooden church with bell and tower was also built on the compound.

The station had its own fire-fighting equipment, with engine house and pressure pumps to pump water from the sea in case of fire. This equipment was installed by a company called Merryweather of London. There were stables with two horses and a covered wagon with a full-time stableman, a cartage man, a battery man and a man to attend to the lighting system, thereby giving full-time

Ballinskelligs Cable Station

employment to four local people. A cook with four domestic servants was in charge of the mess and kitchens, providing meals for the staff and those operators who lived in the unmarried quarters. The housekeeper was Margaret Shea from Kenneigh near Waterville, and the cook was Mary O'Sullivan from Boolakeel. Michael Sugrue of Dungeagan was the local butcher who supplied the fresh mutton and other meats. The bulk of their vegetables were grown locally.

Their recreation consisted of an up-to-date billiards room and lawns for their tennis club. With their families in residence, the entire group would average eighty to a hundred persons. The place was kept very neat with many gardens, flowerbeds and shrubs. A boathouse on the beach provided shelter for sailing yachts and fishing equipment. The superintendent's residence was in another location apart from the station. It was a modern, three-storeyed English building like that provided for a country squire, with gateways and a driveway. I remember some names of the officials and staff.

Superintendents: Mr Topping; Mr Blenheim; Mr Lloyd. Head Operators: Mr Main (Falkirk); Mr Armstrong (English Midlands); Mr Waterstone; Mr Cobley; Mr Stone; Mr Seekins; Mr Westbrook; Mr Faircloud; Mr McMichael; Mr Ratton. Censors: Mr Spencer; Mr Nash; Mr Higgs; Mr Watson; Mr Moore; Mr Harty; Mr Cornwall; Mr Drum; Mr Sullivan; Mr Keating; Mr Golden; Mr Thompson – resident carpenter; Mr Foil; Mr Broderick; Mr Rickard; Mr W. Goggin (Ballinskelligs) – battery attendant, later transferred to Fanning Island in the Pacific Ocean, where the company maintained another cable station. Mr Sugrue, operator, was a native of Valentia Island. Mr O'Connell and Mr Jerome Sullivan were natives of the locality. Mr O'Connell's son later became the first clerk of Dáil Éireann.

The earliest repair ship involved in cable laying, that I can remember, was a ship called the *Buccaneer*. I heard my father say that a pilot from Valentia named McCrohan would come over land to Ballinskelligs, where a local crew awaited him at the old fishing pier to meet the ship as she rounded into the mouth of Ballinskelligs Bay. My father, being one of the crew, told me how the pilot would sit in the stern and steer them towards the ship and he would chant a little rhyme in rhythm with each oar stroke: 'Pull boys pull, there's smoke off the Bull'; meaning, of course, that he, the pilot, saw the black smoke from her funnels appearing near the Bull Rock. The *Great Eastern* was the ship that laid the cable through the deepest part of the Atlantic, and only came to the mouth of the bay, where the shore end leading to Ballinskelligs beach was connected to the Atlantic through a smaller diameter cable. I remember seeing a ship called the *Colonia* and a smaller inshore repair ship, *Lady of the Isles*. The *Lord Kelvin* was a great four thousand tonner. Other ships of one thousand tons were the *John W. MacKay*, the *George Ward* and the *Marie Louise MacKay*. Those latter-named ships were all used for coastal repair.

A story is told about the day when the first shore end was brought onto the beach in the spring of 1875. The big ship manoeuvred as close to the beach as possible, taking advantage of the high water peak of a spring tide. The cumbersome, heavy cable was coiled onto flat, raft-like boats, which would float into shallow water. Large numbers of peasantry were assembled on the beach, watching the wonder of a transatlantic cable being brought ashore. The foreman in charge of the operation had harnessed two local draught horses to a rope attached to the end of the cable. All went well, until strain was applied to the rope and, helped by a gentle swell, the nearest float to the shore overturned, spilling the coiled cable into six feet of water. At this stage, the horses proved very ineffective because of soft sand. The foreman, being a very astute person, stumbled on another bright idea.

Ballinskelligs Cable Station

Seeing the potent pulling power of the large crowd, he proceeded to bargain with them. Every able-bodied man who would help pull the cable ashore was to be paid two shillings and six pence. He would need forty men, and as an incentive the first man who would lay hands on the cable was to be given a half sovereign in gold. No sooner said than done. The hired men rushed headlong into the broken wave where the cable lay.

One man outstripped them all with a mighty leap and dived into the sea. Grasping the end, he tore it loose from the coil and helped by the rest of the hired team pulled the cable up the sandy beach in front of the cable buildings. True to his word, the foreman paid each person two and six pence, and calling for the man who merited the gold coin, asked for his name and address. The man in question was Denis O'Leary from Ballinskelligs. In presenting him with the coin and holding O'Leary's arm aloft in a gesture of victory, the foreman announced that henceforward the cable would be called 'Cable O'Leary'. The name stuck – not on the cable, but on Denis, who was known as 'the Cable' from then on. The next generation inherited the name and to this day their progeny are referred to as the 'Cable O'Learys'. The family was already famous, being the last to fight the rack-rent bailiffs, the sheriff and the redcoats with pitchforks during their eviction in 1864. I saw pictures of the eviction taken by a photographer, one Mr Cuthbert, who was connected with the construction of the cable company. The pictures, in sepia tones on a glossy tin plate, showed the peasantry of the time in their wretched clothing, barefoot people wearing long unkempt hair. Those noble but crestfallen people were my ancestors.

The station flourished for more than half a century. Many tales were told by old people, who could not understand a word of the clipped English accent and whose means of communication was 'the sweet and kindly' Irish. One of the cable superintendents was a Mr Topping; he kept a huge Saint Bernard. A breed of dog which is usually very docile, this specimen had a ferocious bark and a mean-looking face. In fact, the local people lived in fear of the animal, which was known to the Irish-speaking community as *gadhar mór Topping*, or 'Topping's big dog'.

At that time we had a change of clergymen, a new curate and Parish Priest both at the same time. The curate was a very gentle priest, always speaking about the good influence of the Holy Spirit in our lives. The P.P. by contrast was very gruff and spoke in a booming, threatening voice. One day when the new curate visited our school he asked the children how they liked their new pastors. The teacher wished that the ground would swallow him on hearing one little fellow tell the astonished curate, he had heard his father say that one was like the Holy Ghost and the other had a bark like Topping's dog.

Another old lady, who had but few words of English, told me how she was collecting carrageen moss among the rocks, on the shore near the cable station when she heard a conversation in English between two men. One was the captain of a small steamboat, whose anchor got badly fouled on the newly laid cable close to the shore. The crew of the ship were making frantic efforts to release the anchor, while officials of the cable company stood on the shore. Speaking on a loudhailer, they remonstrated with the captain of the ship, shouting: 'Go away and don't smash our cable!' To which the captain would shout back: 'F*** you and your bloody cable.' The old woman told me that she asked her sailor brother what the meaning of this was, to which he replied that it was a word they used whenever they had difficulty with hauling an anchor. She asked me if this was the real meaning of the word concerned and I said that I supposed her brother had given her the correct information.

Ballinskelligs Cable Station

When the 1914 war broke out, the British government took precautions in protecting the station, with an impenetrable barrier of barbed wire. The barrier was ten feet across, with wooden oak stakes eight feet high, driven deeply into the ground. The wire was coiled in spirals, in a fashion that made it impossible for a human to crawl through, without cutting himself every inch of the way. The entire compound was surrounded on all sides, guarded day and night by a platoon of twenty-one men and officers who lived in wooden quarters built within the area. Three sentry boxes were occupied full-time, one guarding the beach and two on the approaching roads.

The first platoon – the infamous Scottish Borders – wore kilts, and then there were the Sherwood Foresters, who crawled up Sackville Street in 1916 to quell the Irish Rebels. Later on I saw veterans of the Munster Fusiliers, who were given a stint of a couple of months in Ireland, before returning to the trenches. I saw them march eleven dusty miles from the railhead in Cahersiveen to Ballinskelligs, each wearing full pack and rifle; old hardened war dogs, who had served the empire well, sometimes dubbed by the British Tommies, 'the Dirty Shirts'. This very regiment were the men who covered themselves with glory by breaking the German line with fixed bayonets and saving the guns at the Battle of Mons. The old ballad is sung in their praise: 'Who saved the guns that day at Mons? The Munster Fusiliers!'

Some very beautiful English girls lived in the cable station. I remember some of their names like Florrie Westbrook, Inez Cornwall, Kathleen McMichael, Beatty Stone and several Armstrong girls, one maiden more beautiful than the other. Natalie Lloyd, the superintendent's daughter, and of course the Main girls, were beautiful and distinctive looking, not forgetting the spouses of the officials, who were all fine specimens of womanhood.

Skelligs Haul

The tennis club took part in tournaments between Waterville and Valentia cable stations. A nice wooden Protestant church was built on the grounds. It was used by the community for Sunday school and for regular service, held by the Reverend Parson Fahy who resided in Waterville and travelled to Ballinskelligs by pony and trap. Some Irish operators were discharged from service on suspicion that their families were sympathetic towards Sinn Féin during the 1916 Rising. The cable community kept very much aloof from the local peasantry and preferred not to mix, sometimes organizing their own private entertainment such as garden parties and private dances.

During the war years the cable office was eternally busy working in shifts, night and day, in communication with the United States and the Colonies. All messages were scrutinized by official censors placed on the station. The company, owned by American and British millionaires MacKay and Bennett, was terminated in 1918. The cables were connected to Penzance and to the British and French network. Some operators retained their jobs, being transferred to Penzance, some to Key West, Miami, and others to the United States and London. Afterwards, the buildings were used for summer Irish Language courses, and later were totally demolished.

I worked for the commercial cable company of Waterville doing interior decoration. This gave me a certain knowledge regarding the interior of a transatlantic operating station. There were large, wet battery rooms, heated rooms, keeping certain instruments at proper temperature, dark rooms with cable-testing equipment, rooms showing large charts of the Atlantic seabed. With the advent of Teletype, television and telex, computers, the internet, e-mail, etc., these new technologies make those instruments look like pieces from the Stone Age. One computer can now operate and control an entire floor, where hitherto twenty operators

Ballinskelligs Cable Station

were employed to take and send signals of communication. In another decade of centuries, I have no doubt, man will have discovered telepathy and how to harness the subconscious mind. Then one might ask the question, 'Whither goest thou, *Homo sapiens*?'

I have in my possession a dated and brassbound section of the transatlantic submarine cable which was laid into Ballinskelligs Bay in 1875 and 1896; also transmitting form No. 3 of the Direct United States Cable Co. Ltd, showing a copy of a message received at Ballinskelligs Cable Station on 3 September 1894; the receiving clerk was Mr Cobley. There is also a copy of a code message from New York to Paris, dated 14 February 1923, and specimen recorder slips of tape, showing direct, main-cable duplex signals.

It is said that Cable Company personnel generally ignored the local peasantry, whom they considered too low a class with which to fraternize. This is not surprising because the surrounding area at that period was designated a Congested Districts area, having no industries, a large population, bad housing and small holdings of land carrying high rent and rates. Many people lived very close to the poverty line. The Realm was not interested in the welfare of the peasantry of the locality, and this state of administration only led to the inevitable Rebellion of 1916.

A member of the Armstrong family, Herbert, who was born in Ballinskelligs and died in Vernon, British Columbia, Canada, presented the above items to me. His father John Garnet Armstrong, an Englishman born in Carlisle, Cumbria, beside the Scottish border, was a Catholic. John married Margaret Harty, a member of a well-respected local farming family. He died at the early age of forty-nine, leaving a large family of eleven.

I am pleased to say that John Armstrong's attitude towards the local people was on the most friendly of terms. He wrote numerous letters to government departments, and attended meetings on behalf of the rights of the needy. Another very popular English man was Mr Westbrook, who died in his native England, living to the fine old age of one hundred and one years.

The Seekins family were also well respected. William George Seekins died in Miami at age eighty-five. He was born in London and began working as a boy at the Cable Station in Ballinskelligs under the tuition of his father. He was later transferred to the station in Newfoundland, Halifax, where he received from England the message that the *Titanic* had sunk, on 15 April 1912, with a loss of 1517 lives. He was the first to relay the fatal message to New York and the New World. He was later transferred from Halifax, Nova Scotia, to Miami Beach Station, where he served as superintendent for twenty-five years.

Not all the clerks at the Cable Station were competent to man the receiving signals on tape. Mr Cobley was one of the best, but Mortimer O'Connell was the best operator for speed and accuracy. There were no typewriters in those days and the superintendent always gave O'Connell the task of writing all official letters to the Headquarters of the Cable Company in London. Herbert Armstrong states in a letter from Vernon, June 1976, speaking in praise of O'Connell: 'In all my life I have never seen such beautiful handwriting.'

John Garnet Armstrong was one of the first technicians of his time; along with taking part in transmitting and receiving messages, he was also the only man on the staff at Ballinskelligs who could fix the various instruments in those days of comparatively primitive machines. Trouble from magnetic and electrical interference, called induction, caused distorted cable signals that in turn reduced the efficient working of the entire system. A number of experiments were carried out by John Armstrong, and when applied, they greatly increased the quality of the cable signal to Ballinskelligs. John Armstrong's idea became standard

Ballinskelligs Cable Station

practice on all Atlantic cables and in the course of time was improved upon. His theory was that every electric signal, whether phone or telegraph, creates a magnetic field, and any conductor picks up this and causes interference.

My dear friend Herbert Armstrong worked in the Valentia Cable Station for several years, until shortly after the Easter Rising of 1916. Valentia was originally the Anglo-American Cable Company but was gobbled up by the giant American company, the Western Union Telegraph Company. There were five cables going out from Valentia and six from Waterville and Ballinskelligs. A few days after the Easter Rebellion in 1916, the British government sent several censors to each cable station in Ireland. To quote my friend, every day for the whole twenty-four hours one of the censors was stationed at our side checking every word transmitted over the cables, all through World War One. They did not trust Irishmen working in cable stations in Ireland. The outside world knew nothing about the Rising until it was completely crushed and all the leaders executed. Some Irish operators tried to get a message through to the Irish in New York, but the censor was alert and clamped down on the transmission switch. This created quite a scare in British quarters, with the result that all the young Irishmen were transferred to different cable stations outside of Ireland, out of harm's way.

Those pioneers of cable communication were giants in their own right. Prior to the submarine cable, sailing ships took many weeks to bring mail messages across the Atlantic. The cable station cut the message time to minutes.

We have many unsung heroes, but a tribute to the cable men of the south coast of Ireland, Ballinskelligs, Waterville and Valentia! Your memory must never fail.

Boy and Man

AN EARLY SCHOOLING
Skelligside

Whether by desire, design, or accident on the part of my good parents, I squawked and squalled my way in 1906 into the Gaeltacht of Ballinskelligs on the southern shore of the beautiful Iveragh peninsula. Sleeping and crying as a child, laughing and talking as a boy, the constant music of the Gaelic tongue fell softly on my ear. The language of the Sasanach was seldom used in our family or among the neighbours.

At national school I experienced a new set of growing pains, pains of a physical as well as a mental nature. The master was a stickler for accuracy, and when English was in session he would growl and wield his hazel wand, shouting 'Watch your grammar!' I learned English not through curiosity or love, but in fear and trembling.

I have tried to write with honesty and from the heart, presenting to the reader a picture in story of rural life in Ballinskelligs during the first half of the twentieth century. Many of the little things which fitted into the jigsaw of our daily lives have now, alas, become only a memory. [...]

My mother, Mary Cremin, told me that no professional medical aid was available on the night I was born. A local woman, who knew the traditional skills of midwifery given to her from generations, gently directed and delivered me over the threshold of the womb into this world. I drew my first breath on 31 May 1906. I was the last of the little clutch of five boys and two girls.

Skelligs Haul

At the age of five I was sent to school. I remember being neatly dressed in a skirt of blue frieze, and a frilled pinafore tied with white tape across my back. Few wore boots and trousers in my class. The master, Cornelius Shanahan, entered my name in the school roll and kindly presented me with a penny. But alas, on that same day I came to grief. While playing in the schoolyard I fell across a shallow pool and lost that first penny. My sister Sheila took my hand in hers and led me home with soothing words. Thus ended my first day at school.

As time went by I got used to school routine, though I was not in love with learning yet. The master's snake-like hazel rod was eternally busy. Because of my slow rate of progress in arithmetic, the portion of my anatomy between ribcage and buttocks was massaged by that same rod. I would rather see the devil himself than the long tot on the blackboard: I often reached the top figure helped by several applications of hazel.

Everything about my schooldays now seems to belong to the Stone Age, even the blue-black slates we used instead of copybooks, with pencils of the same material. Pupils had to stand back-to-back in twos to prevent copying, though we would sometimes whisper words or figures to each other when the teacher was not looking. [...]

The teacher warned us not to loiter on our way home after school. We were fond of delaying near an old ruined house by the roadside, where we played various harmless games such as long leap, hop step and jump, and frog's leap. One particular contest led to our undoing. This was a competition to find the boy who could piss the highest. It meant pissing over the wall of the old ruin which had different levels and was ideally suited for the purpose.

Some busybody who had seen the boys at play told the teacher of our pranks, and he punished us and informed

An Early Schooling

our parents. My mother was appalled. She exhorted me to change my evil ways and to confess my sins immediately. I lived in terrible fear of God, though to me He seemed a much nicer person than the teacher or the priest. We did not consider our competition to be so sinful or obscene. It was great fun while the water lasted. I do not know if any records were broken. One boy pissed sideways, so because of his poor aim he was barred from the contest. It was not considered safe to stand near him while competing. We called him Paddy Sideways. Later on, we were bombarded with hell-fire, brimstone and eternal damnation. We were labelled as young blackguards by the breast-thumping, holy-water hens who were usually whispering into the ear of the village pump. They foretold we would eventually bring ruin and shame on our respectable parents.

For me there was a second fall from grace during that school year. I was coming nine years old. My mother kept a flock of Rhode Island Red hens, and with them a beautiful strutting rooster. The creature had a curved tail like a golden rainbow with a few blue-green feathers for decoration, two bright looping gills hung like rubies from his jowl, and his slender yellow legs were adorned with formidable spurs. I think he was my mother's 'sacred cow'. He would perform a pirouette in front of her when she fed the hens.

One evening as I arrived home from school he was standing supreme on the doorstep of our kitchen. I tried to walk past but he attacked me by flying in my face. I aimed a kick at him and blurted out, 'Be off, or I'll kick your bloody arse!' My mother nearly fainted upon hearing my new language. She took me inside and started to wig my ears. My father, who was weaving a lobster pot, intervened. 'Don't be harsh,' he said, 'he is only learning.' Looking back now, we were a group of young mischievous scallywags who were wont to break the standards of behaviour required by the strict rules of the time.

Skelligs Haul

Ballinskelligs National School was built in the year 1867, employing four teachers and consisting of two separate adjoining schools for male and female within the one building. A hedge school catered for the locality until then. On the first day of July 1909, the school was allowed bilingual status. The region was densely populated before the Great War of 1914, and all the people spoke the melodious and subtle Irish of the region. English Schools' Inspectors conducted all examinations in those years – Dalc, Welply, Lehane, Alexander and Cussen. I often saw the teacher grow pale on their arrival in the classroom: he would not expect an iota of pity from these grim-faced taskmasters.

Examinations on Religious Instruction took place once a year. The inspector was usually a Catholic priest who often conducted the examination in English. Some of the senior boys were showing poetic talent by composing light religious poetry:

'Who made the world?'
'Paddy Fitzgerald
With a spade
and a shovel.'

The infant class was not slow at learning from its elders, so the Reverend Examiner was astonished to hear from the smaller children that Paddy Fitzgerald was a powerful deity, much to the consternation of the teacher, who seemed to suffer hot flushes. I remember one question put to a pupil in my class: 'Did God create the devil, my child?' The answer came in faltering English: 'He warn't any devil when He made him, Father.' Another question: 'When were you born, my child?' brought the reply: 'The night of the Biddy, Father!' The child meant she was born on the feast of Saint Brigid. Nevertheless, we had a good grasp of the catechism and all aspects of the faith, and the priest usually gave us good marks.

Neither priest nor monk, father nor mother, nor even the teacher himself told us anything about the birds and the bees. It was not right for us to mention sexual matters. I did not know exactly where I came from. Now, when my body was growing and my sexual organs were awakening, I thought something very strange was happening to me.

I understood from the faint whisperings that sex was very sinful – sinful to speak of, to think of, to look at, to touch, to read about or listen to. That very same sex was swallowing souls into hell every moment. An old man I questioned about it said, 'Blind people are a great pity.' Everything about sex was a mysterious secret in my youthful days. Those who fell victim then to the pleasures of the flesh caused a public scandal.

I remember the first time I laid my eyes on a naked young woman. She was having a swim nearby one summer's day. Every vein in my body burst into flame. Beauty drew me to her, a beauty kept secret from me until then. Then a sudden fear possessed me. Is this original sin, the seed of all sin? Is it Satan who creates this desire in me – a deadly mortal sin in front of me? Oh, blind people are a great pity! So the old man said.

TUG OF WAR IN THE CLASSROOM

This account of Michael Kirby's schooldays is drawn from *Skelligside* and *Skelligs Sunset*.

My name was entered on the school roll in 1911 at the early age of five years. My only book was called The First Book, and it contained little words like 'at', 'cat', 'bat', 'rat' and so on. I do not remember other books. I heard my parents speak of a book called the Readamaidaisy or Reading Made Easy, which was its proper title. Another book called The Three Rs they called Readin', 'Ritin' and 'Rithmitic.

I remember being transferred from infant grade to first class. I now possessed a lovely small paper table-book that I soon learned to sing like a song: 'One and one is two, two and two is four,' and so on. The teacher helped me to write, showing me how to balance the pencil between the forefinger and the thumb, by placing his open palm over my small hand, guiding my pencil across the page and forming the contour of my first letters. Gaelic lettering was different, having more tails. I found the contrast between Irish and English scripts a bit confusing. I had no difficulty in understanding Gaelic, it being our most used language at home and in the workplace.

Our principal teacher was not a native Irish speaker, making communication with his native-speaking class more difficult and perhaps a little ridiculous from the pupil's point of view. Looking back over that period of my life with what modern jargon terms hindsight, I have come to realize that our teachers had difficulty in dealing with us. They referred to our natural behaviour with such names as 'ignorant rustics, lunatics and clowns', often softening the blow by declaring that the clown was the smartest man in the circus. It must be said, in all fairness to our teachers, that we were the uneducated product, given to them to mould in our formative years into something of value – a formidable task by any standard.

The attendance reached 120 boys at Ballinskelligs National School, a large rural population coming from a congested district area where the average acreage of a smallholding was six to twelve acres. Large native-speaking families were living in poverty-line conditions. Our family owned one milch cow on six acres of cutaway bog. Among

Tug of War in the Classroom

many more like us, we did not pity ourselves, but just accepted what we were born into. As a school-goer, I was totally devoid of logical thought as to what the future held or might hold for me. We stayed in school until we were confirmed; after that our future was bleak. We could be classified by the Church as perfect Christians but in digging a ditch the necessary qualifications amounted to a strong back and a weak mind.

Our teacher, a squat, square figure of mellowing bachelorhood, instilled fear into his pupils. He always kept a stockpile of strong hazel birches in the press or locker, and was brutally cruel in his administration of punishment. I witnessed stalwart youths who stood erect with outstretched palms, never flinching from each thudding, swishing cut of the strong hazel birch. I can still see the pallor of agonizing pain from fierce cuts across each open palm being endured manfully. I watched the teacher's face grow pale and deadly serious, as if he really meant to reduce his helpless victim to a mere human wreck, such was his expression of fury. In latter years, I read of the birch being used on convicts, but in our school you daren't miss your homework.

Our school had a goodly supply of open rat holes because of its wooden floors. We formed a conspiracy that at every chance available to us, the hazel rods would be pushed into the rat-hole cavities beneath the floor. 'Operation Rat Hole' seemed to succeed for a time, much to the bewilderment of the teacher. Then one day the brewing storm broke, and a long, latent fury spilled over. This happened when the last hazel rod mysteriously vanished; schoolwork was suspended in the main classroom. Our teacher ordered 'Silence and attention!' while he stood behind the old rostrum, which looked very like the magistrate's desk in the local courtroom. Calling the boys in turn, he questioned each in a low tone regarding the disappearance of the rods.

When the enquiry produced only angelic innocence, the teacher decided on mass punishment for the whole class: ten strokes, five on each palm. But where would he find a suitable rod? Ah, a broom handle! The sweeping brooms had long, rounded, polished handles. Choosing one, he extracted it from the socket of the broom. The first boy to receive his baptism from the heavier weapon withstood the ordeal with valour, grinning at the master through a mask of near laughter and pain, seeming only to infuriate the administrator; whereupon the broom handle snapped into two nearly equal parts, giving the wielder much more control of balance and stroke. We all received our reward for taking part in 'Operation Rat Hole', and it was only a matter of time before we became strong and perfect Christians.

Another form of punishment meant the curtailment of our recreational period prescribed by the Department of Education. The master would keep the senior class involved in maths within the school while he leisurely examined copies. This curtailment of our freedom seemed to hurt more than corporal punishment.

A number of boys suffered from speech impediments. One particular boy who had a most severe speech problem was constantly at loggerheads with the master, who was convinced he could cure the boy's stammer by holding his head high and making him sing the words as he read them. Each day's session of the master's speech therapy and vocal chord exercises ended in disaster. The boy became more and more emotionally conscious of his problem and dreaded each session of speech training. The master could be heard shouting in a loud voice: 'Sing it, you clown! Out with it!'

'The night was dark and dreary ... ah ... bup ... bup!'

'Out with it!'

One day the boy – let's call him John – decided he had to fight back. He grabbed hold of the hazel stick, then

Tug of War in the Classroom

started a tug o' war. In the ensuing struggle, the master's spectacles became dislodged, bringing the bout to a sudden end. The master ordered John to get back to his seat. Relations remained strained from then on, until one day, hostilities broke out again because John was slow at mathematics. This time he refused to extend his hand for the usual punishment. The master prepared for the fury by removing his spectacles, but he did not reckon with John's next move. The master always wore a heavy gold chain, complete with bar and ornate medallion, looped across his waistcoat. On the chain was his heavy silver watch. I am sure he was proud of this fine piece of jewellery as I often saw him fondle the beautiful chain and subconsciously run it through his fingers. Grabbing John by the arm, the master asked him once more to hold out his hand, but more quickly John grabbed a loop of the gold chain and started to pull. In astonishment, the teacher dropped the birch, saying: 'Oh! No, no, Johnny, go back to your seat.' Replacing his glasses, peace was restored. On another occasion the master made the observation that Johnny was, by nature of his impediment, 'a very highly strung person'. But Johnny was the only boy in our class who was logical enough to know that attack was the better part of defence.

We all paid a few pence twice a year towards 'stationery money'. This helped pay for copybooks, pencils and writing pens with red wooden handles mounted with steel nib and holder. We also contributed towards the winter fuel. Each pupil brought two sods (bricks) of turf peat each morning until the fuel store was full. The master made sure that each pupil contributed his fair share. [...]

Christian Doctrine involved learning about our faith in both English and Gaelic. We had no Bible, except for short lessons in Bible history and explanatory catechism. The Bible seemed to be for the more enlightened, or rather smacked of Protestantism. We were not allowed partake in Protestant rituals, funerals, etc. Marrying a Protestant would require a dispensation from the pope. The rules were very strict.

I remember one occasion when the parish priest visited our school in the run-up to confirmation. He took the senior class for a short examination while the teacher stood aside. The purpose of his visit was to find out how we would answer questions on faith and morals when confronted by the bishop. The questions centred on the Ten Commandments. All went well until the sixth commandment: 'Thou shalt not commit adultery.' One by one we were asked what constituted adultery. We did not have a clue. One boy suggested it had to do with a woman. Another gave him some ridiculous answer, whereupon the priestly catechist lost his cool and, folding up his broad-leafed, soft felt hat into a baton-like weapon, proceeded to lambaste us, his budding Christians, about the ears. When the priest had departed the teacher tried to unravel the hitherto unexplained mystery of adultery in the following vague manner: 'Supposing a girl was on her way over the hill and a man met her in a lonely place and knocked her down with the intention of committing adultery ...' All went well until confirmation day. The good bishop grew a little tired after he had examined several classes. He ordered a canon to finish the examination. A boy from our group was asked what was covered by the sixth commandment, to which he answered: 'If a girl was coming over a hill, Father, and a man knocked her down ...'

'Very good, my child! God bless you.'

He then went on to another child, much to the relief of all concerned.

We were issued with copybooks that cost only a penny each and carried a beautiful specimen headline in perfect copperplate writing, bearing such captions as: 'All that glitters is not gold', 'Discretion is the better part of valour'

Tug of War in the Classroom

and 'The darkest hour is that before the dawn', which we would try to imitate by writing the sentence repeatedly until near-perfection was attained. I had trouble with the bottom loop of the letter 'f', which remains added to my legacy of human imperfections. Even to the present moment, I carry with me a most vivid recollection of receiving a violent blow with an open palm, which thereby compressed the air within my eardrum, causing searing pain and deafness that I never revealed to my parents because of a fear on my own part. The violence and sudden impact of the blow seems like a happening of yesterday.

Watches were only for rich people, anchored within breast pockets with gold or silver chains, and looped across the noble breasts of lawyers, churchmen, tavern keepers, doctors, teachers and landlords. The first German alarm clocks appeared in the shop fronts of Cahersiveen in the first decade of the last century. Their prices ranged from two-and-six to five shillings. The school clock stood in an elevated position on top of the tall press built into the wall. The clock was manufactured in the USA by the Ansonia Clock Company in New Haven, Connecticut. It replaced the old clock with weights and chains and had a spring-wound mechanism that struck the hours. The master adjusted the time by moving the hands backwards or forwards, by reaching up with a long stick kept for that purpose.

Our senior class consisted of some very bright, mischievous boys who decided to set the clock forward by five minutes while the master accompanied the parish priest to the school gate, where the two would stand discussing matters in private. That evening we closed school five minutes earlier than usual. Pranks like this went on until the master became suspicious and decided to take action. He left the schoolroom, apparently to inspect the latrines situated at the rear of the school. Tom Sullivan, a very fine strapping lad, stepped up to the rostrum and, wielding the long stick, proceeded to adjust the hands of the clock at least fifteen minutes ahead. Suddenly, a loud, tapping noise attracted our attention, and the master's scowling face appeared at the back of the window with a wagging finger. Tom Sullivan scampered back to his seat in expectation of severe punishment. When he entered the room all our eyes focused on the master who, to our astonishment, stood before the class smiling broadly. He called on Tom Sullivan to come forward. Tom approached the master with trepidation and was asked the question: 'Now, Tom did you interfere with the clock?'

'I did, sir!'

'Why?'

'For you to let us home early, sir!'

'By how many minutes did you alter the clock, Tom?'

'Fifteen minutes, sir!'

The master glanced at his pocket watch and looked in turn at the school clock. 'Exactly, Tom! Now go back to your seat and I will give you a set of problems to occupy your time for an extra fifteen minutes, and every time the clock is interfered with, you will stay in school until you change your ways!'

That was the last time we interfered with the new school clock. The master had won that round. He had his good points as well, like the little girl in the poem: 'When she was good, she was very, very good, but when she was bad, she was horrid.'

It is sad to think that the old school clock with its weights and chains has lost its place with the maelstrom of the rapid advance in modern technology. It is now a museum exhibit of the not-so-distant past. No longer does it wag its pendulum like a welcoming, faithful canine greeting its master, or emit a leisurely, soothing tick, tock, tick, tock. Now only a small battery inserted within its interior controls the almost empty space. No winding key is required anymore. For a

Tug of War in the Classroom

piece that emerged from the shadow of the sun cast on a beautifully engraved rock in a rich man's garden, I mourn your passing. They left you with no guts to live.

The grown boys played football in the little field attached to the school. The ball was made of long cloth strips, wound solidly and hand-sewn with every conceivable kind of twine. It had a certain amount of dull bounce, and it made do. Many boys wore long flannel skirts, often pleated like the Scottish kilt. Sometimes it was impossible to differentiate between the sexes, except when the boys held up their skirts to water the lawn.

We contributed threepence each towards a leather football that cost twelve shillings. The master contributed four shillings. He kept the inflated ball in the schoolroom. He acted as referee and organized inter-school games. He also gave physical drill instruction in the school. During play hour a team was picked of ten a side. The game waxed fast and furious, no quarter given and no quarter called for, no referee, no set rules, the pupils on the sideline urging on their favourites. After the game it was not unusual to notice some of the warriors nursing minor injuries: maybe a bloody nose, or a pendant of flesh hanging from a bare foot, where a big toe had been stubbed against a jutting ground-stone. Our teacher, a kind-hearted man who missed no opportunity to perform a good deed, would immediately apply some ointments he kept stored in a cupboard for such emergencies. [...]

At a later date our football became a source of annoyance to the teacher. Because of our playground being in close proximity to Seamus O'Leary's oat field, the ball would occasionally soar over the boundary fence. It would become lost for a while among the yet green, unripened crop of standing oat stalks. A number of boys would go over to retrieve the ball. Owing to the damage to his oat crop created by repeated trampling, O'Leary, having given several warnings, decided he must take some action.

One day, when class had resumed after our play hour, we were all engrossed in various tasks. Suddenly, the door swung violently open, revealing the form of a wild, dishevelled man standing like a pillar of salt in the doorway, shirt sleeves folded to the elbow, with a gorilla-like chest, pale and unshaven face, a hook nose and greying tangle of once-dark, bedraggled hair falling around his ears. Standing there with a reaping hook in hand, his leering eyebrows and his fierce blue eyes seemed to penetrate the room. Our teacher rushed towards him saying: 'Oh, no, no! You can't enter the school, James! Please go at once!' The master found himself suddenly pushed aside and into a corner by Seamus who spoke in Gaelic, saying, '*Má chuireann tú lámh orm, bainfidh mé an ceann díot!*' ('If you put a hand on me, I'll cut your head off!') while making a looping gesture with the reaping hook. Turning towards the class, he spied a little heap of peat sods near the fireplace and proceeded to pelt us with fury. We all dived for cover beneath our desks. The map of Europe hung on the back wall. One peat sod landed on the shores of the Black Sea, leaving a little crater, in the grain-growing regions of the Ukraine. O'Leary, having vented his fury, gave a strong warning in Gaelic before departing: if we caused any further damage to his crop, he would return.

The master arranged with the assistant teacher, who owned a small farm not far from the school premises, to let us play football in his property, thereby avoiding any further contact with O'Leary, who, in all fairness, had suffered much loss to his oat crop.

As a matter of interest, the aggrieved Seamus O'Leary, my friend and next-door neighbour, was the last surviving member of the O'Leary family who were cruelly evicted and brutally treated by the Crown forces when the last eviction took place in South Iveragh, County Kerry, in the year 1864.

Tug of War in the Classroom

Our teacher grew beautiful geraniums in red clay pots. He would send us out on the roadway to collect a bucket of fresh horse droppings. To these we added water, pounding and mixing until it dissolved into a rich dark-brown liquid, which the master poured into a beaker jug. This solution was used very effectively as a fertilizer to grow a fine crop of geraniums. No doubt medics today would shrink in horror at handling horse manure without protection. He was a very good music teacher. We liked the way he used a steel tuning fork to find the note. He taught us many songs, in both Gaelic and English, and we had an excellent school choir.

Some schoolbooks, both in Gaelic and English, were wonderfully informative and interesting. A Gaelic book entitled *An Treas Leabhar* had some beautiful Gaelic poems like 'Bán Chnoic Éireann Ó' ('The Fair Hills of Erin') and '*An Díbirtheach ó Éirinn*'.

Tháinig chun an taoide díbirtheach ó Éirinn ...

There came to the beach a poor exile of Erin,
The dew on his thin robe was heavy and chill,
For his country he sighed when at twilight repairing,
To wander alone by a wind-beaten hill.

The Gaelic prose was precise and difficult for the country boy who came from a native Irish-speaking fireside. There appeared to be a wide gap between the Gaelic he listened to at home and that which he was obliged to read from the school reader, which bore the imprimatur of the academy.

I do not wish to find fault with high standards, and only relate a factual experience of my school days. The English readers had many beautiful essays and poems. The last book we were introduced to was *Macbeth*, and we read it aloud. Connie Curran, Paddy Connor and I read the parts of the three witches. I was the first witch. I remember we would read it in turn. We had already devoured the long poem, 'The Rime of the Ancient Mariner'. There were so many verses in it to learn by rote. The first night I brought it home I left the book down out of my hands and our young pup chewed it. Two other unusual books we had were *Around the World in Eighty Days* and *Twenty Thousand Leagues Under the Sea*.

Elementary science was taught in the year or two before we left school. There was a grant given for the teaching of rural science. I had a special love for chemistry.

After confirmation, further education seemed futile. We could read and write and do a few simple problems in maths, and had a fair, general knowledge of geography, natural science and poetry.

The secondary school was situated in Cahersiveen, staffed by Christian Brothers who were established there before the turn of the century. That school was out of bounds. We had no means of transport. Our parents could not afford to pay for digs in Cahersiveen and bicycles were non-existent. Some boys were fortunate to have relatives in America who sent passage money for the New World. The classes that had attended Ballinskelligs National School during the end of the nineteenth century could sit for the King's scholarship. Many became engineers in the Colonial Service and served in responsible posts in India, Malaysia and Argentina. One was chief of police in Malaysia, one in charge of the grain stores in Buenos Aires and another a major in the British army in India. Many more became rich men in Canada, the United States of America, Australia and New Zealand. This goes to show that the Irish peasantry had brains to burn, but the opportunity for work or employment did not exist.

All my boyhood school companions have gone to their reward. The majority rest in foreign soil, where they found employment and threw in their lot with others for better or worse. Gone also are our teachers, who in our best interests had the unenviable task of trying to fit us for at least a menial part in the emerging society of this country. May they rest in peace.

Sadly, the schoolhouse is now closed.

PENANCE AND GRACE

Skelligside

As far back as I can remember we had the parish retreat. We called it mission time. It usually lasted for two weeks and was an occasion for penance always observed with great reverence and devotion. We would come home early from working in the bog, in time for attending evening sermon and devotions. One such evening we happened to meet one of the reverend fathers, who greeted us very cordially.

'Evening, boys! I suppose you have worked very hard today. Are you all coming to devotion this evening?'

We assured him that was why we had suspended work so early.

'Oh!' he said, 'excellent! Very good. Have you the turf saved for the winter fuel?'

'Yes, Father,' we said, 'it is all saved and fit for bringing home.'

'Are you all quite sure that the turf is saved?'

'Why yes, Father, we are certain.'

Then came the serious question: 'Have you your souls saved?'

We looked at one another and said in all simplicity that we did not know or we were not quite sure if our souls were saved.

The priest's countenance suddenly changed. His features now seemed grave and serious, and turning to us he said: 'I'm disappointed in you fellows. You make perfectly sure that that turf is saved, but make light of the most important harvest of all, the saving of your souls. Good evening to you, and make sure that you come to evening devotions.'

One of the boys observed that Father seemed to be getting a bit vexed. Another said perhaps he knew we were damned anyway! A third said, sure where was the use if we saved our souls that week, maybe we'd be as bad as ever the next week. However, it set us thinking about the seriousness of mortal sin and the salvation of our souls.

The mission fathers were usually of the Redemptorist Order. One would deliver mild sympathetic sermons about the love and mercy of God, while the other would thunder blood, fire and brimstone, exposing the influence of evil that we sometimes fail to notice in our lives, and the mercy of God's love which we take for granted. One evening I walked home with my neighbour, who was then an old man, after listening to a sermon on the seventh commandment. He seemed disheartened, and told me about having stolen a box of boots when he was working as a deckhand among general cargo on a ship in New York harbour. After breaking open the box, he found that it contained boots which were several sizes too small for him, and on sudden impulse he dumped the box of boots into the Hudson River under cover of darkness. Several times, he said, he mentioned this in confession, only to be told by the priest in New York that he must make restitution. He said in all sincerity that he was too poor ever to be able to make restitution for a whole box of boots that had rotted in the bottom of the Hudson long years ago. I tried to tell him that God would understand how the poor are tempted to steal, but he had a different way of thinking. His argument was that poverty was a trap set for the poor, which leads them to commit sin.

Penance and Grace

The Redemptorists preached in soul-scorching terms about illicit sexual relations: the evils of the dancing hall, the dark ways home, and the frivolous parents whose failure to enforce discipline led to loose moral behaviour. Company-keeping was frowned upon in any shape or form: the only cure for illicit courting was to be salted in fasting and in penance. The girls were exhorted to forsake their lovers, and to refrain from meeting in the darkness of forbidden trysting places.

Confessions were usually heard on specially appointed days about half-way through the retreat. All the adult population availed of this opportunity. Confessions would also be heard after the evening sermon, to facilitate those who could not attend on the day appointed. A mixed queue would form outside the confessional. My teenage daughter was awaiting her turn on a certain evening. I had arranged to wait for her outside the church as it was now approaching twilight. When at last she emerged, I found she could not express herself coherently because of sudden bursts of laughter.

'Please tell me what's so funny. Did you get confession?' I asked.

'Oh yes,' she made reply, 'but something very amusing happened. When my turn came to enter the confessional, a wizened little man jumped the queue, and scooted into the box in front of me. When I walked back and took my place in the queue once more, the man standing behind me tapped on my shoulder, saying in a loud voice, "Listen girleen! Why on earth did you let that bloody bastard get ahead of you?" '

The queue shook with suppressed laughter. Even in such solemn moments, perhaps it is good for us to laugh.

Another story is told about an old couple, whom we will call Mike and Brigid. They had listened to a paint-stripping sermon on forbidden sexual relations, and were on their way homeward to their cottage under the shadow of the mountain. Mike puffed on his turned-down briar pipe, while Brigid walked beside him in pensive mood, her shawl folded across her shoulders, occasionally heaving a deep sigh. They were nearing the end of their journey when at last Brigid broke the silence.

'Mike! Did we have sexual relations?'

Mike slowly removed the pipe from his mouth and aimed a spit at the hedgerow.

'By Gemini, we did, Biddy! And not a damn one of them came to your mother's wake or funeral.'

The parish retreat usually concluded with everyone feeling better off in mind and body. The penance, the discipline, and most of all the grace of the Holy Spirit worked wonders in our lives.

I heard a wise old matron give her reasoning about large families in rural areas of Ireland and especially among the poor. We had no other form of entertainment during the long winter nights, no cinema, no dancing, nothing except going to bed with husband or wife, and the result was a large family to care for.

One of the earliest churches in our parish of Prior was a long, low, thatched house, the ruins of which were to be seen at the eastern end of Ballinskelligs beach. A little stream which runs down from Kinard East and enters the sea at this point was called The Stream of the Old Church. A tale is told of how the roof was being blown off the church one very stormy Sunday. The priest celebrating Mass became anxious and asked his congregation, 'Is there not one good man amongst you who will go out into the storm and make an effort to save your church?'

Some time elapsed before anyone made a move, as each neighbour looked at the next, waiting for the 'one good man' to arise and go out, but no one stirred, until the priest renewed his appeal to his flock. Only then did a man come forward saying feebly: 'I am here, Father!'

The congregation burst into laughter, for this was God's fool, the man whom they said was not the full shilling, so thin and emaciated he could hide behind the handle of a garden rake. One shoulder drooped and his hair was long and unkempt. He was born thus, but he was still God's example of 'the good man'. The laughter was short-lived, as each strong man, young and old, followed God's fool out into the storm.

Times have changed. The simple faith is being challenged. Questions are being asked. Winds are blowing, some gentle, some harsh. People are looking for truth, some almost despairingly, and only death remains constant. At eighty-four years of age, sifting through accumulated beliefs, it is difficult to adjust to new formulations without having to question my own conscience, and spring-cleaning is not easy.

* * *

Paul and his mother came to Ballinskelligs last summer. She rented a cottage at the bend of the road, by the stream which tumbles down through the townland and into the bay. Paul had only just celebrated his seventh birthday and was his mother's only child. Each day he busied himself like a duckling in the shallow pool of the roadside stream. I asked him why he spent so much time in the stream. I got only a serious fleeting glance for an answer. It was plain that the child was building bridges with small stones and short pieces of stick.

The stream had only a couple of inches of water owing to the summer drought. Paul always wore red Wellingtons. One day I sat on the bank of the stream close to where the child amused himself. He did not seem to notice my presence, and continued to build his little walls of stone. I could see that Paul was having great difficulty in constructing a bridge. Something happened every time: the stones either slipped out of place or the sticks were too short, and the walls would come tumbling down. Still, with indomitable courage, the little fellow would start all over again.

Once more, I ventured to make friends with the child. Choosing my words and speaking gently, I told him in a light-hearted way that I myself was an expert in bridge-building, and boastfully claimed that I could build any kind of bridge under the sun. I asked him if he would let me work with him at his task. After looking at me for some time, I noticed the serious indifferent look leave his childish features, and the light of a soft smile spread over his face.

Together we constructed beautiful miniature bridges across the shallow stream. With my pocket knife I cut short willow sticks which served to span the little walls, which we then covered with fine sandy clay. I became a friend to the child, who kept up a constant flow of speech, some of which I didn't understand because of the short London city accent.

That evening he took my hand and we went to meet his mother, who thanked me for being so friendly to her son. I promised I would come for an hour the following day to show him how to make little boats. Next day we built a loop into the side of the stream, representing a harbour with two headlands. I made boats, some of paper, others of felistrim from the fronds of the yellow iris. We used thorns of French furze for nails. When all was finished, I could see the child was delighted, and though the little bridges were so small, in Paul's eyes and in mine they seemed as important as Westminster, or Brooklyn Bridge. An old neighbour who noticed us declared, 'Mike! You're reaching your second childhood! Maybe you're doting!'

I could see the sunrise of joy shining in the face of the child I had thought to be lonely. The privilege of making friends with Paul and watching him admire the masterpiece of his dreams gave me a wonderful sense of satisfaction. I bade him goodbye until tomorrow.

That night a summer thunderstorm broke over Ballinskelligs. The clouds burst and torrents cascaded from the mountains. I went out at about ten o'clock next morning to find the crystal stream of the day before swollen into a frothy flood. Every trace of the miniature harbour and bridges had been swept away, leaving only a muddy pool. Paul stood by my side, with his hand in mine, and I saw two tears slip slowly down his cheek. What had happened to his *Tír na nÓg*, his Land of Youth? I felt a lump in my throat as I said goodbye to Paul and his mother, who were returning to the great city. I thanked God for my friendship with the child. For a short while it brought me back once more to my own childhood one late April when my Cremin grandmother took my hand in hers and led me across green fields to a knoll beside this same stream to pick sweet-scented bluebells and primroses.

GAMES AND PASTIMES OF MY BOYHOOD

Skelligside

Many and varied were the games played in ancient Ireland. Hurling now takes pride of place and has reached its prime position as our national pastime. It is a game of great skill and endurance, played in almost every county in Ireland, culminating in an All-Ireland final between the best two unbeaten teams, who do battle for the MacCarthy Cup before a crowd of eighty thousand people in our national stadium, Croke Park.

The crooked stick of seasoned ash is fashioned with oval or rounded handgrip; the heel, or striking part, is crooked and flat. The stick derives its name from the Gaelic word *cam-ann, camán*, meaning having a crook or twist. The best hurleys are the sticks taken from branches that have a natural twisted growth.

Many games were played with stone, such as casting a stone from the shoulder. The cast was made from a special mark. The weight of the stone varied from light to medium to heavy; three pounds, six pounds or eight pounds. The stone was usually round, clumsy and smooth, making it difficult for any one contestant to grasp. The throw or cast had to come straight from the shoulder. Any step over the line meant disqualification. It is said that activity beats strength: the muscular, brawny contestant was sometimes defeated by a lean, scrawny participant, much to the delight of the onlookers.

I remember a game called rounders being played by the school children. I do not recall the rules of the game, but it was not unlike cricket, the English game. I heard people say that the early Irish emigrants took the game to the USA: hence the game called American baseball. I can say that the several players stood in the formation of a wide ring using a round bat or stick and, after a strike, a series of runs took place before the ball of crude, sewn leather, filled with sand or clay, was retrieved.

We played a game called 'Ducks Off', which was extremely dangerous for both spectators and participants. The ducks were pieces of round, hard stone about three or four pounds in weight. A flat table of rough stone called the granny was placed about fifty feet from the line where each throw was made. The ducks were rolled towards the flat table by a team of six boys. The boy whose stone was found to be the farthest away from the granny was obliged to place his duck on the granny, to be shot at by

Games and Pastimes of My Boyhood

the other boys. A scramble would ensue for the boys to get back to the line if the stone remained stationary on the table and was not knocked off. The game had many rules and was both intricate and dangerous. One of our players suffered a blow to the head which made him temporarily unconscious. Before collapsing, he put his hand to his head and exclaimed 'Oh boys, I am dead forever!' The teacher frowned on it being played and punished us accordingly for taking part.

The game of 'Gobs' was played by girls with five rounded pebbles carefully selected from the bed of a stream, or gravel rounded by the action of the waves on the beach. The pebble game had many stages of skill, namely scatters, knobs, strillions and cruvs.

The leather inflated ball introduced a radical change, making football much more exciting and attractive to both players and the general public. Hurling and Gaelic football are now played at national level. Great sums of money are paid to watch the games.

Other pastimes were the hunt or the chase. The hunt for the wild boar is mentioned in sagas about the Fianna, the mythical warriors of destiny. Wild boars were found in the Glen of Prior, looking westwards on the Great Skellig. The Glen is called *Gleann Orcáin, orc* being the Gaelic for boar. The stag was also hunted and became the subject of a great epic poem immortalized by Walter Scott:

> The antlered monarch of the waste
> Sprung from his heathery couch in haste.
> But ere his fleet career he took,
> The dewdrops from his flanks he shook.

The stag referred to by Scott was hunted in the Highlands of Scotland but it is interesting to note that the last retreat of the great red deer was the mountains of Kerry.

Skelligs Haul

Beagle hunting has been a favourite sport in Ballinskelligs for as long as I can remember. Only the rich landlords kept kennels and packs of beagles. The local gentry kept horses at Portmagee, at Fermoyle Castle in Prior parish and at Derrynane. The terrain was not suitable for horse-riding in pursuit of the fox. Still, it was indulged in by those country squires.

The Ballinskelligs beagle clubs existed back in the 1700s. My grandfather was known as Tadhg na nGadhar, 'Tim of the dogs'. For some short time he was the kennel keeper to a certain knight squireen of the clanging hoof and horn, whose hundred dogs bayed deep and strong. My grandfather loved dogs and had a way with them. When the kennels of the Big House were opened in Portmagee, the dogs would come all the way across the mountains in the early morning to wait outside the door of his little thatched cottage in Ballinskelligs.

Gone are the halcyon days of the Big House, gone too are the masters of the hunt in creaking calfskin saddles, who plied the scourge and steel. In their stead the local peasantry still keep beagles for hare hunting. The hare-hunting beagle is a much larger breed of dog than that of the fox chase. Hare hunting is not a blood sport. The club members will not allow a hare to be killed. Rather, it is an endurance test to find the best dog. When the hare is seen to falter and is showing signs of exhaustion, the dogs are called off by a blast of the huntsman's horn. A closed season is declared to allow the hares to breed and bring forth their young, called leverets. It is during this period that the hunters organize a series of beagle races called drag hunts. A scent is laid down by a special set of runners over a fifteen-mile course, over moorland, mountain streams and rough obstacles. Each runner will pull a scented piece of meat or sack tied on the end of a length of rope from a starting point to a finishing gateway, where the judges await the winning beagles. The winning owners are rewarded with substantial trophies and money prizes. Some beagles are black with tan ears, said to be of the Hubert breed. Others vary in colour from speckled to blue-grey, chocolate and white. South Kerry beagles are much sought after and fetch good prices. [...]

HEART ATTACK AND THE DRUNKEN BALLET DANCERS
Skelligs Sunset

Almost thirty years ago came another milestone in my life. I was still working hard, this time preparing a chimneybreast to take a much larger fireplace, a job that entailed cutting away some very hard concrete with steel chisels. My arms ached but I didn't want to admit that I felt tired, until the Easter Sunday morning that I tried to stop a stubborn cow getting onto the roadway as the Circuit of Ireland Motor Rally was passing by. Then it struck: a sudden pain in both wrists, a bursting, breathtaking pain in the centre of my chest. If only I could pass some gas up or down, what a relief it would give. But no, a giant vice-grip held my heart, refusing to let go. I knew enough about life that I never took death seriously. I also knew that panic was not the best medicine for a heart attack. This brings to mind a fisherman skipper, who observed from his wheelhouse that his crew seemed excited about fishing gear that was badly entangled on deck. He emerged from the wheelhouse and said in a loud voice: 'Now men, if there is to be panic, let it be orderly.' When Dr O'Shea arrived, he gave me an injection and asked me how I felt, saying: 'You know, Mike, you could die!' I told him in rather blasphemous terms what I thought of the Grim Reaper.

The fifty-mile journey to Tralee Hospital was the 'slow boat to hell'. Strapped to a steel ladder-like stretcher, I felt every pothole, bump and hollow. It seemed more like being strapped to the back of a farmer's harrow when sewing spring oats. I conked out on two occasions. The ambulance pulled into the roadside and I was given oxygen. My daughter Anne and a nurse were with me. Anne whispered: 'We are entering the hospital grounds, Dad. You are a very patient man, you never complained or panicked.' I was too ill to tell her I had used orderly panic. The hospital doctor gave me a further injection. I was attached to a monitor and made comfortable. The pain was abating and 'peace came dropping slow'. Anne said: 'Goodnight, Dad. I'll see you tomorrow.' To quote Coleridge's Ancient Mariner:

> To Mary Queen the praise be given!
> She sent the gentle sleep from Heaven,
> That slid into my soul.

Several times during the night, the watchful eye of the 'lady in white' lingered close to the pallet of the stricken hero, listening to my breathing and glancing at the wavy lines of my heartbeat on the screen of the monitor.

'Are you feeling all right?'

'Yes, thank you, nurse!'

Another day dawned. I felt weak but comfortable and they put a needle in my arm, tubed to a bottle. This, I was told, was the drip. My wife Peggy and my family visited me often. I now began to realize how fortunate I was to be alive. A farmer in middle age was brought in, but only lasted a few hours. A travelling man was recovering but refused to give a blood sample because of some old custom in his clan.

After several days in the intensive-care ward, I was transferred to the general ward. I wondered at first if I had

Heart Attack and the Drunken Ballet Dancers

been moved to some mental institution. I was astonished to see, in the dim night light of the ward, two pyjama-clad figures waltzing on a highly polished floor, to the accompaniment of their singing – 'Daisy, Daisy, give me your answer, do!' I was not prepared for entertainment such as this. I sat bolt upright in my bed. The man in the neighbouring bed leaned over and said: 'That's the French sailor and Jimmy Kelly. They found a bottle of whiskey somewhere. They waited until the lights were dimmed to drink it. They are harmless young lads. The sailor is being treated for pneumonia. Kelly is to be treated for his back.' By the look of him, there was nothing wrong with his back. The waltzing became more hilarious when the Frenchman started a ballet-like South American dance. The man next to me, whom I got to know later as Johnny, exclaimed: 'I own to Christ, if someone happens to fall, he'll break his bloody arse!' At that moment a night nurse entered the ward and tried to get the dancers back to bed. The sailor was quick to obey, but Jimmy kept insisting that the nurse dance with him. She went across the room and spoke briefly on the phone. Two men in white coats entered the ward and asked Jimmy to behave and go back to bed. By this time Jimmy was losing his cool, only to find himself swiftly held prone on the bed like a trussed fowl while an injection was administered. In a few short minutes Jimmy seemed to get very drowsy. Between yawns he kept singing little snatches of: 'The songs that were sung' ... yawn ... 'the days when we were young' ... yawn! Jimmy's head hit the pillow. The nurse wheeled up a cot with a high railing. Jimmy was placed carefully inside and made comfortable. The rails were closed, leaving Waltzing Matilda to sleep it off. Not a peep was heard from the French sailor.

The day nurses arrived early, as dawn was breaking. They had some difficulty in waking Johnny. 'Wake up, John!

Skelligs Haul

It's six o'clock. We must make your bed.' John opened his eyes and gave a prolonged yawn: 'Excuse me, nurse, it was one long whore of a night.' The good nurse didn't seem to hear. I was being educated and entertained. An old bachelor farmer's bed was lined up near that of the sailor. They never seemed to hit it off. The Frenchman would say: 'If you give me your address, I can get you a nice French wife.'

The farmer would retort: 'I don't want your French wife, or any wife for that matter.'

'Oh! French girl keep you warm. Maybe she kiss you! She make love all night! Do you hear?'

'I hear you! Shut up! You're only fit for telling lies.'

Some of the exchanges were special gems of *craic* and banter. The matron carried out an inspection of all the lockers because of the drunken ballet dancers. The empty Paddy bottle was found standing by the wall, but dead men tell no tales.

Jimmy would come over and sit on the end of my bed. The sailor also became a very good friend. We had a lot in common to talk about. A friend from Dublin brought me a bottle of whiskey, which I shared with the sailor and Kelly. This time we divided the beverage into Lucozade bottles and hid the empty bottle in the rubbish bin. One nurse said the ward smelled like a brewery.

Day by day I felt stronger, until eventually I was discharged. I was told I had angina and that I would have to live with it. I was to walk two and a half miles per day. I was to take two Trasicor, one Aldactide, one Centyl K and three Lanoxin a day. I had damaged my heart, but the heart is a wonder, sometimes building itself up again. If I was careful I might live three years or more – a consoling thought! I was also advised to get my things in order: paperwork etc. Having at least three years to get my paperwork done, the first job I did was to paper the front room, just in case I might snuff it!

Heart Attack and the Drunken Ballet Dancers

I was called to my first check-up in Tralee. A young Indian doctor checked my heart and blood pressure. He assured me that I didn't have angina. I was to take more exercise and walk five miles a day. From that day onwards I decided I would change my lifestyle. First things first: I stopped smoking for good, gave up mutton, ate very little butter or sugar. I also tried to be careful about salt. A beef stew once a week using no frying pan and very little bacon, plenty of white cabbage, boiled onions, oatmeal gruel, carrots and parsnips. I never spilled the water of any vegetable down the sink: I drank all the juices. I ate mackerel in any form, fresh and smoked; white fish and salmon; chicken, skinned and roasted; raw celery; garlic; parsley and turnips; whole grapefruit; no junk foods or biscuits; only homemade bread.

I can make fish soups from any kind of shellfish: limpets, crab, razor and all types of clams, mussels and lobsters. I love the common wrasse and skinned gurnard. Even several kinds of edible seaweed can be added to soup, with segments of sea urchin. Crab claws give edge to the appetite, but do not allay hunger. Fish roe of herring, cod and whiting are full of minerals as are, in fact, the roe of all fish. A mackerel in season should cook in its own oil. Too much mineral oil and cooking fat are to be avoided. Fish oil will never create wax or clog the arteries. I drink the water in which salmon is boiled, mixed with a little onion and garlic, with a touch of black pepper and salt. It is very savoury. Only very lean beef should be consumed. I cut out all fudge, cream, cakes and fizzy drinks. I like an occasional drink of whiskey, never brandy. Citrus fruits, grapes, pears, plums and apples must never be taken in excess: they may trigger severe acid indigestion. Along with natural sugar and vitamins, fruit also contains a high degree of acid. Christmas plum pudding, chocolate, whipped cream, tinned fruits and fancy buns only remind me of splitting headaches – they are not for people with wonky hearts!

Skelligs Haul

When I told my doctor of the things I had eliminated from my diet he said: 'You're surely for the birds, Mike! If you cut out any more, you'll starve to death!'

Walking against the hill must be practised with patience, in order to put a little workload on the heart. Deep breathing of pure fresh air, a good sleep and a good hearty laugh can help you cheat the impending heart attack and the Grim Reaper himself.

A PAINTING IS BORN

Skelligs Sunset

To me all nature – sea, land, clouds, mountains, valleys, rocks, flowering plants and grasses – is an enigma. I feel that I too am part of nature's picture.

Maybe the awesome immensity of the plan becomes too weighty for my curious, mundane intrusion. Then why do I not close the window of my niggling curiosity to be enveloped again in the darkness of my coming, lest the light that has illuminated my birth becomes the torment of my going? At present, I stay with the Psalmist, saying: 'O Lord, I love the beauty of thy house and the place where thy glory dwelleth.' Now, having wrestled with myself, words and mind trying to outwit my inquisitive investigation, I find myself bogged down on beholding the bountiful things that surround me in their natural beauty.

What part do I play in this plan? Am I, like Shakespeare's Hamlet, only 'a poor player that struts and frets his hour upon the stage'? Does my life culminate in dusty death, as he suggests? Please, Willie, let poor Yorick escape at least from the gloom of a paradise lost! I do not want the jackpot, only some of the peace and tranquillity that is here for the taking.

I assume that no two humans have the same minds. During the time I earned my living fishing in the company of other fishermen, hundreds and thousands of mackerel passed by and through our hands. We often tried to find a pair of mackerel with the exact same skin patterns, but failed. Scientists tell us that no two snow crystals are the same. Does this prove that we are part and parcel of nature's specially graded species? I think it is only fair, if we are all somewhat different, that we should refrain from sermonizing to each other from our divergent points of view.

Snow crystals become the silken, shimmering, glittering raiment of the mighty peaks of mountains. Man's false ego may tempt him to disturb the beauty of a glacier filled with snow crystals. Too often he becomes engulfed in an avalanche of nature's beauty or perhaps of his own vain ego. Beauty in the eye of the beholder may become a Hydra-headed monster, creating greed and desire. I only ponder, wonder and wait for a little chink in the armour of this beautiful, unending yet terrifying, infinite cosmos. I can only hope to learn that I, puny man, am part of the enigma of nature.

Now, why did I attempt to paint a picture in the first place? Truly it came from within. Maybe a pregnancy of the mind, wanting to emulate with the crudest strokes of a brush the mountains and landscape that surround me daily. The phenomenal, ever-changing kaleidoscope of light and shade when clouds momentarily obscure the sun, instantly changing the colour of the landscape into a sequence of different hues, adds to the difficulty of the artist who aspires to imitate.

On a summer's day can be seen the serenity and bloom of meadows and mountains in a distant dreamy, hazy, bluish shade of purple; clouds of cumuli in perfect complementary colour, all blending harmoniously into the ethereal arch of infinity. Surely the scene is composed by the divine will of some god-artist, painter of nature and of our very being. On the other side of the canvas we see the awesome power, yet terrifying grandeur, of a violent storm, in which little waves become mountainous crashing seas, venting, washing, spilling and spending a spume-blown, foaming fury on shingle beaches and rock-bound headlands. A good ship can be seen wallowing between breaking billows, her patient master anxiously guiding, tending, shepherding, and finally bringing her back from the brink of impending doom.

On reaching my seventieth birthday I finally decided to satisfy the consuming, pent-up desire to paint the beautiful scene that had confronted me since my childhood. If memory serves me right I pondered, mulled and minded what kind of materials I would need. Having decided, I murmured to my wife Peggy: 'Here goes nothing.' Clomping out of the back door, I caught the end of her retort: 'At this hour of your life, it's your prayers you should be thinking of!'

In a shed at the back of the house I kept all kinds of bric-a-brac. Faithfully awaiting me on a shelf I found some small tubes of oils that I had bought some time previously, and also several rusted tins of paint, some of which had only a few inches of thickened paint in the bottom. I suddenly imagined the ghost of Little Boy Blue standing in the attic surveying his toys, some covered with dust and rust, and the beautiful ending of the poem depicting his childhood innocence: 'Ay, faithful to Little Boy Blue they stand, / Since he kissed them and put them there.' Alas, I fit, not into the category of childhood innocence, but the category of 'gone with the wind'! I found a saw and a piece of hardboard that my son was using. He obligingly cut me a rectangular piece, twenty inches by eighteen inches. I told him I was

A Painting is Born

to become the new Picasso. He didn't seem surprised, just said: 'Why not!'

My paints, as I remember, were a motley mix of colours. I used raw linseed oil and some turpentine and a drying agent called terpene. After a long period of stirring, pouring, thinning, mixing and experimenting, at last I painted a sky of hazy, light blue-green. Not a cloud in view; I called it eggshell blue, but for the life of me I could never tell what species of bird laid that colour egg. I waited several days for my cloudless sky to dry out. Probably it suffered a hangover from my generosity with raw linseed, plus my trial and error.

Next morning I gazed longingly at the mountains beyond Ballinskelligs Bay that I knew so well: Hog's Head and the curving hills stretching eastward and upward; to the south the majestic mountains of Beara nodding their heads with chieftain-bearing pride in the background; Deenish Island and Scariff Island westward, sheltering the entrance to the bay. I employed some makeshift tools of my own, such as a half-inch black bristle brush used for painting windows and an old steel writing pen with a wooden handle that I found effective for drawing lines. Pieces of rag and scraps of foam came into play and as I progressed I even tried using the tip of my right forefinger. This tended to lead to a somewhat messy kind of art, and so I was obliged to demote the promoted finger back to its original index position.

I painted the near hills with every colour I thought possible. To match the scene I painted in some little blotches like clouds of grey and white, and a very calm serene sea with glossy reflections. All in all, I felt pleased with my first effort. I did not receive any great recognition or encouragement from anybody, except friendly remarks such as: 'I suppose it's nice!' 'Well, I wouldn't know really!'

Skelligs Haul

and 'Are they pictures of cows in the sky?' This was the last straw, enough to make poor Picasso take a flying jump into the bay. Months passed. My masterpiece stood nakedly without frame, fame or recognition in a dim corner near the fireplace. My enthusiasm for future creativity in the world of painting seemed to suffer a deflective downward curve. Despite that, a fervour and an ardent flame still burned within my mind.

I confess to feeling pangs of regret on the day that Peggy and I decided that the picture had served its purpose and it was now to be consigned to its original birthplace in the shed behind the house, and to the limbo of my unfulfilled dream. On my way out to dispose of the painting, Peggy said: 'Wait a moment, I see somebody at the front door.' I laid the painting on the kitchen table, face upwards, before opening the door. Two men stood there, and upon inviting them inside, they told me that they were interested in information regarding Skelligs Rock and the possibility of a boat trip there. After exchanging some pleasantries and graciously thanking me, much to my surprise one of the men approached the kitchen table and, taking the picture in his hands, he asked: 'Who painted this?'

He introduced himself as a person who held a distinction from an academy of art, and accompanying him was a student from that school. I humbly asked for his evaluation of the work. His reply was as follows: 'If I was asked to give an evaluation, I would have to give it full marks for colour, blending and distribution, including natural perspective of mountains.' He then asked if anyone had given me tuition, to which question I truthfully answered in the negative. The good man advised me to study nature as it appeared to me and not depend on books. His words and generous appreciation helped to free my mind. Immediately I became

My Garden

part of the sea, wind and shadow of the hillside. I felt free. I could sing again:

> Oh! Had I the wings of a dove,
> To soar through the blue, sunny sky,
> By what breeze would my pinions be stirred?
> To what beautiful land should I fly?
> Would the gorgeous East allure,
> With the light of its golden eyes ...
> In vain would I roam from my island home,
> For skies more fair!
> (Denis Florence MacCarthy)

Thus ends the narrative of my initial experimental involvement with oil painting, from which I have received so much joy and intense pleasure, seeking to emulate the beauty of nature, the elusive mystery of the now and hereafter. That first painting is one of my most treasured possessions, now hanging in pride of place over the fireplace in my living room.

MY GARDEN

Skelligs Sunset

> The kiss of the sun for pardon,
> The song of the birds for mirth,
> One is nearer God's heart in a garden
> Than anywhere else on earth.

I have forgotten who composed this poem [Dorothy Frances Gurney did – ed.] or where I first heard the words, but it became indelibly stored in some cell of my brain. It surfaced immediately when my mind or inner-something triggered the idea: why not write an essay describing a country garden? Then suddenly up popped the poem that I use here as an introduction. Perhaps an eminent brain surgeon will produce some breakthrough data on the grey matter.

Now, in the evening of my days, and especially when road-walking has become so hazardous, the confines of my garden are more than a safe haven. I regard it as a peaceful, God-given sanctuary, a place where I have time to rest, to reflect and to observe the little things that I didn't even have a thought for; the trivial natural happenings that I was too busy to observe, being too concerned earning the crust of that daily bread. For that matter, isn't our entire island a garden? The Garden of Eden? Please, do not bring that one up. I do not want any serpents. I do not want to get evicted by some belted earl landlord of the British Empire, the Irish Republic, the EEC or any other global, dominating empires that say they want peace in the garden. Yes! I have bushes in my garden, but my garden is a Kerry garden.

I have discovered some very important things in my garden, most of all peace of mind; time to listen to faint little twitterings, different notes and sudden flutterings near at hand. I discovered that I also had inquisitive company when a red robin came bobbing along one day. I fed it with breadcrumbs and other titbits of fat. Then it introduced its little fledgling to join in this unorthodox hospitality, call it what you will, Simon Community or meals on wheels. Well, it worked. The offspring thrived. The breast feathers soon became pink, losing the drab colour of a fledgling. Then a blackbird discovered what was happening in the garden. No doubt some loose bird-talk spread the news! Magpies, jackdaws and crows converged on the scene and would stand daringly, letting off steam in a scolding, chattering chorus of criticism and indignation, or perhaps pleading to

My Garden

be fed. However, my diplomatic department has failed to crack the code of bird-talk and for that alone I am thankful. If Big Brother ever gets that far, all wild birds will have to stick their beaks in the sand.

Now, the blackbird with the yellow bill was clever. He introduced his wife to the freeloading. By the way, his wife's name in Gaelic is *céirseach*. She is not too much concerned with music and wears very drab clothes, not the shiny velvet black of her musical husband, *londubh*. I have no doubt she is a most diligent, hard-working housewife, always feeding and taking care of the children; a real homemaker. I cannot understand how she married him in the first place, who made the match, where she came from or whether Mr Londubh was cast into a deep sleep and a rib taken from his side. If so, he is stuck with her for good. I will not ask Darwin or Einstein. Perhaps their answer is outdated. I remember a little rhyme from my schoolbook:

Birdie with the yellow bill,
Hopped upon my window sill
Cocked his shining eye and said,
'Ain't you shamed, you sleepy head?'

(R.L. Stevenson)

Now, perhaps I am guilty of rash judgment. If so, I crave forgiveness. I have heard from sources of authority that the male blackbird assists in the construction of the nest, the feeding of both wife and chicks, taking a turn to sit on the eggs to keep them at their proper temperature. If *céirseach* needs exercise or food during the hatching period, the male will sing not directly over the nest but at a distance, which misleads predators seeking to find its exact location. If a predator comes too near, the bird will utter a loud, chattering alarm cry and will attack if possible.

Skelligs Haul

In my garden was a pair of wrens of our smallest species, the gold-crested wren. They were very elusive. Our brown wren, *dreoilín* in Gaelic, can burst into sweet, short bouts of song. The magpie is a murderous, ferocious pirate who will hunt, destroy and consume young chicks and eggs. Other enemies are stoats, grey-back crows and cats. I do my best to protect my songsters. Last summer, after having read some humbug treatise dealing with reincarnation, while sitting in my garden seat, there was my robin staring me in the face. I concluded that it was time to issue a warning. Addressing the bird, I said: 'If you are my good mother Mary Cremin, RIP, you better get the hell out of here or you could wind up in the belly of the cat!' However, it didn't seem to work with my robin.

Not alone is bird life interesting, one must also consider insects. The honeybee seems to be attracted to a special dahlia. The bees in question are light brown in colour. I watched as they seemed to work in unending relays, tanking up and flying away I noticed they always flew in a southerly direction, while others kept coming in from the same direction. This sequence continued until late evening. They certainly work late and early, gathering honey for the hive. I also noticed some bees crawling near the plant as if they were half-asleep and after a period of time they would come to life and fly off. This was explained to me by a professional beekeeper. He said they were young bees that suffered from consuming too much nectar. They become intoxicated and suffer from a slight hangover, from which they have to rest for a while until they recover and fly back to the hive. I did not invent this; I have to believe the authority that explains it.

I have tried to meditate by closing my eyes and ears to all worldly anxiety, attempting to release myself from the material woe of the existing universe, transcending to a higher plane, praying and repeating a mantra. I usually drop off to sleep. It seemed to me that I was peering down

My Garden

into a vast tunnel of dark, peaceful emptiness. Maybe if I continue in my search for the light I will find it. Presently I will trust and say, like John Henry Newman: 'Lead kindly light ... the night is dark and I am far from home.'

Having awakened from my fanciful garden dream, I noticed a flying insect cut circular pieces from the green leaves of rose bushes and fly off. Imagine a wasp-like fly, using a sharp saw or serrated tool, cutting out a piece of leaf to be used, I have been informed, as a lining for its nest. It is very fastidious about which leaves it carves. Dangerous area, my garden! I could have my leg amputated!

Of course my garden is a very private, peaceful place, or at least it is meant to be. I admit that this is not always the case. Only yesterday I had to intervene in a real free-for-all between what I assume were two cock robins engaged in mortal combat. On my intervention they grudgingly flew off with some rumpled feathers and bloody beaks. Were they fighting for territory, or was there some dispute concerning marital relations or maybe girlfriends? It is sad to think that the urge to kill is the ultimate solution.

Soft April showers and bright mayflowers will bring the summer back again, also the aphids, and many species of blackfly and greenfly that produce spores and fungus, bringing disease and decay to many beautiful flowers and shrubs. The gardener must also deal with several different species of snails and slugs, with acid rain and salt spray thrown in. All is not rosy in the garden or in wild nature. We hear about the balance of nature. Was there ever a perfect balance or is it a perpetual fight for survival? I do not know the answer; I am only asking myself.

I sincerely believe that each individual is entitled to a period of undisturbed sleep, be it by night or day. Now, one night when a serene tranquillity enveloped my garden and I was fast asleep, I was rudely awakened by a wild, piercing shriek. I found that I was disturbed by the caterwauling of the feline species. Why do they make such an outcry? Some define this as 'catting', others say it is the ineffable rapture of lovemaking. Feline sex suggests to me a rapacious form of procreation. Why all the rampaging, rip-roaring rumpus, culminating in a wild, unearthly shriek causing every canine in the neighbourhood to bark and howl?

Nature has many strange, mysterious ways of dealing with the procreation of the species. I do not want to create a border between male and female cats but I honestly think that a case could be made for compromise on both sides: females on neutral ground and toms bound to a curfew and ceasefire. If this could be implemented, poor unfortunate Humpty-Dumpty might enjoy a good sleep and not become a somnambulist.

One is never really sure what to expect in a garden. Only last year I was regaled by a nocturnal visitor in the form of a screech owl. Fortunately, it was before bedtime. I directed a flashlight on the branch where it perched cat-faced, looking down at me. When I attempted to mimic the wise visitor, it was more than it could take and, giving me a departing half-hoot, half-screech, it flapped its great wings, disappearing into the night.

> A wise old owl stood on an oak,
> The more it heard, the less it spoke.
> The less it spoke, the more it heard.
> Let's imitate this wise old bird.

At the start of this essay I described my garden as a God-given sanctuary, a place where I could rest, find peace and time to reflect. Now, on second thoughts or perhaps awakening from my reverie, I must accuse myself of floundering in a morass of sheer hypocrisy. I think I have read somewhere in the Bible: 'What hast thou got that was not given unto thee?' I do not realize my errors, finding myself in direct conflict with nature itself, thinking myself secure within my greedy, begrudging self-made enclave, lording it over the fowl and the brute. I only wanted special birds, special animals, special flowers, roses and shrubs, special everything in my garden. I had no time for love-cats, owls, jackdaws, magpies and ravens. I could not tolerate nature's wild whims disturbing my sleep, never even giving a thought to the fact that I had entombed myself within a fortress of self-gratification, when suddenly I was confronted with a startling truth: 'Behold the lilies of the field, they neither reap nor spin. Yet Solomon in all his glory was not clothed as one of these.' (Matthew 6: 28)

Now descending from my thinly gilded throne, admitting my faults with humility, I arrive full circle back at the beginning of my composition: 'One is nearer God's heart in a garden / Than anywhere else on earth.' […]

A GARDEN: IN THE WANING LIGHT OF MY YEARS
Skelligs Sunset

Time was when I walked the highways and byways, the hills and valleys of my native townland without let or hindrance, carefree, young and healthy. I did not notice the flowers, the trees, birds or bees, even myself. I never gave a thought to who I was, except that I strutted by on two legs. All other animated creatures shunned my presence. In a lighter vein I could be likened to Topsy in *Uncle Tom's Cabin*, who, when asked where she came from, retorted: 'I 'spect I growed.' A friend of mine in Nova Scotia, when asked where she came from, said: 'I think we were here always.'

Skelligs Haul

The fact of the matter is that I am now old and frail. I glimpse the Grim Reaper stalking his prey. I await the inevitable:

> Sceptre and Crown must tumble down,
> And in the dust be equal made.
> (James Shirley)

In front of my cottage by the roadside is a postage-stamp lawn, sheltered on both sides by privet and hawthorn hedges, with a couple of fir trees here and there. The only furniture is an old wooden garden seat where I rest and often droop into the sleep of the ending, as foretold in Gaelic folklore:

> *Deireadh fir a shuan*
> *Agus an bhean á faire féin suas.*

> The man sleeping his last
> And the woman alert in the sleep of the ending.

The old road is now a modern two-lane highway with no space for pedestrians, especially those who have three legs at eventide. Once again the old Gaelic riddle comes to mind:

> *Ceithre chosa ar maidin*
> *Dhá chos i lár an lae*
> *Agus trí chois um thráthnóna.*

The folklorist condenses the lifespan of an aged person into one day:

> On all fours as a child in the morning of life,
> Two legs at midday
> Three legs at eventide, an old person walking with the aid of a stick.

A Garden: In the Waning Light of My Years

Now in the waning light of my years on this planet named Earth, I prepare for the natural departure that awaits all life, including the most dominant and exceedingly clever human being called by anthropologists and scientists *Homo sapiens, Homo erectus*, etc. I respect and try to understand the wisdom of these great scholars as best I can, sure of one reality: that I too will disappear into the mist of timelessness. My piece of animated clay will return into the earth from where it was formed, hoping that the spirit will return to its creator. Life seems so vainglorious, the answers still 'blowing in the wind'. Nevertheless, it brings to mind many fanciful echoes of youth and memories of the past.

Now confined to my garden seat, I put up the shutters and close my eyes, repeat a mantra and try to find God somewhere out there in the unending, perpetual tunnel of darkness of my own doubting mind. In this unresponsive, lethargic mood, Morpheus, the Roman god of sleep, must have intervened. I awakened, startled by a dream, to find it was already twilight. I regard dreams as foolish fantasies of the mind, but not this one. Deep within the darkening shadows of failing light I could imagine a lone, kneeling figure with upraised hands, imploring and crying out to His Father for help to ease His physical suffering. Could I not watch one hour with Him? I had slept peacefully through it all, abandoning Him in his anguish. Was this the garden that triggered memories of far-flung days of my youth? Father Colm O'Riordan and Father Andrew Collins, two Jesuit priests, often visited and sat with me outside my roadside cottage while on holidays in Ballinskelligs. One worked the mission fields of Rhodesia. The other gave his all in a dreadful leper colony. Farewell, you warriors of Christ! Enjoy your paradise. Nobody said it was going to be easy.

Family and Local Folk

OUR HOUSE
Skelligside

During the long winter nights, it was good to sit around the open hearth in the warmth of a blazing turf fire. Our house had an open fireplace and chimney-back with built-in stone hob seats on each side. The front wall of the chimney-breast was supported by a great wooden beam which my father said came in on the tide just in time for the building of the house. No matter where the wind blew from, our open chimney never smoked. Our kitchen was lime-washed, and even the walls near the fire were as white as snow every day of the year. Sometimes a change in the weather would bring a lump of soot down from the chimney, to be pounced upon by my watchful mother.

We were all proud of our thatched cottage. There were two bedrooms with a kitchen in between, and space for another bed in the half-loft reached by a ladder. A division of painted boarding separated the kitchen from the bedrooms. The kitchen had a dresser hung with row after row of ware, sometimes in white with a blue and gold pattern. I remember the beautiful china jugs with floral designs which were once full of delicious-tasting red fruity jam. Country people always bought 'the jam in the jug' in preference to the jam in the plain pottery crock. The container helped to adorn the country dresser, and woe betide any slovenly butter-fingers who would break or damage a piece of the precious collection! The kitchen walls were decorated with a picture of Christ and the Virgin Mary, and a piece of Blessed Palm after each Palm Sunday.

Skelligs Haul

A great wicker basket was kept full of turf in its corner at the far end of the kitchen. The fire, continually fed with pieces of pine bogdeal, stayed in until bedtime. It made a lovely blaze and gave off a fragrant smoke. My father dug for these roots, which were found deep in the bogs. The wood, preserved for two thousand years or more, was resinous and inflammable. It was once used for interior lighting, but now made a fine torchlight for spearing fish on rivers, as well as the traditional yule-log at Christmas. Each night a bucket of spring water was brought in for the next morning's breakfast and for drinking. I never drank water more pure and invigorating than the blue crystal from the Bog of the Hummocks. Even in summer it was as cold as ice.

A large wooden peg driven into the wall high up in the corner of the chimney, well out of view, held a supply of salted cod. After about a week the fish would be stiff and dry and flavoured with turf smoke, which gave it a sweet taste. We always ate the smoked cod on Christmas Eve, with a white sauce my mother made from flour, milk and onions and other finely chopped vegetables. During my youth, we did not eat much meat except on feast-days. Pork was cheap and plentiful, and pigs' feet were a penny each, but that penny was hard to come by. A pig's head and a large pot of cabbage, turnips and potatoes, washed down by a flood of fresh buttermilk, seemed like food for a king. On the other hand, we were lucky in having the choicest of fish, both cured and fresh: nourishing casks of pickled herring with the full roe left in, not to mention mackerel, cod, bream, whiting and other varieties. Our diet varied from time to time as we took advantage of the great tides which exposed the clams, razor clams, escallop and cockles, which we would dig by the bucketful. My mother boiled, cleaned and minced a selection of these mixed with herbs, salt and pepper. This was a mouth-watering clam chowder.

Our House

The old skinflint with one leg in the grave who drank a cupful of this savoury potion would feel like living again.

All the neighbours kept flocks of geese and had roast and stuffed goose for Christmas and Easter. A goose market was held in Cahersiveen before Christmas. One shilling and sixpence was a good price for a fat goose, while a five-week-old piglet sold for four shillings – a fortune in those days. My mother kept up to forty small yellow hens of an old breed called *Sicily Buí*, as well as small black hens with a few speckled feathers on the wings, called Black Minorca, before Rhode Island Reds were introduced to Ballinskelligs. We also kept a dozen or more ducks with a great mallard-like drake. Eggs were plentiful and cheap when all the hens were laying, and fetched thirty-six or forty pence for one hundred and twenty. The cock rarely announces daybreak in the countryside now. As one old-timer put it, on hearing the cock crow after a sleepless night: '*Tar slán, a mhic na circe!*' 'A health to you, son of the hen!'

My father had seven acres which seemed over-stocked. They fed two milch cows, always of the Black Kerry breed, and two calves which were sold as yearlings. We kept a donkey and cart, with a creel to bring home the turf. Every inch of those seven acres had to be utilized, to grow potatoes, oats, and hay for winter fodder. The cattle and the donkey were left with little room for grazing. The annual rent on the seven acres was three pounds ten shillings, payable to the Mary O'Mahony Estate of Dromore, and later to the Irish Land Commission, until the parcel of land was finally redeemed by the occupying tenant.

Ballinskelligs and the surrounding countryside of Iveragh was vested in the O'Mahony and Fitzgerald families. Other parts were owned by Trinity College, Dublin, and by the Marquis of Lansdowne. Landlords did not have a good name. If a tenant was unable to pay his rent he slept by the roadside. An old widow was evicted from a little cabin whose ruins are still visible on the roadside near Canuig, Ballinskelligs. As the sheriff and bailiffs threw her from her miserable holding, the widow cursed in Irish, 'May a funeral of demons escort your soul to Hell!' Some of my neighbours suffered a similar fate. A platoon of Redcoats with guns and fixed bayonets travelled from Tralee to Ballinskelligs, where they wreaked vengeance on the O'Leary family, who were in arrears to the Crown to the sum of a few paltry shillings. Denis O'Leary, his daughter Brigid and three sons resisted with pitchforks, and it was only on the intervention of the parish priest that the old man's life was spared. Because the Chief Constable was injured in the fray, old Denis was put in irons and taken fifty miles to Tralee, bound like some wild animal, bruised and broken in both soul and body.

The land of Ballinskelligs was divided into small uneconomic holdings, and the region was registered with the Congested Districts' Board. In the entire parish perhaps only ten people would own enough land to farm twenty cows and keep a pair of horses. These 'strong' farmers, who cultivated an air of independence and pride, were sometimes referred to as 'squireens'. A great social barrier existed between them and the poor men or women struggling to survive on a few acres.

HASTE TO THE WEDDING

Skelligs Sunset

A far cry from the lavishness, flair and showy extravagance of today were the Shrovetide weddings of my youth. When my relative Tom Fenton from Coom married Margaret McCarthy from the Glen, the wedding was to remain indelible in my memory, I being only seven years and some months. That morning I was given in care to the local postman, who would pass by the wedding house on his daily delivery. This extra duty, on the instructions of my mother, was to escort me to and leave me safely at the Fenton dwelling. My mother would follow later and help other women to prepare the wedding feast.

Ned Walsh was the postman's name and a more kind and loving person you could not wish for. He made my journey comfortable and exciting by sitting me astride the saddle of the first bicycle I can remember seeing in the locality. Rural postmen were not supplied with any means of transport and mail was delivered on foot. How Ned came by the bicycle I do not know, as bicycles were a very scarce commodity for years to come. The road to Coom was of rough, loose stone called gravel and was very steep, but we arrived safely at my cousin's house. Ned was invited to the wedding, being an able performer on the melodeon. He could play all night long set tunes, jigs, reels, hornpipes and old-time waltzes. Later in life, I heard him play such tunes as 'Haste to the Wedding', 'Bean ag Baint Duileasc' ('The Woman Cutting Dulse'), 'You Broke my Cups and Saucers', 'Garden of Daisies', 'Boney's Retreat' and others, too numerous to mention here.

On reaching the Fenton farmhouse I saw many women neighbours preparing the wedding feast. I was very relieved to see my mother arriving and working with them later on. Some were busy tending to great black iron pots. One contained rich savoury beef broth, hanging on the swing crane within the chimney breast. Another pot was full of floury potatoes, bursting their jackets. Several kitchen tables lent by neighbours for the feast were placed end to end. Ned was given a *tomhaisín* (a little measure) of whiskey and also a big dark glass of porter with a white collar of rich, creamy foam. We were both seated to table, each with a generous supply of corned beef and cabbage and a plentiful amount of delicious beef broth and potatoes. Ned noticed that I seemed very shy. He would occasionally whisper and say: 'Don't be shy! Eat up, boy, or you'll never grow up if you don't eat up!' When all the tables were set, fancy tablecloths were not displayed, but all tables scrubbed white and laden with great portions of roast goose and mutton on beautiful patterned earthenware plates. There was a choice of good, wholesome food, from home-cured bacon and cabbage to the entire pig's head, complete with snout and ears scraped clean.

All was ready for the wedding party, which would soon arrive, after celebrating at Paddy Keating's or at Haren's licensed premises in Ballinskelligs. Another spare table was heaped with several loaves of homemade bread, some known as curranty cakes and baked several days previously, in the round oven on the hearthstone covered with live coals. Also a plentiful supply of baker's bread called *builíní bána*, white loaves dubbed by us country folk as 'shop bread'. There was plenty of red jam in earthenware crocks and china jugs and a supply of homemade fresh butter.

The wedding party could now be seen appearing around the road leading into Coom. This bend is known by the Gaelic word, *An Lúb* (the bend). I remember seeing several jaunting cars and farm carts coming into view, also single riders on saddle horses. The strains of sweet music from a melodeon drifted upwards along the valley from the homeward cavalcade, giving the evening a joyful air of festivity. The kitchen soon filled with guests, who were mostly small farmers, their wives, a few fishermen and a good few young boys and girls. A special table was set up in the centre for the bride and groom. The bride wore a long skirt of heavy blue material, the hem of which helped sweep the floor. Her footwear was not totally visible, except for little glimpses of soft, polished black leather. Margaret was a very handsome woman who had spent some time in America. She was dressed in a white blouse with a very high collar reaching under her chin, sleeves that were long, wide and full, covering the wrists and the back of her hands, and a bright brooch with brilliant, flashing eyes adorning the front of her neck. All flesh was left to the imagination of the beholder, in contrast to the modern creations of our present fashion, making brides and mothers of that era look like packages labelled 'not to be opened till Christmas'. The bride's coiffure was her crowning glory. Her fair auburn hair was coiled into plaited rings turban-like on the back slope of her head, supported by ornate combs with sparkling coloured eyes, which were beads of glass. Looking back now, I think the dress had a genteel suggestion of Victorianism.

When the meal was finished the tables were stowed to make room for dancing, singing and drinking; also perhaps some furtive courtship. Two wooden casks of stout, with very thick oak staves, stood on a table in the back porch, attended by a special, trustworthy person, a neighbour or close relative of the family. The drink was distributed in pint-glass measures and care taken that some were not favoured more than others. It was well known that a bucketful of stout could disappear mysteriously into the night to regale a stag party held secretly behind the barn or a haystack in the haggard. Therefore the person in charge had to be vigilant, lest any fast ones were pulled. In latter years I heard drinkers praise the viscosity of the black beverage of those days, saying: 'Sure there was eating and drinking in it!' 'Wouldn't the glass stick to the counter!' and 'It was like black honey compared to what we're drinking now, pure bog water (*uisce na gcos*), and look at the price of it!'

The young unmarried women wore their hair long and plaited, but were dressed much the same as the older women. All wore black woollen shawls. A few yellow or brown shawls were in vogue later on. Some young girls were wearing white blouses. Fashion was changing from 1912 onwards.

The dance commenced with old-time sets and four-hand reels. Nano Roche, the groom's mother, took off her leather shoes and danced a superb Irish reel in her vamps. The hearth flagstone had a hollow sound. Some said it was laid across an empty iron pot in order to give a staccato effect to the tap dancing. Paddy Lawlor, whom I knew in later life, was a young man then. He danced 'The Sailor's Hornpipe'. Others danced jigs, making a merry drumming sound of hollow reverberations. All footwear was fashioned by local shoemakers, who vied with each other as to who won the most customers. Men's footwear, whether light or heavy, had in most cases iron-tipped heels. Some women wore buckled shoes.

Invariably the petticoat was woollen and the colour very often was a bright red of finely woven flannel. The woman with the red petticoat complete with apron was a common sight during my growing years. As the night wore on, songs were sung. An old man would take the singer's hand in his, rocking the arm to and fro in rhythm with the air of the song. This was called *sean nós* (old style). My brother Paddy sang a song called 'The Shamrock Shore'.

> In the blooming spring when the small birds sing,
> And lambs did sport and play,
> My way I took and friends forsook,
> Till I came to Dublin Quay,
> I entered on board as a passenger,
> To England I sailed o'er.
> I bid farewell to all my friends,
> Round the dear old Shamrock Shore.

Another beautiful song was sung in Gaelic by Maurice Fenton, 'An Buachaill Caol Dubh', about a maiden lamenting the loss of her 'Slender Dark Boy'. John Fitzgerald from Horse Island sang a very old English song, which I heard many times in later life, and which has never lost its charm, called 'After the Ball Was Over'. Annie Fenton from Caherdaniel sang a very old song called 'Lucky Jim', and 'Siúil, A Rún'.

> I would I were on yonder hill,
> 'Tis there I'd sit and cry my fill,
> And every tear would turn a mill,
> *Is go dté tú, mo mhuirnín, slán.*
> I'll dye my petticoats, I'll dye them red,
> And round the world I'll beg my bread,
> Until my parents shall wish me dead,
> *Is go dté tú, mo mhuirnín, slán.*

Weddings are an occasion of rejoicing and happiness but there is always the danger of arguments if Bacchus is allowed to influence rational thinking. In this case two neighbours got involved in a silly argument relating to the best method of castrating calves and piglets, which was practised by lay people. One accused the other jocosely of bringing home the testicles and grilling them on the fire tongs as tasty morsels. The jocose word spoken without malice can often contain the germ of offence, which can perchance lead to fiery emotion. In this case, a free-for-all was avoided by the intervention of their good spouses, who prevailed on their bellicose husbands to shake hands and have a little common sense, thus avoiding an outbreak of hostilities among good neighbours.

The feasting continued until early dawn. Food was again prepared for all the guests, who were called to the table in turn. A table in the parlour had several brass candlesticks with wax candles lighting. I remember drooping slowly to sleep in a soft chair beside my mother. All I can recall is that my eyes faltered, and I was seeing beautiful coloured rainbows of light encircling each candle flame. The miracle of suspended consciousness being so deep, I was surprised to wake in my own bed in Ballinskelligs, late next day. How I arrived there is only known to my good and caring mother who moulded my growing years!

As I grew in age I was present at other weddings, which followed much the same pattern. Local boys would dress in costumes consisting of funny tunics and hats made entirely from sheaves of oaten straw. A group of those young boys and girls visited the wedding house without invitation. They were always treated with tolerance and courtesy, given refreshments and allowed to dance with the bride. They also carried their own musical instruments. This was an old traditional custom in most parish communities, to go 'strawing'.

A story is told of a girl who was forced into a marriage of loveless convenience by her parents. On her wedding night, when festivities were at their height, her lover came disguised as a straw-boy, complete in his costume and mask. During the dance with the bride, who recognized him as her former sweetheart, she whispered: 'Please come for me before dawn breaks and bring your horse.' The story tells how the horse was found cropping grass peacefully on the roadside somewhere near Cork city. A farewell note with the following poem and a straw-boy's hat were found attached to the bridle:

> America lies far away,
> A place we soon will be.
> Let those be damned forever,
> Who would part my love from me.

People who could not provide transport were satisfied to walk to church and home again, to partake of whatever fare they were able to afford. They raised fine families, living good Christian lives and were mostly contented with their lot. Some weddings were frowned upon by one or both sets of parents. It is said that 'marriages are made in heaven', but I venture to say a number of very doubtful ones are made on earth. That a marriage should be valid it was most important that the mutual consent of the contracting parties was fully observed. Eloping couples were very few. Only a courageous girl would throw a bundle of her wearing apparel into the night, and follow by wriggling out through a narrow gable window and down a short ladder provided for her, into the waiting arms of her swain. Perhaps the next letter received by her distraught parents would come from lovers on their way to the New World. However, marriage was not always by the mutual consent of the contracting parties. Some couples were forced into marriage by domineering parents and clergy, who would not tolerate a hint of pregnancy, let alone illegitimacy in their families. The edict pertaining to such a transgression was marry or abscond, or else risk becoming a social pariah among the self-righteous parish Pharisees.

> The night of the wedding,
> The night of the fun,
> The night of the wedding,
> She had a young son.

Young women were usually left holding the burden of blame and so-called shame. They became the sacrificial lambs on the altar of a slowly emerging, modern, democratic, partly Christian society. Many never entered the marriage bed but cursed the day they were joined in dubious wedlock. Who has not heard of the shotgun wedding!

A story is told of a young man who denied being responsible for a young girl with whom he was friendly, but who now appeared to be pregnant. In good faith their parents and the local parish priest used their good influence to persuade the couple to marry. The matchmakers considered that the pair should do the decent thing and thereby avoid a scandal. When all seemed serene on the nuptial morning, as the bride approached the church accompanied by her parents, she was seen to suddenly swoon and fall to the ground. The priest was immediately summoned to her side, and he in turn ordered medical attention. The doctor performed an on-the-spot diagnosis, declaring that the girl was not pregnant and in his opinion she had nothing more exciting inside her at that moment than an excessive amount of superfluous gas trapped within her intestines. So ended what otherwise could be termed a mild case of shotgun pressure, much to the relief of the proud parents.

At my uncle's wedding, a local woman named Kate was detailed to attend to the milking of the cows that evening. Night had fallen at six o'clock and it was dark in the byre where the cows were tied in their stalls. Six cows were in one byre and in another smaller house were tied two cows and a mule. I was to accompany her with extra buckets and a lantern – a rough type of carriage lamp with a candle and glass sides. All went well while she milked the six cows. We took the pails of milk to the dairy and strained it through a muslin cloth into the tubs where it accumulated for churning. In the dairy standing on a small table was a barrel of stout, with a tap and a white enamel bucket ready with several pint measures to treat the guests when the wedding party arrived. Each time we visited the dairy Kate would fill herself a pint glass of porter. I know she drank it with gusto because of the smacking sounds she made with her lips and a satisfied exhalation of her breathing ending in an 'Ah! Ah!' of relish. She offered me some to drink. When I declined she said it was good for me.

Lastly we entered the small byre where the other two cows and the mule were in their stalls. On handing her the little milking stool, it was at this juncture that some sudden gust of air puffed out the candle flame within the lantern, leaving us in complete darkness. I groped and fumbled with the matchbox, in a hurry to strike a light. In the meantime I heard Kate chuckle to herself, saying: 'Hurry boy, light the candle quick. There is something strange here. I think this cow has a pair of balls.' I heard her shout of laughter as I got the lantern going. She had mistaken the mule for a cow in the darkness. Kate was a jolly, warm-hearted person, very good-humoured and loved a joke.

A few summers ago I was a guest at a wedding with much of the modern trappings. The dinner and reception were held at a special venue. In contrast with the old-style country weddings, for me it was a repetitious, uninteresting and boring affair. We listened to impromptu speeches extolling the qualities of one or other of the newlyweds, punctuated with intervals of readings from telegrams, cards, etc. The hired band played blaring, ear-splitting disco music, making ordinary conversation barely audible. The antics on the dance floor seemed not so much good physical exercise as a carbon copy of some ritual dance performed at a tribal feast in Africa. Gone were the old-time jigs, reels and Irish dancing.

THE LADY OF HORSE ISLAND

Skelligside

My aunt Julia Kirby lived on Horse Island. She was a tall broad-shouldered swarthy woman of the *Uí Chiarmhaic* clan. She well matched her name in the flesh, for *Ciarmhac* means 'son of the dark one' and her eyes and hair were as black as the fruit of the sloe thorn. She married David Fitzgerald of Horse Island some time in the eighteen-sixties. Her husband died suddenly of pneumonia, leaving her with six young children, and my father went across to the island and helped her rear the young family.

Many were the tales she told of the hardship and privations suffered by the smallholders of that time. In early spring and autumn Breton fishermen arrived in sailing boats from Brest, Saint Malo and Concarnau to fish for the much-coveted mackerel found in abundance off the south-west coast of Ireland. They kept casks and salt on board and cured some of their catch for the Irish market. They were as destitute as were the Irish at that time, coming ashore on the island to collect bucketfuls of the striped chocolate and cream snail-shells, and filling my aunt's little kitchen where they roasted the snail-shells on the coals of the open fire. They would break the snails open, add a little salt and eat them from the palm of the hand, offering her some snails and addressing her as Mother. 'Oh Mother!' they would exclaim, 'snails plenty goot for the Mungi, they are just like butta!' They would also bring her sour black wine kept in casks, which they called 'vino claret'. The sailors virtually lived on the snails which still abound in the island's stone fences, where can be seen the brown thrushes knocking them against the rocks. Perhaps we miss out on this delicacy. The sailors all wore wooden shoes like clogs, carved from solid blocks of wood, some of them very ornate. They would row over to the mainland when the weather was suitable and pick buckets of winkles and limpets from the reefs when the tide had receded. They also fished for wrasse from the rocks and would exchange dark French tobacco with the locals for fresh milk and eggs. When the weather was not fit for fishing, they repaired their nets and sails, without which they could not operate. They often took to the fields on the

The Lady of Horse Island

shore to walk for exercise, and would sit for hours on the beach playing a card game.

One old man from Ballinskelligs called Seamus Jack would sit beside them every day while they played cards. Old Seamus seemed fascinated by hearing a foreign language, and vowed that he understood every word the sailors said, maintaining that anyone who could speak Irish well could also understand French. When asked to translate some of the games he would answer readily. One game the sailors played was just like the Irish '*Dáir an bhó*', so it meant 'Bull the cow', and the French name for the ace of hearts was '*cloch i dtóin chait*' or 'a pebble in a cat's arse'. With roguish braggadocio, he continued to show off, speaking French to himself and to others in the neighbourhood.

Julia Kirby was very devout. Rain, hail or shine, she would assemble her little flock to recite the Rosary. On many evenings, the sailors from Brittany joined her in prayer. When reciting the Confiteor, they answered in Latin, striking their breasts, '*Mea culpa! Mea culpa! Mea maxima culpa!*' They became fast friends, the old lady of the island and the Breton fishermen.

Julia told a tale of a lone fisherman who lived on a hooker anchored in the harbour. He would arrive unexpectedly, stay for some time – perhaps days or weeks – and vanish again without trace, always putting to sea at night. He was quite deaf, but could lip-read and speak. Aunt Julia called him '*Bodhaire*' or 'the deaf one'. He lived entirely on fish, which he was expert in curing and drying. He would row himself to the island in a small dinghy he kept on board, and walked with a severe limp. *Terra firma* seemed to upset him. The children were amused with his weaving, rolling gait. Some fishermen called him 'Old Stormy': he could be seen far out to sea in very foul weather. He had a smattering of other tongues as well as Irish, but he never divulged his identity though he was constantly muttering in monotone.

One night while *Bodhaire*'s hooker lay anchored in the shelter of the island in early October, a fierce hurricane struck the coast. Later that night when the storm had abated, Julia Kirby peered out into the feeble spume-filled moonlight of the harbour but failed to see the hooker. It was gone, swept away by the power of the storm. The good lady of the island said a prayer for the old man of the sea before retiring. Later that night she was awakened by a knock on the door. She lit a candle, and asked who was outside, but received no reply. Then came a knock on the window pane, and there she beheld the half-drowned figure of old *Bodhaire* like an apparition from the deep. She opened the door and he stumbled into the kitchen, dishevelled as a wet hen, his fingers torn and bleeding and his scanty clothing in shreds. Breaking into a mournful sobbing, he repeated over and over in Irish, 'Mo *bháidín, mo bháidín*,' 'My boat, my little boat, I've lost my boat!' His hooker had been dashed to pieces but he escaped miraculously by climbing the cliff face. Julia Kirby made him comfortable while he stayed with the family, until one day he was taken on board a French boat on her way to Saint John's, Newfoundland, to fish for cod.

The good lady of the island lived to enjoy helping to raise her grandchildren in old age. She often went to the mainland to take up vigil beside the sick, the lonely, and the dying, bringing succour to many bent on their last journey. She suffered patiently in her own last years from an incurable infected foot. This seemed part of the pathway to sainthood: the golden domes, the jewel-studded shrines, the carved angels standing guard by the marble tombs are but dross beside a cup of water given in His Name.

Horse Island is now deserted, where generations of healthy, happy families were once reared. Present-day economics make island life impossible.

A FAMILY WAKE
Skelligside

The old man tormented and grey will die,
And die will the beautiful lark of the hill,
The youth will go and his wisdom leave behind,
And all who live shall vanish into everlasting time.

I first became acquainted with death on the evening that my grandmother Mary Fitzgerald Cremin died. Her house was near ours, only two acres or so to the west. I was with my mother at her bedside. The date was 17 September 1915. She was eighty-nine years old, and even if the signs of feeble age said that death had conquered, the lines of a once gentle maiden were still in evidence. The priest had left, having anointed her and administered the last rites. Her face had assumed a dark greyish colour. A parchment mask seemed to cover her features and the grin of the unmerciful reaper was plain to be seen on her cheeks. Several neighbouring women attended at her deathbed. They said the Rosary aloud while one of them held a lighted blessed candle in her hand. The flickering of the candle-flame was the only light in the bedroom, and ghostly shadows danced across the lime-washed walls. In the centre of the bed I could see my grandmother's face. It had now changed completely: the dark mask of death had vanished and she looked radiant with peace and grace, her fine features of polished marble like a sleeping queen's, her breath coming in a series of short sighs, with no death-rattle, no prolonged agony. My grandmother died like a baby going to sleep.

My uncle Aindí Fada and a neighbour Tadhg Phats were busy hanging white sheets on the side walls near the back door. They then placed two tables end to end and covered them with more sheets and a plentiful supply of pillows, some edged with beautiful homemade lace. When all was in order, my grandmother's bier was like a scene from the time of the Pharaohs. My aunt Nell, who had just arrived home from America, told us that the undertakers over there were using paint and powder for many a day.

Some time later, I noticed the women going into a huddle and whispering. They were preparing for keening the loved one who had just died. They then approached the corpse and in unison started the mournful lamentation or *caoineadh*. The cry would reach a climax, hover for a brief moment at the highest note, then descend to the depths of desolate heart-rending lamentation, each sob getting weaker and shorter until it became a stuttering moan. Being only nine years old and having never experienced keening of the dead, I became so frightened that I went through the kitchen door like a bolt of lightning, and God never stayed me until I was safe and sound again on my father's hearth. He was in the kitchen, saw my distress and sat near me to explain gently that keening the dead was a very old custom, and maybe if the truth were known most of these women were not sad at all nor shedding real tears, but putting on a show to perpetuate an old custom. At first, I thought it an odd explanation, but it did not take me many years to understand that my father was right.

My mother came looking for me and took me back o the wake. Uncle Aindí and Tadhg Phats had arrived back with a large cask of porter, a box of white clay pipes and several blocks of plug tobacco. In another box I saw some bottles of red whiskey and loaves of baker's bread and crocks of red jam. The women and the men were given tea and baker's loaf with plenty of fresh butter and jam. Some men arranged seating with stools and wide thick planks of wood. The neighbours filled the last inch of space inside the

A Family Wake

kitchen. Two boys were kept busy shredding tobacco and filling clay pipes which were presented one to each person. Very soon clouds of tobacco smoke filled the room.

Some time later Aindí and Tadhg Phats came in carrying two large buckets of porter with white caps of creamy foam. Every man was given a pint glass of it. It was good to watch them swallowing great draughts, which sometimes left a beard of foam on their chins. I got a terrible longing to taste a drop of it myself, as the sweet scent of apples seemed to fill the kitchen. Not one word of English was spoken at grandmother's wake that night. The girls and the older women wore long skirts, black woollen stockings to the knee, and black shawls, with the odd brown or yellow shawl among them.

I remember listening to Aindí Fada and Tadhg Phats discussing local affairs. They both liked their drop, and usually waxed eloquent and philosophical – I suspect they were helping themselves generously from the buckets. Merry or not, they were the essence of conviviality. When all the old topics were exhausted – gardening, fishing, women, even horse-racing and regattas – and I thought that the last word was said, my uncle Aindí uttered a yawning moan, so deep and sad that one would think it came from the nethermost end of his gut. '*Ochón*,' he sighed. 'I wonder who will be here to wake us when we die?'

'Maybe, Aindí,' said Tadhg Phats, 'you won't need any wake or funeral.'

'How could that happen?' asked Aindí.

'Well,' said Tadhg Phats, 'supposing you were lost at sea and your body wasn't found: maybe only the porpoise and the spike dogfish would be at your wake.'

'Now Tadhg,' exclaimed Aindí, 'don't talk like that. If you were a proper Christian you would never drown, and you would never fear the sea pigs, the dolphins or the dogfish.'

'What connection has Christianity with the subject?' asked Tadhg Phats.

'Hold on now,' said Aindí. 'It's like this. Peter the Apostle was able to walk on the water while he had confidence in Christ.'

Tadhg Phats answered with a great burst of laughter. 'On my soul, Aindí, whatever Saint Peter may have done, it will be a long time before we see you walking ashore from the Skelligs.'

The neighbours were enjoying this talk and they all laughed. At that moment my mother announced she was going to say the Rosary of the Virgin Mary. It was now midnight and she led the neighbours through each decade and then the Litany, imploring the saints in Heaven to intercede for the departed souls. The night was now getting late and I was feeling tired, so my mother took me home, but grandmother's death stayed planted in my memory until this present day. May you have a bed in Paradise, grandmother.

THE JOURNEYWORKERS

Skelligside

My thoughts go back once more to the long winter nights of my early boyhood – the floor swept clean, Mom putting an apronful of black turf from *Gob an Dá Chaol* into the fire, the day's work finished till tomorrow. After supper the neighbours would visit each other, a custom called cabin hunting, night rambling and other such terms in Irish. It gave neighbours a chance to relax from the tensions of their daily lives and chat about topical affairs.

The Journeyworkers

I remember Tomáisín, a regular caller to our house, as an old man of nearly eighty. Although he attended only a hedge school, he was able to read and write, do mental arithmetic and discuss things. He preferred the clay pipe to the wooden one, and he would often ask my mother for the loan of a knitting needle to free the stem. My mother hated the smell of tobacco, and when she would see the men rubbing the knitting needle in their trousers afterwards, she would say to them in Irish, 'You are a bloody dirty lot!'

Another neighbour who often came was Andy Gow O'Sullivan. Andy was an old man when I got to know him. He owned a thatched cabin about fifty paces west of our house. The land he had would not make a graveyard for a wren – it consisted only of the pathway to his door. He was one of the journeymen workers called the *spailpíní fánacha*. The tools of their trade were the spade, shovel and reaping sickle. I have often heard Andy telling stories about the great harvest and grain reaped by the special harvest *meitheal* or work party, and about the skilled use of the reaping sickle and the implements for preparing potato and vegetable beds. The journeymen of the past were specialists in their own way. Their work was neat and produced an excellent crop yield.

Seasonal migration from Ballinskelligs became traditional after the Famine. Workers travelled on foot to Tralee, their spades on their shoulders as a sign of their trade. If they got no work there, they would continue their walk, to the markets in Limerick city or Tipperary town. After a hard journey, in poor clothes and bad shoes and with little to eat, these fine workers were easily hired at a low wage by the rich farmers.

Andy would describe the beautiful country mansions owned by big farmers and also told tales of the horsy people who owned packs of hounds for fox hunting. According to him, any worker hired to become a hand at the Big House would consider himself fortunate. Whenever Andy became slightly inebriated he would talk about the beautiful women who made up his youthful love life. Without a doubt he would have been a dashing young blade: he was yet tall and handsome even in the evening of his days.

While I write about the travelling work parties, it is only just and right that I fill the page with knowledge of the past that my dear mother handed down to me. My mother Mary Cremin and Eileen Connell of Dungeagan travelled to County Limerick in the year 1877. They left Ballinskelligs with another group in the late spring of that year, walking most of the long journey, and they worked for nine months before returning home barefoot in deep snow. My mother was only eighteen, and Nelly O'Connell one year her senior. They were fortunate in meeting with good people who hired both of them at the market-place in Limerick city: rich farmers owning acres broad and free which were used mostly for dairying. The girls were put in company with other girls, under the management of a stewardess, and stayed in a special house near the dairy. It was a hard life, constantly milking evening and morning. The milking started at five o'clock. Afterwards the great churns were set up for the hand churning, which was heavy work. There was other work too: food had to be prepared for pigs, potatoes harvested, washing and ironing done. My mother said she often felt so exhausted going to her bed that it was terrible to think of another day's work starting at the dawn. Sunday was no different from any other day: there was no day of rest. They only wore their shoes going to Mass, because they had to last for a year at least. Their entire wages for nine months were eight pounds. This was the grim story my mother told about the life of the seasonal workers.

Many fine young men who went over the hills with their spades were never to return. Some were hired by unscrupulous farmers and had to sleep in cold lofts over the stables, where they contracted illnesses and died as a result. Many others joined the army: they wanted to be freed forever from the misery of the journeyworker's life and they did not care that it was a change from the house of Horror to the house of Hate. There was little choice between being a private in the king's army and being a beggar and a journeyman. An Irish poem called 'An Spailpín Fánach' or 'The Journeyworker' is sung to a haunting air. A translation of its first verse will give an idea of its richness …

> Never, never more shall I go to Cashel,
> Selling or wasting my manhood
> At the market-place
> By the hiring wall,
> Like a pauper on the sidewalk.
> Churlish landlords
> Arriving on steeds,
> Inquiring if I am for hiring,
> Oh come let us go,
> For the road is long,
> Come away with the *Spailpín Fánach*.

BEACHCOMBERS

Skelligs Calling

Was it because I had read Defoe's *Robinson Crusoe*, Ballantyne's *Coral Island* or Stevenson's *Treasure Island* that I wished to walk alone on a stretch of clean sandy beach, especially in the full of the moon? On a night such as this when the waves, breaking and trooping shoreward, have turned to a brilliant silver and when the sand and the sea take on a polished reflection, giving an added exhilaration to the expectations of the beachcomber, the thrill of finding a great spar of wood or a cask washed ashore is linked with the beauty of the night. Beachcombing can become habitual and also exciting. It held a sense of allurement for me.

A variety of flotsam, helped by ocean currents, drifted onto the South Kerry beaches during the World Wars. Wreckage was the result of the dreadful torpedo and various other devices of destruction. All kinds of valuable planks and broken wood came ashore. Ships' life-rafts and abandoned lifeboats, casks of petroleum and kerosene, large iron barrels of a liquid called acetone, lubricating oil and great wooden casks of yellow palm-oil butter. Every household had a plentiful supply of palm oil. The casks weighed half a ton. Many casks were smashed on the rocks and great lumps of the solidified oil remained on the seashore, there for the taking. The oil had many uses. It was used for chapped hands, stiff joints, infected cuts, waterproofing heavy, hobnailed, leather boots and even for axle grease on farm carts. Bales of raw rubber and cotton were commonplace. Packs of rubber contraceptive devices of American manufacture also became victim to the torpedo blast. The caves and beaches were strewn with what present-day society call condoms. I heard one old man ask his son, 'What kind of damn things are these?'

All wreckage was to be surrendered to the Revenue Commissioners under the Merchant Shipping Act of 1800. This law was never observed by the beachcombers, if at all possible. In the gospel of the beachcomber, the great Caesar was not to be rendered to, or become a beneficiary. The Royal Irish Constabulary kept a very watchful eye on such illegal activity. Nevertheless, some of the rank and file constables proved unfaithful to His Majesty by helping the natives move barrels to a secret rendezvous, where a buyer would pick them up. All was done in strict secrecy for a deserving share of the loot. The constables wore civilian garb for these nocturnal deceptions. The natives used a code of names, such as 'washtub' when referring to the wreckage of casks washed up on the shore. Planks were 'sticks', iron casks were 'drums' and poles were 'bullets'. Some casks of rum and whiskey were washed ashore. Most dangerous of all were the large floating mines, bedecked with horned, sensitive detonators.

Two neighbours of mine, Jamesie Stock and Paddy Tom, were beachcombers of a different kind. They were perpetually on the prowl, dawn to dusk or midnight – whenever wind or tides favoured them. They could smell a barnacled object that had floated ashore in the darkness of night. They had found, salvaged and sold what other folk would leave behind. Jamesie Stock lived alone in a cottage overlooking the beach and, like a cormorant on a rock, not even a bottle floated ashore but Jamesie's watchful eye floated beside it. Paddy Tom lived with his mother Sheila. Only a green field separated both dwellings. Sheila was a very austere woman. Her husband Thomas had flown the coop with a younger pullet many years earlier. Both disappeared into the oblivion of America, leaving Sheila to bring up her baby Paddy, who was now showing a few extra wrinkles above the eyebrows, still unmarried, but still Mom's kinky-headed little boy.

One night while Jamesie and Paddy were having one last prowl on the beach before departing for their separate homes, Jamesie observed what seemed to be a cask bobbing among the breakers, coming nearer the shore until they could see it more clearly. Wading into the sea, they rolled it onto the hard sand until they were well beyond high-water mark. On examining the wooden cask with lighted matches, they concluded from the markings that it contained some kind of alcohol.

'Where do we put it?' asked Jamesie.

'We can't take it home,' said Paddy. 'My mother would mess up everything.'

'I know where we'll hide it,' said Jamesie, 'in *Poll a' Chait.*'

'The entrance to that place is overgrown for years and besides, the cave is full of wild cats,' countered Paddy.

'The last wild cat I heard tell of must be as old as the hag of Beara,' said Jamesie.

'I'll bring the wheelbarrow,' replied Paddy. 'It will take some *mulliking* to bring it up the *cumar* (ravine).'

'That's a desperate cross place,' said Jamesie. 'Bring the auger and the brass tap. Don't forget the hurricane lantern. It will be dark in *Poll a' Chait.*'

Jamesie stood guard until Paddy arrived with the barrow. They both lifted the cask and set it in a reclining position on the small vehicle. *Poll a' Chait* was about two hundred yards above high-water mark. The way leading up to the little cave, hidden in the ravine, was the bed of a rivulet, which ran dry in hot summers. It was strewn with rough stones and boulders. During the ages the little mountain stream had gouged out a fissure with clay walls to a depth of twenty feet in some parts. The mouth of the cave was difficult to find as it was entirely obscured with wild sally, brambles, furze, briars and ferns.

After much puffing and panting, swaying and stumbling in the dim half-light, the undaunted pair eventually arrived at the entrance of *Poll a' Chait*. Jamesie decided they must rest awhile before entering the cave. Leaving the barrow outside, it was with some trepidation that the anxious beachcombers lit the hurricane lamp and crawled into the cave. The interior was spacious and dry, with a rocky ceiling. The floor was on a higher level than the bed of the ravine, and reaching back some distance. The light revealed a rusty skillet pot. The staves and hoops of a collapsed cask were evidence of past occupation.

Just as Paddy bent down to examine the old skillet, a large otter slithered by, making for the exit. Paddy jumped with fright saying, 'I thought it was a wild cat.' 'Come let us get the cask inside,' said Jamesie, 'it is getting late.' There was just enough space to ease the cask through the doorway. They brought some large stones from the rear of the cave, forming an improvised platform on which they set the barrel. Producing the auger, Jamesie chose the exact position on the cask, where he instantly bored and inserted the brass tap with a few deft blows from a piece of rock that he used as a mallet. He successfully avoided spilling any of the yet unknown contents. Tapping a barrel can go very wrong and is not a job for the inexperienced.

At last came the moment of truth. The long-awaited suspense and curiosity as to what the cask contained would soon be over. Surely it had to be whiskey! It was marked to contain thirty gallons, constructed of thick oak staves and bound with brass hoops. It seemed as if it had drifted in the ocean for a considerable time, where it accumulated a short, fuzzy, marine growth. This made it slippery and difficult to handle. Paddy held the tin mug while Jamesie opened the brass tap ever so easily. Soon a slender stream of dark, honey-coloured fluid gurgled slowly downward, until the tin mug was about half full. Jamesie said, 'It must be rum, it smells like wild honey.' Paddy dipped his forefinger in the liquid and proceeded to lick it like a cat, relishing each lick. 'Oh boy, but this is powerful stuff,' he said.

Jamesie who could contain himself no longer, brought the mug to his lips and took a deep slug whereupon he immediately bent double, gagged and became breathless. He spluttered and coughed until finally regaining normal breathing, helped by Paddy's backslapping. 'By God this is a dangerous brew, it has cleared the skin from my tonsils,' exclaimed Jamesie. 'It must be diluted with three times as much boiling water.'

Skelligs Haul

Paddy took a careful sip, saying, 'I feel it travelling out to the tips of my toes. It will make great punch. I love punch with lump sugar – you can't beat the P.P.'s nightcap.'

'Forget about your punch, we must decide how best to dispose of it, we can't drink a barrel of rum,' said Jamesie. 'Furthermore, we must be careful with the sale – remember what happened to the barrels of lard, it could also happen to us. I don't want to wind up in court – jealous neighbours are bad news, boy.'

'Leave the sale of it to me,' said Paddy. 'I have a plan.'

'It better be good,' said Jamesie. 'I'm all ears.'

'We'll make a deal with Dan the Pedlar,' continued Paddy. 'He's the safest man this side of the grave. He sells *poitín* at every fair in Kerry and was never pulled over yet.'

Now, Dan sold everything from flypaper to snuff, little bottles of seawater mixed with pepper and sugar as cough medicine. He sold a host of items, including *poitín*, for which he took secret orders. He never delivered the stuff himself but acted the perfect commercial traveller very successfully. The police never took him seriously, regarding him as a half-wit, which he feigned to an amazing degree of perfection. Having agreed to make a deal with Dan, Jamesie and Paddy both decided to call it a night. Putting the barrow inside the cave and carefully concealing the entrance with brambles, they walked together across the field. 'Your mother has light in her window yet. No doubt she'll want to know if we found something in the washtub. Don't let her smell your breath.'

When Dan the Pedlar was contacted, a bargain was drawn up and approved in strict secrecy. The rum was to be diluted and sold in bottles, half pint and smaller, containing one or two glasses each. These bottles could easily be concealed on your person. The half pint was sold at four shillings, the next, three shillings and the smallest for two shillings. Dan the Pedlar gave the new product a trade name of its own, as distinct from *poitín*, calling it 'American Moonshine'. Dan's reward was a third, as equal partner. The venture proved very successful. The beverage received a whispered acclaim among the 'under the counter' customers, a cure for almost any malady.

All went well, without a hitch, until the Feast of Michaelmas. Then came the first hiccup, which happened at a dance in a local country house. The large kitchen filled to overflowing with local folk and with pilgrims who usually came to pray at Saint Michael's Well on 'Pattern' (Patron) Day. They also took part in the ensuing mixture of revelry, dancing, drinking and praying. Among the crowd could be seen Dan the Pedlar, busily plying his wares with his usual stealthy confidence. American Moonshine was disposed of among pilgrim, prayerful and local faithful.

As the night wore on, nocturnal revelry reached a crescendo of sound, so much so that the local RIC police on night patrol decided to investigate the source of the singing and shouting. To their consternation, they found many in various stages of intoxication. One youth had virtually fallen by the wayside; he had lost all orientation relating to the perpendicular. Footless and incoherent, he could only answer feebly, 'American Moonshine.' The police took him into custody, until he was sufficiently sober. When questioned as to where he acquired the alcohol, he vaguely remembered a stranger giving him a small bottle of what he termed American Moonshine. He told the police he saw everybody swigging it, but nobody seemed to know much about it, except for its name.

The police were not convinced. They took Dan the Pedlar in for questioning, all to no avail. Dan played the part of dreamy blankness to perfection, with an expressionless vacuity, giving answers so woolly and unrelated as to cause mirthful laughter among the questioning constables. The head constable was heard to observe, regarding the homeless 'knight of the roads', that he was 'either a confounding rascal or has a tin can and pebble for a brain.' Nevertheless the police searched the entire locality, every dyke and farmyard, excepting *Poll a' Chait*, which place was so obscured by undergrowth as to be unnoticeable.

Jamesie and Paddy decided to play 'possum' for a while, by suspending all commercial marketing of the American Moonshine Company until they felt sure all police activity had ceased. They would sneak into *Poll a' Chait* for a couple of hours each night, make themselves a mug of punch on a mini oil flame. Every rainy day they would retire to the cave, where they drank, smoked and slept comfortably on beds of dry withered bracken. In slang terms they were, 'having a ball' – what more could they ask for than owning their own 'local' and drinks for free? In a short time their capacity to absorb more alcohol became evident. They were under the spell of that powerful Greco-Roman deity called Bacchus.

All proceeded happily until Paddy's mother Sheila became uneasy and worried as to the whereabouts of Paddy and Jamesie, who had now been on the absent list for three long days and nights. As time went by, Sheila pondered on the best course of action to take, deciding as a first step she must notify the police of their disappearance, when, lo and behold, as she happened to glance momentarily through the kitchen window during her worried musings, she recognized the figure of her son staggering across the meadow in front of the house.

Paddy staggered to a halt, falling prostrate to the ground. His mother rushed to his aid uttering a startled cry. With all the strength of a loving mother, she helped him find his unstable footing, supporting each tottering step in his lurching gait, until she laid him on the kitchen settle. Two neighbours arrived at the same time. One carried the semi-conscious Jamesie on his back helped by Dan the Pedlar.

They laid him on a rug spread on the kitchen floor. Dan the Pedlar assured Paddy's mother that all would come right, saying they had only a drop too much and he had already ordered the doctor. Jamesie was incoherent and rambling, but two words were clear among the disjointed verbiage: 'American Moonshine'. When the doctor arrived he pumped out the excess alcohol from the tanks and administered an antidote to counteract toxic poisoning. After a bout of vomiting and concurrent explosions of superfluous gas from their exhaust valves, they both improved rapidly.

When Sheila was made aware of the full story and where the cask was hidden, she ordered Dan the Pedlar to bring the pickaxe saying, 'You plot-scheming old shagger, come with me to *Poll a' Chait*.' Dan knew better than to risk the ire of obduracy personified, so he obeyed meekly, despite his feeble protestations to save some of the blessed stuff. He watched the Amazonian Sheila reducing the cask to a little heap of staves and brass hoops with each swing of the heavy pickaxe, leaving the amber liquid flow into the ravine. Thus ended the commercial venture of the beachcombers.

SILENCE! SILENCE IN THE COURT!
Skelligs Sunset

Minor law cases before and after the Famine were held in the magistrate's court or the court of petty sessions, usually in the local courthouse. In my locality the sessions were held in a building in Portmagee. Petty crime consisted mostly of unlighted vehicles – vehicles were classified as farm carts of all descriptions – including side carriages and tub-traps. Bicycles and motor cars had not yet arrived. Other offences brought before the courts included inebriation and disorderly conduct; wandering animals; arrears of rent; non-payment of money due; theft; trespassing; claims of malicious damage; failure to obtain dog licences; breaches of the School Attendance Act; parental neglect of children; unshod animals and poaching. It was compulsory for the owner of a farm cart to display his name and that of the townland wherein he resided on the right-hand shaft of the vehicle, in clear English lettering. Defying the edict of the Crown, my brothers printed my father's name in bold Gaelic lettering, *Seán Ua Ciarmhaic, Baile 'n Sceilg*. For this my father was fined ten shillings, and ten shillings was not easily come by in those days. Henceforth the name was displayed in both languages. Perhaps our ass-cart could be recorded in some book as being the first to acquire bilingual status.

Many funny tales were told of how the court and its officers operated. Country folk would attend in force to hear the pleadings presented by the plaintiff and defendant in lawsuits between neighbours. The clerk of the court was usually a minor civil servant with some scant knowledge of law. An old man from Ballinskelligs, whom people said was not the full shilling, held the conviction that he was a reincarnated lawman of some kind. He would never miss being present when the court was in session. The old man, always dressed in his Sunday best, would call for order in the court and bow to the judge. The magistrate accepted him as part of the judicial system and, to boost the old man's ego, he was provided with a special chair in the courtroom. On a day when the clerk of the court was absent, the magistrate had occasion to go to the men's room. The policeman in charge failed to quell the pandemonium that arose out of the general hubbub of loud conversation among the local neighbours, until the old man lost his patience. Rushing over to the judge's bench, taking the gavel and striking the bell, he declared in a loud voice: 'Silence! Silence in court while the barrister is pissing!' This tale I heard from old Gaelic speakers while I was yet a very young boy, from folk who could only manage the *cúpla focal* of English.

Another hilarious tale I heard from the lips of a farmhand who was called to give evidence in a case between two neighbouring farmers. Mickey was getting on in years when I heard him relate the story, now more than seventy years ago. The aggrieved party employed him as a servant boy and farm-hand. He was called to give evidence supporting a charge of trespass, claimed to have been committed by his neighbour within the yard of the hay-barn. Mickey was called to the witness stand and cross-examined by the solicitor for the defence.

'Now, my good man, do you remember the morning of the seventh of January?'

'I do, sir!'

'Did you notice the nuisance at the foot of the ladder?'

Mickey made no reply. The magistrate then intervened, reminding him that a witness was obliged by law to answer the question, to which Mickey replied: 'What is a nuisance, your honour?'

The magistrate said: 'Turn around and ask somebody at the back of you.'

Mickey turned and looked into the eyes of a colleague named Dan.

'What is a nuisance, Dan?'

Dan whispered behind a slanted palm: 'Something that has a bad smell, Mickey!'

One could hear a pin drop in the court. The magistrate asked: 'Do you now understand the meaning of the question?'

'No, your honour!'

'Why, Michael?'

'Because there was no bad smell, your honour!'

The magistrate spluttered and coughed and, owing to a very boisterous outburst of laughter among the peasantry, ordered the court to be cleared.

Another old story that goes back to the start of the 1800s went the rounds and was always told in Gaelic. It concerned a young man from Valentia who was purported to have raped a neighbouring farmer's daughter before joining a French fishing schooner that was short-handed and bound for Labrador to fish for halibut and cod. It was not unusual for French fishing vessels to stop at Valentia on their way to Newfoundland. Their method of fishing was to attach baited lines to long hickory fishing rods. Dozens of rods would be arrayed in holders along the ship's side. In those days the coast of Labrador teemed with fish. It was only a matter of hauling the fish on board. Part of the crew was given to attending to the fishing rods and part of the crew to curing the fish and storing it in sealed wooden casks. When the last cask was filled it was time to return.

It seems our Seán was a long-rod fisherman attending to several lines when required. The time to return depended very much on the Atlantic weather. The coast of Nova Scotia can be very treacherous sometimes, with thick dense fog or perhaps a freezing gale blowing from the direction of Iceland. Therefore leaving France in springtime and returning by early or late autumn was always a hazardous undertaking, fraught with danger. The trip could take ten to eleven months.

It was late autumn when Seán's ship returned to Valentia harbour. He found to his consternation that a warrant had been issued for his immediate arrest, supported by the sworn evidence of a woman who claimed he was the father of her child because of an assault on her by him at a given date. Seán was incarcerated in the local gaol pending the hearing of his case. Penalties were severe in those days. Transportation to Van Diemen's Land for stealing a

Silence! Silence in the Court!

sheep was a normal penalty. Who has not heard sung that beautiful Gaelic ballad of transportation, 'The Connerys'!

On the day, the trial was presided over by the magistrate at the local courthouse. As usual, the courtroom was filled to capacity. Seán's relatives and friends sat silently listening to a damning sequence of lies piling up against him, while Seán stood pale and unshaven. His fate seemed sealed until his counsellor stood up in court. Asking for silence, he approached the judge, giving him a piece of paper that was an extract copied from the schooner's logbook and signed by the French captain. The document showed the date of the ship's arrival in Labrador to be one month earlier than the date the girl testified the offence had taken place. There was great jubilation in Seán's household when he was set free. It is said that his old grandmother, on hearing of his release, exclaimed in Gaelic: 'I never doubted you my grandson, you were the greatest fisherman of all, who was able to stretch his fishing rod from Labrador to Valentia!'

Graft and Craft

THE GIANT'S GRAVE AT COOM
Skelligs Sunset

It all started with me when my brother-in-law Jack Sullivan entered the field where I was busy digging potatoes and without further ado asked if I was interested in a job. If so, I was to report next Monday morning, at a certain field on his farm, where a team of experts from the National University were to undertake the excavation of a megalithic tomb dating back to the early Bronze Age.

This, he told me, was archaeology – a most frightening word – which was not for someone whose education was limited to sixth form in the national school. It seemed as if there was something very spooky about the great word that could only be discussed by bespectacled professors wearing weirdly flat, tasselled hats in some inner sanctum, and even they were sworn to secrecy.

I was glad to avail of any work, spooky or otherwise, and if there was money for ignorance, surely I could not fail to qualify for the job. I arrived at the site early on Monday morning complete with employment cards from the local exchange, some sandwiches and a flask of tea. Immediately I reported to the professor, a doctor of archaeology, who was to conduct the excavation along with a group of students who were receiving archaeological field training. I was then signed on, becoming one of four labourers whose function was to dig with a spade. Our names, starting with mine, were Mike, Jack, Con and Florrie. All of them, except myself, are now deceased.

Skelligs Haul

Before starting our first workday we were assembled in classroom order in the shed, which served as the professor's office and that of the students. Bespectacled, he sat behind his desk and lectured us on how he expected us to behave during the period of excavation. We stood meekly, cap in hand, all except Florrie who still wore his cap at an alarmingly acute angle. I always expected it to become disengaged, but somehow it still clung there. Flor wore it too well; to see him decapped would be like seeing a bishop without his mitre.

The professor spoke to us at length about the people who had supposedly built this wedge-shaped tomb of the early Bronze Age; mysterious people who were the first settlers in Ireland. Describing the expected finds, he said: 'We may find pieces of honey-coloured flint, tiny arrow heads, perhaps shards of red, thin pottery or an urn, beaker-shaped, which always, whenever found, stands mouth downwards, under which might be fragments of human charred bone or ash. For want of a better name, we could call their owners 'Beaker People' and evidence would suggest that they voyaged from the shores of Brittany four thousand years ago.'

When it rained we were not allowed to come within the wooden tool-shed and we were told that we could build our own improvised shelter with sods of clay, which leaked incessantly like a sieve. We were also told bluntly not to answer any questions put to us by any visitors or newspaper men, because we were not qualified to speak about our work to anyone in the outside world. I suddenly realized that the old adage was brutally true: officers do not drink with the men.

KELP AND POTATOES
Skelligside

My brother Paddy awakened me at daybreak. Giving me a gentle shake, he said, 'Get up! Patas Curran and I are going west to the island sound for a boatload of stripe to manure the potatoes. We will need you to keep the boat free from water.'

On hearing this, I jumped out of my warm bed, knowing I would not have to attend school. I hated school, anyway. I was now eleven years old, tall, with spindly legs, barefooted and bareheaded. My mother objected, but Paddy impressed on her the importance of my job, which was to bail out water which would be taken on board with the kelp. My mother advised Paddy not to overload the boat, and to distribute the seaweed evenly. Before we departed, she gave us her blessing, and sprinkled us with Holy Water. I carried a gallon canister and a tin bucket for bailing the boat.

Patas Curran was waiting for us on the beach, the great crooked sickle with its long handle on his shoulder. The kelp-cutting sickle is a blunt instrument. Were it too sharp it would not bring the kelp to the surface in the loop of its mouth. The boat was near the pier, a four-oar craft, twenty-five feet long. It was built by 'Pardner' Galvin, who was expert at building a seaworthy and shapely boat. An old fisherman christened her the *Glassy Gander* and the name stuck. When we went on board Paddy took up the stern sheeting to inspect the water plug in the bilge. The tide was still ebbing, and the sea was like a sheet of opaque glass. This was the great spring tide: it would not reach out so far again until autumn. Patas pulled on the bow oar, while my brother rowed in the second berth. Under both oars, the *Glassy Gander* moved easily westward, like a phantom floating on air.

Skelligs Haul

This was the life I loved, the freedom of the sea and the smell of salt, phosphorous and iodine. The morning sun shone into the Cave of the Rock Doves on our right, producing a roseate enamel blending with tints of pink and light purple. It was as if I were looking through a giant kaleidoscope. Who would be imprisoned in a musty schoolroom on a morning such as this?

The oarsmen changed course, to avoid the light ground or shallow on the shoulder of Mike Shea's reef. A large area of drowning man's laces covered the shallow part of the Sound. It was impossible to row between the long matted sea strings which grew long and dense. A swimmer in this area would have no chance of survival. Still, it was a good position for mooring a trammel net, for the mullet and sea bass were often found in abundance among the sea strings. Sea trout also like to swim among the cords. Of course it was unlawful for us to catch a young salmon or sea trout when fishing for mullet. Even though we didn't invite the fish to get caught in mullet meshes it was a crime to keep or eat illegally caught fish of this description, and perhaps we were also in danger of hell-fire, so like good Christians we always put them back where they came from.

We slipped silently to the left of *Carraig an Phollóig*, the Pollack Rock. The water was receding quickly, so the jagged sunken reef of the Sound was showing. The double-headed kelp and the great black sea rods, some broken and naked after the winter storms, pushed their heads above the water. We were now floating on top of a vast submarine forest. The water rose and fell as the round heads of the sea rods appeared momentarily above the surface. We could have filled several boats with them, but were only interested in the long yellow ribbon kelp and in the heavy belted dark brown stripe, which grew long and slender. We also cut the short-stemmed whip kelp and the serrated kelp. My brother

Kelp and Potatoes

and Patas brought the boat into a fixed position near the reef where the side was fair and deep. They divested themselves of their woollen *geansaí* and of their inside shirts and put on sleeveless jackets and old trousers.

Each took turns at the cutting sickle, one bringing great armfuls of brown kelp to the surface while the other took the long streamers from the mouth of the crooked sickle. Much water was taken on board with the dripping weed. I managed to keep the main floor of the boat bailed. Paddy was the architect responsible for distributing the kelp evenly. Each armful he laid carefully in its place, making it flat and laying it clockwise, just as in making a rick of hay. The *Gander* settled lower into the water under the weight of the cargo of black-brown velvet streamers which we had won from the unpolluted waters. We now had little more than six inches of freeboard to spare, but the sea was calm as glass.

My brother Paddy said we had taken enough on board. Patas jumped onto a flat rock by our side, taking the tin bucket with him, and choosing a suitable piece of stone, he began to chip loose the great flat *bairneachs* or limpets which are seldom exposed to the sunlight. This limpet is related to the 'Chinese hat', and is not tidal. It has a pale buttery colour, is fat and makes an excellent soup. In no time, he had collected nearly a pailful of them, which he gave to me as a gift. Paddy kept the boat steady until Patas came on board. The tide had now turned to flow while they rowed the *Gander* gently by *Cloigeann an Chrainn*. With the kelp stowed high and square over her gunwale, she resembled a Venetian gondola as we berthed safely at the pier. The harvest provided enough fertilizer to nourish the potato crop for that year, and the memory of that happy morning remains with me still, even though more than seventy years have flown. My brother and Patas have now passed over the divide. May they rest in peace, Patas in the

Old Priory burial-ground, which was once Saint Michael's Abbey, and my brother Paddy in a cemetery beneath the lovely hills of Connecticut, U.S.A.

The potato plot was treated with a liberal coating of sea kelp, which was in plentiful supply along the south-western coast where it was cast ashore by the winter storms. When mixed with farmyard manure, the decayed residue of winter bedding of cattle housed in the byre, this fertilizer was rich in mineral elements, making it an excellent dressing for potatoes. Most of the work on the smallholdings was done with a special iron spade which could be bought in any ironmonger's store. It was sold in separate parts: the iron spade, the treadle, and the ash handle. The parts would be taken to an experienced joiner, who carefully assembled the parts to suit the workman, right or left-handed as the case might be. A good spade worker would plant a bed of potatoes one hundred yards long by three feet wide each day. It was slow, laborious work, but by this method more potatoes were produced on the smallholdings than on some of the larger estates. The small cottiers did not keep horses and therefore did not have ploughs.

Many varieties of potato were grown. An early variety which survived the blight of the Great Famine was a round dark purple-skinned potato called the 'stouter'. This would be ready for the table in mid-May. In my youth, anybody worth his salt would have cultivated a bed of early 'stouters'. The main crop was a yellow-fleshed tuber called 'champion'; this was a dry floury potato with a very sweet taste. Housewives described them when boiled as bursting their jackets with goodness. Another long tuber was called the 'peeler'. This was a soft and soapy white potato, easily cultivated and used mostly for animal feeding.

The potato fields were a pretty sight when seen in full blossom, after being earthed and manured with guano, a powerful fertilizer imported from the Pacific and South

Atlantic. A strong solution of sulphate of copper mixed with soda crystals made a forty-gallon barrel of wash. The knapsack sprayer was not yet on the market, so in those early years we sprayed with little hand brooms, taking the wash in an open bucket and walking through the furrows. This was a crude method, but it kept at bay the dreaded fungus spores which attacked the potato holms.

GROWING FLAX
Skelligside

About the year 1875 my mother was sixteen years old. She told me that flax was sown and grown in the locality in plentiful supply, and that there was no lovelier sight than the small fields of blue blossom in full bloom. From her I heard the story of its growing and processing. Some of the information, alas, is gone, because it never occurred to me that the wasp should ever goad me so deeply in later life that I would plough a blank field of parchment and seed it with my thought. Flax was easily grown. It required little fertilizer, or else the crop would grow too rank and produce too much soft bark on the stem. A flax which had no commercial value was called 'the flax of the fairy women'. People would have nothing to do with this, and it was considered a bad omen to have it growing among the good crop.

When the blossom faded the flax ripened into seed and became fit for reaping. The seed was taken out with little flails made for the purpose. Linseed oil was used for the relief of constipation in farm animals. Meal was also made from the seed and fed to young calves.

Each farmer had his own special pond of fresh water in which the sheaves were soaked, until the outer hard skin became soft and brittle. The flax was then taken from the pond to be placed on a wooden bench, where the sheaves drip-dried. The stems were beaten gently with a wooden mallet to crack the bark, and the sheaves once more opened and spread under the sun to dry. At this stage, the *sistealóir* or flax dresser took over. He had special instruments, such as the flax comb, the hackle and the tongs, and removed the now-brittle bark, the cockle, and any other rough growth, without damaging the core of silvery threads. He prepared the flax for spinning, and there was plenty of demand for his skills as he travelled from village to village.

Because flax looked so much like the silken tresses of women, a traditional system of measuring was devised. One handful of unspun flax was a *scoithín*, or lock of hair, twelve handfuls or locks equalled one tress, or *treisleán*, and twelve tresses made one ball of twine weighing one pound and some ounces. This was a crude yet effective measurement. A special spinning wheel used for flax was called the fast wheel, or *luadaire*. Many Irish poems referred to flax. The speaker in this poem is a woman whose lover is going to the wars:

> I'll sell my rock and I'll sell my reel,
> And sell my only spinning-wheel.
> I spun the flax and I sold it well;
> I bought for my love a sword of steel.

Hempen twine was homespun. The women knitted fishing nets for coarse bottom fishing of hake and various other fish. The thread was coarse but hard-wearing. Weavers made clothing from it but it was cold to the touch and it never ousted woollen fabric from the market.

CUTTING THE TURF
Skelligside

Today very few people in Ballinskelligs use the traditional turf spade called a *sleán*. The machine is now doing the work of the *meitheal*, a working party of neighbours who helped each other to harvest a winter's fuel. Now you must buy turf from the person who owns the bogland – if you have the two or three hundred pounds you need in your fist. As the Gaelic poet said about money:

> A fool can keep me,
> A wise man may spend me,
> Gather some of me,
> And you will have a lot of me.

Money did not count during the turf harvest when I was young. Neighbours always helped each other. There were acres of bogland in every locality along South Iveragh. Each family from Cahersiveen to Bolus had its own turfbank. The fuel was of very good quality, dense, dark and brown. For an annual rent of between ten shillings and two pounds, you could cut enough turf for a year. Woe to him who could not provide enough turf for the winter's fire, for that individual was either bone-lazy or not worth his salt. In Gaelic tradition, a fire was as important as food, and saving the winter's turf was a very important job. In the poem 'Raca Breá Mo Chinn', or 'My Beautiful Head Comb' the maiden entreats a young man to marry her in the following words:

> 'It is a good time to marry,
> My young boy,' said she,

Skelligs Haul

'Ere the rest of the harvest comes,
And we will have stored the turf.'

Uneasy would be the man of the house until the turf was cut. Each man in the community gave a day's work for a day in return. People were friendly, kindly neighbours, who liked to be in partnership not alone on the day of the turf cutting but at any time of urgent necessity.

I remember how stirred with joy we were when turf-cutting day came around. We did not have to go to school that day. The lunch basket was all packed the night before. My mother would prepare large oven-baked loaves, plenty of hen eggs, fresh butter and sweet jam, a big can of spring water, a can of fresh milk, the big kettle, and two ounces of plug tobacco as a gift for the pipe-smokers. The turf pikes, the *sleáin* and the ordinary garden spades and shovels were all ready long since, and the local men notified. There was no fear of any man ignoring his neighbour's *meitheal*, unless something urgent prevented his attendance.

Four men usually followed each *sleán*: the man who was cutting, the man who took the sods, called the brincher, the man on the brink of the trench, and a fourth who spread the sods to dry. It was good to watch them working in unison, with no fear of wasted, broken or trampled turf.

The first thing we did on reaching the turf-bank was to choose a sheltered place where the lunch could be prepared for the workmen. A great glowing turf fire was lit, the kettle was brought to the boil, with several teapots brewing and a small pot with perhaps a score of eggs inside bubbling on the live coals. Brown and white loaves were cut into thick slices, which some men plastered with great blobs of home-churned butter. The men could eat as many eggs as they requested, and would wash down the meal with big mugs of sweetened tea. After feasting, the team would rest for some time on the gorse and heather sward, and as they resumed their work one could hear the rasping noise from emissions of superfluous gas:

> It is a good horse that will fart at noon time,
> But it is a better horse who will fart at eventide;
> And better is the work which causes the horse to fart.

As evening approached, the heath was covered with an array of turf sods neatly spread, each cube lying on the shoulder of its neighbour, waiting for wind and summer sun to make it ready for next winter's fuel.

When the last sod was cut and the task complete, the men looked with satisfaction at the work they had all taken part in. The man of the house would then address them, saying he wished them God's blessing and not as much as a germ of sickness in the years to come. The answer always came back 'that the wish may also be yours'. A man who has never heard that loving wish after a day's co-operation with his neighbour is the poorer for it.

The sound of the modern machine can now be heard on *Réidh na gCúl*, on *Currach na nDamh* and at *Gob an Dá Chaol*. The raw smell of diesel oil comes easy on the wind. There are only three men now where once there were twenty. The machine has no conscience, no faith, no soul. It is a cold, serious, business-like master, interested only in profit. A new Caesar with a heart as cold as iron has taken the turf cutting away from the *meitheal*. Caesar must be paid, or it is with the 'fire of the fox' – *tine an mhadra rua* – that the old and feeble will have to face the winter.

An ancient Irish folk-tale tells how one frosty morning a vixen and her cubs were travelling across barren land. The cold and hungry cubs were bewailing the intense cold, until Mother Fox urinated on an icy flagstone. A white vapour rose into the morning air, whereupon the cubs stopped complaining and huddled together around the source of heat, and Mother Fox was heard to say, 'Hush, my beauties! We shall soon have a fire.' And so, a green or slow fire is still referred to as the 'fire of the fox'.

OATS AND HAY
Skelligside

I remember seeing my father and our neighbour Pat O'Connell reap a three-quarter-acre field of oats with sickle hooks about seventy years ago. In the morning before they set out to reap, they tied makeshift pads to their knees. It was fascinating to watch how rapid was their progress, and how skilled they were in the use of the sickle. One reaper moved a few yards ahead of the other and they laid the oats in perfect rows, ready for binding. I tried my hand at using the reaping hook, only to inflict a nasty cut on my little finger, the mark of which is plainly visible to the present day. Later on, the scythe came onto the market with its long crooked wooden handle, mounted and turned by the local blacksmith. The scythe blades were manufactured in Sheffield from steel of excellent quality, honed and ground. They were razor-sharp and would slice through the long grass, when used by an expert. Good mowers would cut an acre of hay per day for the princely sum of ten shillings. The scythe was sharpened with a flat piece of wood, eighteen inches long and three inches wide, whose sides were coated with emery grains cemented to the wood. These pieces were called scythe-boards and sold for sixpence. In later years, the more expensive carborundum sharpening-stone was imported from England. The modern version of the scythe is sold in a ready-to-assemble pack, complete with iron tubular handle. It is a handy instrument for the lawn gardener, but not for mowing an acre of hay per day.

Oats and Hay

Making hay was laborious work in the old days, especially if there was broken showery weather which might delay the drying process. The first little heaps were called grasscocks. The young folk who were being trained in the art of making the perfect grasscock were exhorted to put only the minimum amount of grass into its construction. I heard of one old farmer who lost his patience with his pupils and said in desperation: 'I want you to make the grasscocks only just about the size of a hen's shit. Now can you understand?'

The next stage was a larger cock which would contain a couple of hundredweight of hay. Those cocks were allowed to age for several days before being spread out under wind and sun until the hay was perfectly dry, to be made into what were called 'wynds'.

A wynd or meadowcock had to be properly made. It would contain about a half-ton of hay. Then came the final day for the great haggard cocks. The haggard enclosure would be cleared of any nettles or other growth, and the stone foundation where the great conical ricks were to be built made exact in circumference, and raised above the ground level.

The great storecock would contain as many as twenty-five meadow wynds – eleven or twelve tons of hay. The cock would taper outwards and upwards, until it reached its greatest circumference, which would be in the region of fifty feet. From this point, it became slowly conical, culminating in a point like an inverted spinning-top. It was imperative that the hay be perfectly dry to prevent pressure heating or fermentation. To construct a storecock of these dimensions would need at least ten workmen. Three experienced men worked in the rick, and three more on the ground kept them supplied with great forkfuls of hay. The men in the rick laid and distributed the hay, layering it evenly in a clockwise direction, making sure that the great centre was kept very solid underfoot with no humps or hollows. Two neighbours with horse carts drew loads from the meadows to keep the haggard in good supply, and with them would be two others who filled the loads and helped tie the ropes. One man had the most onerous job of all: his task was to keep the outer wall in perfect geometric balance. This man was the architect whose experienced eye oversaw the whole operation.

A good dinner would be laid on and, as it was thirsty work, the men would be supplied at intervals with a drink of black porter. Those workers were usually in serious mood when constructing the big top of hay, for each wanted it to be the showpiece of the neighbourhood. The housewife would have prepared a cap of sackcloth with which to cover the point of the rick from rain. The last job was the raking down of all loose or surplus hay and the tying with red fibre ropes spaced at eighteen-inch intervals. When the hay-forks and hay rakes were finished for the season they were laid carefully away, perhaps on the cross rafters of the cow byre, until next year.

The first horse-drawn mowing machines did not reach Ballinskelligs until the early twenties. This machine was manufactured in Ireland, as was also the old hand-turned chopping and pulping machine. In the late nineteen-forties I saw a reaping and binding machine for the first time in the 'beautiful vale of Tralee' and some years later the first threshing machine began operating in South Iveragh.

White and black oats were grown successfully in Ballinskelligs. Great circular stacks with thatched tops were to be seen in every haggard. The great problem was to get at the grain, as it had to be threshed by hand. Our forefathers were trained in the use of the flail stick, but this was before my time.

On the smallholdings I have described, grain was fed to the cattle on the sheaf. Mixed with hay, it provided good winter fodder. Barley and rye were grown in smaller quantities, because certain soils contained too much lime to grow oats successfully. The average smallholding was less than twenty acres, and in most cases, half of this was not arable. The fields on each holding were reduced to small half-acre paddocks. They were usually surrounded by fences of clay, stone and grass about six feet high, with a hedge of French furze on top. In springtime, the French furze was topped with yellow blossom which presented a pretty sight on the green landscape and also provided shelter for the little fields. The seed for this furze was imported from France where it was cultivated because of its high protein content, and was considered good animal feed. The Irish used it more for shelter hedges than for fodder, although I have seen it used in chopped form as feed for horses. In South Iveragh, French furze left unattended grew wild, but with the advent of modern farming it was uprooted and destroyed.

THE GENTLEMAN AT HOME
Skelligside

Taking the cow to the bull was a hush-hush exercise. I was twelve years old when my father asked me to help him with an unruly cow which happened to come to dairy. When my mother's reluctant approval was granted, I was allowed for the first time to witness one of nature's oldest rituals, that of fertility, in a practical form.

The cow was in a heated frenzy. An otherwise placid animal now refused to lead, walk, run, or be drawn. She swung round and round in circles, backed, sulked and bellowed. My father walked ahead with a lead rope while

I took up the rear, striking the cow every now and again with a slender willow rod. After what seemed an eternity, we finally reached the farmyard of Tom 'the bull'. Tom greeted my father, and asked the necessary questions. When did the animal have its last calf? When did it show signs of heat? Tom went into a back yard where he opened a gate, calling out at the top of his voice, 'Jack! Jack! Jack! Wuarra! Wuarra! Wuarra!' To my amazement, Jack, a cross between shepherd and collie, appeared and came trotting after his master, who was armed with a stout pitchfork.

The bull was magnificent: black as coal, broad-backed with a gleaming coat. Unlike the square ferocious-looking cross-breed bulls, this beast had class, of the pure Kerry breed. It snorted and shook its majestic head violently, as if in scorn of us mere humans. The front shoulders were broad, muscular and deep, while the dewlap hung low from its throat like a black velvet drape. One half of the horns was cream-coloured and pointed, looping out and upwards. The animal seemed to exude a savage virility.

The cow turned around, sniffing at the handsome gentleman in his black glossy suit. I think she even approved of their meeting, as she gave him a few licks of her long curling tongue under the ear. With sudden and decisive intensity, and that inborn, primordial power whose object is the renewal of the species, the drama reached its climax. It all happened in such a short time: one wild leap and lunge, and in less than ten seconds, nature had taken its course. Tom 'the bull' gave the signal to take the cow away. The bull would have followed us but Tom, complete with pitchfork and his faithful friend, had already herded the animal back into its own quarters. This was my first experience of procreation. Later on, when I grew older, I had the responsibility of taking matters in my own hands. There is an old saying in Irish: 'The man who owns a cow must be responsible for a cow.'

The Gentleman at Home

One day when I was taking my cow to be served, I approached the farm where the bull was kept. The animal must have anticipated our arrival. The huge Hereford monster broke loose from the paddock where it was kept, and galloped towards me, head lowered in menace, copper ring in its nose. I tried to put the cow between myself and the mountain of horned beef bearing down on us, but the cow panicked and with the excess pressure the leading rope parted. The cow turned tail and raced homewards. I also turned tail and fled towards the farmhouse. I succeeded in leaping over a low sod fence, and into the farmer's field. The bull leaped clumsily, sending green scraws of turf in all directions, as I scrambled over the fence once more and on to the roadway. I gained more ground towards the farmhouse which was about fifty yards distant and ran for my life towards a dry wall of rough fieldstone that surrounded the back yard, my heart pounding, my breath coming in short gasps. The rough stone wall was nearly six feet high and I could feel the brute breathing down my shirt collar. He stood on the outside glowering at me, pulling clods of earth with the pawing of his front hooves and deftly throwing them skyward. Thank God! The back door opened, the farmer's daughter saw what was happening and she alerted her mother. The good woman explained that her husband was at the fair and said I was to be sure and bring back the cow that evening. She told me that the sudden disappearance of the cow had infuriated the animal, which was otherwise very quiet and gentle.

That evening I asked Mickey Bawn, our neighbour, if he would oblige me by taking the cow back. Mickey Bawn made light of anything that flew, crawled or swam, and boasted of having power over animals, especially bad-tempered ones. When he returned with the cow walking quietly in front of him, my mother asked, 'Was everything all right, Mickey? Did you get what you wanted?'

'I did, Ma'am,' said Mickey, 'and he did it in great style too.'

Tom 'the bull' kept a book of every service given, and an exact history of the calves obtained from the service of his bull. He would immediately notice any disease or emaciation in an animal and give advice on how it should be treated. He allowed each cow only one service, and was never known to give what the locals called a second 'lep'. He stuck to his belief that the cow was there not for sexual gratification but at nature's behest, to reproduce. One neighbouring farmer argued that he should allow two services or more to each cow, to which Tom replied hotly, 'No! No, man! Nonsense! You'd only make a whore of your cow.'

Many quaint expressions were heard relating to the subject, though they were never meant to be immoral or offensive. 'Is the gentleman at home, Ma'am?' a neighbour would enquire.

'You mean my husband? He is, Johnny. Do you want him for something, Johnny?'

Johnny shrugs his shoulders and shifts uneasily. 'Yerra, not much, Ma'am, only a few stabs of the bull, that's if he's convainient, Ma'am.'

Some unlucky force seemed to have put a jinx on me as far as bulls and cows were concerned. One Sunday morning it was necessary to have a cow serviced urgently because she was coming late in the autumn. On my arrival, the master of the house told me to take the cow to the field where the bull was grazing. It had the remains of an old quarry at one end. He then told me to let the cow loose, which I did. The bull wanted to make friends with Daisy immediately, but she fobbed him off. The farmer then decided on another plan. We would both hold Daisy by the nose and horns against the upright face of the quarry wall. Daisy squirmed, leaned and stampeded by bending and twisting herself, and gave one last mighty rush as she tried to climb the quarry wall, crushing the knuckles of my left hand against the rock face and leaving me with a nasty gash. Cupid was not shooting straight that morning. After receiving first aid for my wound from the farmer's wife, I took the wayward Daisy home.

BUILDING AND THATCHING
Skelligside

The many skills required and used by the people who lived in my locality were handed down from generation to generation. Thus, the head of the household would be able to lay thatch properly and repair it as the need might arise. In other crafts such as basket weaving, people helped each other to improve their skills. Practical methods were used rather than any show of professionalism or theory.

All the houses in Ballinskelligs were thatched cottages when I was young. The neighbours helped cut the thatching material, bring it to the site and fix it on the roof. Many and various were the kinds of thatch used. The ordinary green rush grew in abundance. It was long and glossy, but when it dried it got so brittle that the soft reed broke in very small sections and was therefore not good material for roofing. Several other kinds of reed grew in the neighbourhood – the forked shorter rush grew in marshland, the needle or spiked rush on the wet margins of salt beaches. Another plant called red sedge, which was short and dense, was in scarce supply except on the marshy slope of a mountain or bogland. Blue sedge was an excellent thatch. It grew on the high sand dunes where it could be seen in great blue tufts, nurtured by the gritty salt sand blown from the sea.

It was dry and sharp and required an extra sharp scythe when cutting. Oaten straw and rye were used as an inside coat. The great Pharaoh bulrush, called *biorrach* in Irish, was strong, tall and bamboo-like, and ideal for thatch, but alas, it did not grow plentifully enough in the area.

Neighbours also helped to build and repair. When a new roof was to be erected this was how the work was done. First, the couples were put up. These were a kind of angular truss with an X on top which held the roof tree. Then came the cross-supports, called collar braces, and the long side laths. Wall plates were not used in the construction of these dwellings. The scraw or skin of certain dry bogland was used to cover the timber work. It was tough, elastic and felt-like when dried. Great strips three feet wide, sixteen feet long and two inches thick were cut to an exact measurement. The strips were left to dry and when ready were rolled up like bales of felt, then laid on the lathing, finally covering the entire roof. Long-stemmed purple heather was placed over this in overlapping layers with the stems pointing upwards. Over the heather was laid the white oaten straw, bunch after bunch, the joints always broken as in slating. The last coat was of sedge. The process was slow and it required an experienced thatcher to make the roof watertight. Wooden oak pegs were driven into the wall at two-foot intervals, and a stout rope secured to them. This anchor rope was very important. All the slender grass ropes would be attached to it, over the back of the entire house, six inches apart. The last ropes, horizontal binding ropes called *traisníní*, were important in providing protection from the storm. The last operation was the trimming of the eaves, which extended six inches over the wall of the cottage.

The old thatched cottage was comfortable and warm in winter, and cool in the summer heat. On stormy nights, you could hear the rafters creaking in the sheer force of the wind. The hurricanes which swept in from the Skelligs

Building and Thatching

caused havoc to those frail houses. My bed was upstairs on the sheeted loft near the chimney breast, where I slept very comfortably. My father often woke me in the middle of a winter's storm, telling me to hurry down to the kitchen in case the roof was carried away. The great gusts of wind coming from afar sounded like the booming of the ocean waves and left behind them a vacuum-like whistling sound. Working at night tying down hay and oats, with the rushing roar of a hurricane thundering its way across the Kerry coast, I have heard eerie noises that seemed to come from the body of the storm, a shrieking like the squeal of tormented hogs. The old people spoke of such things and attributed them to the supernatural for lack of a better explanation. My dear mother, Mary Cremin, was a very pious and devout person. I see her now like a bishop sprinkling Holy Water on the walls. She often gathered us around her in the height of the wind, and we knelt and answered her Rosary to the Virgin asking her to intercede with Jesus to calm the storm. During her petition she never forgot to pray for all the neighbours, including those at sea, that God would shield them from harm.

Several stories are told about the night of the big wind in 1839. Few cottages survived the storm. I heard my father say that ours was demolished, the roof completely blown away. My grandfather Timothy Kirby, his wife Mary Fenton and their family had to seek refuge in a nearby hedge until dawn broke.

Dermot Galvin, a journeyman stonemason, poet and neighbour, was born at Sussa in the parish of Prior. It was he who composed a poem called 'The Spirit', and another called 'The Fairy Horse'. It was a privilege for me to hear them from his lips. I translate here some of 'The Song of the Hurricane', but its real music and depth can be experienced only in the free-flowing rhythm of the Irish original.

Skelligs Haul

The Song of the Hurricane

I will write me a line to the people of Ireland,
To get a true story of the damage and loss;
The thatched homes were shattered and scattered all over;
The rumble of thunder and lightning's red flash.

Weary and sorrowful sad is my story,
Engulfed in the darkness of Thursday's black night:
Each man tying stout ropes, the children all wailing
The mothers all tearful, tormented with fright.

We will all raise an outcry from Cashel to Boyne,
From Corrane to Lohar and over to Sneem;
East to Killarney, from Kanturk to Blarney,
Calling roofmen and slaters to come to the scene.

The mason and planer, the mixer of plaster,
The hawk and the trowel, every tool to its trade.
High stages are rising to skyline so airy,
With a party of young men to trim and fit slate.

New eave chutes from Spain will embellish each building;
Cascading to earth water's torrent will bring.
Each steeple and turret will all be adorned
With large gaping salmon, their beaks to the wind.

Every carpenter, slater and glazier so neatly
On both sides of Erin, this land of great lore,
Will have silver in plentiful heaps to reward them,
Each evening disporting in pleasure and sport.

Coins of copper and silver with notes in abundance
Will fill up our pockets to feast and to dance.
The great king of grace in his will sent the big wind

The Basket-Weaver

That dark Thursday night to our lovely green land,
Which tore down the castles between the high mountains
And every neat village up to Dublin's great town.

THE BASKET-WEAVER
Skelligside

An old Irish saying goes, 'the loaded basket is the burden of misery: to the devil the bundle!' Country people were well versed in weaving: nobody would be depending on someone else to make himself a *cliabh* or a *birdeog*. Neighbours learned the art from each other, though of course the man who had the skill to design and make baskets of all shapes and sizes was the exception. Some were very skilful at making fancy wickerwork. I often watched young men from the village gather in my uncle's kitchen at night-time, making baskets to gamble for in a card game. Eight of them would play, and the stakes were threepence each. That was two shillings for the basket, and the man who won it got it for threepence. They would bring with them a four-inch-deep grassy sod, three feet square, into which the standing rods were pushed, at two-and-a-half-inch intervals, while the slender twigs were woven all round.

The basket was the most important vessel in farming. There were hundreds of uses for it: gathering potatoes, carrying manure, seaweed and turf, taking vegetables, eggs and fish to the market on a fair-day. The large basket, which was carried on the back, had two sides. It was very important that it fitted comfortably between the shoulders and the small of the back, and this was the side for the carrying rope. The other side was semi-circular. Large square pannier-baskets called *úmacha* were made with hinged bottoms which could be dropped to release the contents. Pairs of panniers were used on the backs of horses or donkeys, supported by a stout pad of matted woven straw. Lobster pots were also woven from green osiers and sally branches.

The biggest basket of all was called a *ciseán*. It was round and bulky and could contain one hundredweight of grain or potatoes. The half basket was next in line, then the *purdy* or little basket. A buxom woman who would be extra broad in the beam would be described as having a *ciseán* of an arse on her.

The man who had learned the art and was expert in weaving was called the *caoladóir*. He had various designs, such as the *birdeog*, which had the shape of a *naomhóg*. One end of it was pointed and the other square like a boat transom, and it was used specially for filling sacks. Another basket was completely circular, only eighteen inches high, and with lifting loops woven into the top binding. This was used to measure grain and other commodities. A much smaller basket was called the skiff. It was about ten inches across the middle, two feet long and seven inches deep, tapered to a point at both ends, and had arched handles across the top. The skiff was made in a special way: the sally twigs were boiled to remove all skin and sap and give it a creamy white colour. A well-made skiff was a lovely vessel. The housewives would go to market with skiffs under their arms to carry home their purchases. I also saw a child's cradle made from sallies, complete with canopy and rocking blocks.

At one time, there was an osier plot beside every house. When cultivated, the green osier grew long and tall. It was the most important material used for basket making. Several species of black sally grew wild and were used for weaving the undersides of lobster pots. The twigs and rods were always cut in the dark moon period when the leaves were all gone, and after a few nights' frost had toughened the stems. Osiers cut in the full moon were found to be brittle and less pliable for weaving.

THE COOPER
Skelligside

An old poem about the cooper has a funny twist to it:

What a fool the cooper was
Who hooped his mother
Instead of the cask.

This rhyme I heard as a child, and to this day I cannot understand it fully. Two coopers worked in Ballinskelligs in my youthful days: Seán Jeremiah Moran, from Boolakeel and Thomas O'Connell from Kinard, both professional coopers who were excellent at their trade. Wooden casks, tubs, keelers, milk vats, firkins, half-firkins, buckets, churns: all these wooden vessels were in great demand. Big wooden tubs were made for storing the milk before churning. They had wide mouths to give air to the milk and they were usually placed on wooden trestles a few inches off the ground so that the air could circulate underneath. A story is told about a dairymaid who fell into a tub full of cream and was rescued by the farmer, who said, 'How did you like your swim, Mary?' Mary was not found wanting in her quick and witty reply: 'It was alright, Sir, but I had a greasy passage.'

All the wooden staves were cut and shaped by the cooper. The best wood for the purpose was hard, black oak called *braicín*. The grain of this dark oak ran free without knots and it was easy to split. The cooper would first make rough staves, which he then fashioned, each stave bow-like on the outside and concave inside. This gave the belly-shape to the centre of the cask or churn. The work was done with the cooper's adze, a tool with a curved steel blade set at right angles to a wooden handle. It was so sharp that one slip or careless swing could cause a bad accident, but it was fascinating to watch the cooper using it. How deftly he made the chips fly! Each swinging stroke had a meaning of its own: light, medium and deep, they succeeded each other until the piece of oak had taken a shape pleasing to the eye of the master.

THE BLACKSMITH
Skelligside

The village blacksmith is a hero in folklore not alone in Ireland but in most European countries as well. Tributes are paid to him in song and in story. The blacksmith can make music on his anvil with the hammer, *ding, dong, dédoró ding, dong, déró*. The old saying has it about sharp eyesight:

> The eye of the hound upon the mountain,
> The eye of the hawk above the moor,
> The eye of the blacksmith on the nail,
> The eye of the maiden at the country dance.

When shoeing a horse, the smith had to be careful not to touch the quick with the nail, because this would result in the horse becoming lame. In my young days, two forges close to Ballinskelligs had enough work between them to employ a pair of blacksmiths with helpers. On certain days the forge filled with people from the locality, each with something to make or to mend. The farm horse stood beside the little cob, the pony and the large draught horses. Mules and donkeys were also kept well shod. The law was very strict on working unshod animals. Some horses had to have a special mouthpiece to quieten them while the blacksmith

The Blacksmith

did his work. Of course, mules were most unhelpful and unpredictable, often pointing their rear hooves to heaven.

The smith was usually a mighty man with whiskers on his hands, muscular and unafraid, and possessing a way with animals. He was able to correct the growth of crooked hooves, cure dry decay and let pus from wounds. He treated sprained fetlocks, cured diseased gums and pulled bad teeth. The rough growth which sometimes appeared on horses' gums he cauterized with a white piece of heated steel, before it affected the animal's digestion. Today we have modern cures, but alas, horses have become rare in the farming community and are now regarded as the playthings of the rich. The smith had to be competent in making the tools of his trade. He could fashion all the farm implements, the garden spade, the shovel, the *sleán*, and the turf and hayforks. Some blacksmiths were better than others at making and designing farm and household equipment. The smith fashioned the tongs, the pot hooks, the crane, the crook, the three-legged stand, the griddle for home baking. From the forge too came the hinges for hanging the door and the clasp for closing it. The great sickle for seaweed cutting and the little sickle for reaping the harvest were all a product of the blacksmith's skill. He was able to fuse two pieces of iron into a weld, and temper chisels, hatchets and pickaxe points. The ploughshare with its knife and nose and hitching equipment, the loops and shoes for the swinging bar, the open loops and the great circular loop, all these and more he hammered into shape; he made the tools for the slater – the rippers and slate-trimming knives with punch attached, and slate-nails by the thousand. Whenever an army marched or a navy sailed, it was imperative that a blacksmith be at hand.

Near Ballinskelligs there once lived a blacksmith called Jamesie Fenton, and his forge stood by the stream of the waterfall in Canuig. He was an old-timer and was a relative of my grandmother Mary Fenton: it is two hundred or more years since his anvil sang. A story is told about a man from beyond the hill in the next townland, who died suddenly while coming back from the market in Cahersiveen. Fortunately, he had given a lift in his cart to a woman from Ballinskelligs. It was she who was left with the sad task of guiding the horse homewards with the dead man's body beside her. Some weeks later Jamesie Fenton noticed that the dead man's horse would arrive barebacked and stand near the forge entrance. This became a common occurrence, and the blacksmith seemed unable to send the horse away. One day he noticed that its hooves were in a neglected state, so he took pity on the animal and made it a complete set of new shoes. After giving the horse its freedom, the blacksmith watched it gallop across the hill, happy to think he had cared for the horse who had lost its master. Next day he learned that the horse had died suddenly. The old folk attached a superstitious meaning to its death, not understanding that it was only coincidental.

* * *

I spent some time working on the New York, New Haven and Hartford railroad in the United States during the thirties. One day I was on the main line between New York and Boston, replacing worn and loose bolts with an Italian from the Tyrol. Having completed the job we were left with some spare time on our hands, and my companion asked me if I could tell him an old folk-tale from Ireland, one about ghosts or the nether world. He was a big kindly man, who showed great interest in the past and in the culture of his native Italy which he had left while yet a youth. I could sense that he was bursting to tell his own story. Traditionally, pride of place in storytelling is given to the older man. I explained that, being the elder, he had the honour of telling the first tale. To my astonishment, he started with the

The Blacksmith

Italian folk-tale of *Séadna*, word for word as I had heard it in Irish long years before. At one point in the story, the blacksmith put the devil in the leather bag, laid him across the anvil and began to pound the guts out of him with the big sledge-hammer until the devil could stand it no longer and exploded in a blue flash of flame, taking part of the forge roof with him. When John was telling this part of the story, there were tears of enjoyment in his eyes, and his great frame shook with laughter. I didn't have the heart to admit I had heard the story in my native land.

My Italian workmate was a man with a big heart and a hearty laugh: I felt better for having known him. I told him my own story about a blacksmith, nicknamed 'Tim of the Sparks' who was also the local dentist. He would tie one end of a string to the tooth and the other end to the anvil, then push a brand of flaming steel dangerously close to the face. The resulting jerk backwards of the head to avoid the burning steel meant that the tooth was always found hanging to the anvil. One day it is said Tim extracted a good tooth which grew beside an offending one. When the patient protested, Tim had a ready reply: 'I'm only preparing for the extraction.'

Blacksmiths had an old custom of making pocket knives as gifts for their customers. Seán Brúnach, a poet who lived in Top Street, Cahersiveen, two hundred years ago, composed a poem in honour of the knife, praising the perfection of the gift. This is my translation of a stanza from the poem he composed in Irish:

> It was fashioned from cast steel
> Both burnished and bright;
> From the shaft to the point
> It would sparkle with light;
> The bright smith who drew
> On his anvil the blade,

Would share them as gifts
With the good friends he made.

No longer can a horse, mule or pony be seen hitched to the forge wall. We do not need the tongs, the pot hooks or hanging crook any more. The village smithy is closed for ever. No longer can the bell-like music of the hammer on the anvil, *ding, dong, dédoró ding, dong, déró*, be heard to drift on the morning air.

TAILORS

Skelligside

Only a few years ago five tailors found work in the vicinity of Ballinskelligs. The people were not excited about fashion then as they are today: they only wanted the garment to be roomy and comfortable. Certain modes of fashion were seen in the clothes of the well off – the landed gentry, the legal profession, the doctors, the business people and of course the clergy – but they were outside the choice or scope of the ordinary people.

One garment worn by the better classes was the swallowtail coat. It was tight-fitting at the waist and wide to the knee, and the centre panel was the narrow tail hanging from a half-belt at the back. It had two large ivory or black buttons, one on each side of where the tail started. The buttons were nicknamed 'brookers'. The coat was usually worn with a colourful vest with ivory buttons (which were cheap and plentiful) and knee breeches, white stockings, black patent leather shoes, silk scarf and top hat. The gentry of the period also wore great cloaks lined with silk, and half-cloaks. The country people wore a frieze waistcoat without

Tailors

a collar. Some of their *cotaí móra* or greatcoats also lacked collars, perhaps to save the precious homespun material. Trousers were long and wide with slanting pockets called old men's pockets. The horizontal front opening was called the sailor's fly, or the 'ready come out'. When the buttons were opened, the flap would fall down, so it was also called the half-door.

Tailors were known to be witty and well able to tell a story. They were the journeymen 'knights of the needle' who travelled from village to village. Where work was available they would remain as long as they were needed. Mostly unmarried men were those tailors, and because of their fun-loving characters they often became entangled in the nets of the opposite sex. A well-known Irish song has a line which goes, 'My wife has gone with the merry tailor.'

The sewing-machine gradually put finish to the journeyman tailor. Calico and frieze disappeared as time went by. Fashions became more innovative and glamorous. A new, more colourful and lighter material called woollen serge was imported, and very soon suits of serge were to be seen on the people, with perhaps a bowler hat.

A superstition which was kept alive until the late twenties held that the suit belonging to a deceased person should be worn in church for three consecutive Sundays. Sometimes you would see a boy dressed in his father's suit, complete with hard hat, the trousers and jacket too long or too short, as the case might be. The poor Christian often looked ridiculously like a showman. I sometimes feared that if my dear father passed on the same would happen to me, for the thought of looking like the famous Charlie Chaplin in my Dad's suit and bowler hat was too much for me. But thank God, the parish priest became aware of the custom and put an end to it.

I do not have much knowledge about women's fashion. Black woollen shawls were worn by young girls and older women. Long wide skirts which swept the floor covered red flannel petticoats. There was no danger you could see the calves or knees of a young girl – you might by chance glimpse the big toes of a bare-footed woman. The black woollen shawl came in very useful for courting couples: if a girl had a sweetheart on the sly, the shawl gave shelter and shade to the young man. I remember how the parish priest condemned company-keeping as immoral. He was known to venture out at night on an odd foray along the byways, armed with a stout blackthorn stick. [...]

I heard my mother talk of women tailors who were called mantle-makers. The mantle was a special garment: a loose cloak with a cape or hood which had frills around the edge to encircle the face. This fashion did not prevail in Iveragh but was worn on the south-eastern seaboard. Reference is made in a traditional song called 'Eochaill', or 'Youghal' to the cloak and the high caul cap:

> One Sunday morning into Youghal walking
> I met a fair maid upon the way.
> Her voice was soft as the fairy music,
> Her soft cheeks blushing like dawn of day.
> I laid a hand upon her bosom,
> I asked a kiss but she answered, 'No,
> Kind Sir, be gentle,
> Do not tear my mantle,
> For none in Erin my grief can know.'

Hoops, lace, light cotton and silk fabric came in with Victoria. I remember a story told more than thirty years ago by an old man who had served as coachman to the local landlord. One day while driving a coach-and-four on a sightseeing tour around by Saint Finan's Bay near Ballinskelligs, he had six lady passengers wearing wide

Puffin Island, early 1990s

Iveragh Hills, 2005

*Horse Island and The Priory
(Ballinskelligs Abbey), early 90s*

*Horse Island and The Priory
(Ballinskelligs Abbey), 1997*

*Horse Island and The Priory
(Ballinskelligs Abbey), 2003*

*Horse Island and The Priory
(Ballinskelligs Abbey), 2004*

Sceilg Mhichíl in sunlight, 2003

The Skelligs and Bolus Head, 2000

The Skelligs and Bolus Head, 2002

Moonlight on Glen Strand, 1989

Sceilg Mhichíl from Saint Finan's Bay, 2004

Ballinskelligs Castle by moonlight, 2003

Sea Pinks, 1992

crinoline dresses with large hoops like billowing balloons. The weather suddenly changed and there was a fearful storm. At a narrow bend on the road the horses could not negotiate the very sharp turn. As the old coachman related it: 'We had to unbuckle the horses and with the help of the ladies and a passer-by we managed to pull the empty coach into the clear. It was the will of God that the ladies weren't carried up into the sky by that gale. The great gusts of wind got under their hoops and blew them inside out, silk was torn, hoops broken, beautiful hats blown away. Whenever the ladies attempted to walk they always ended in the embarrassing position of bottoms up. We had a hard job to get the horses into the shafts of the coach again. The road into Ballinskelligs was more sheltered, and we rested a while at a roadside tavern with a hot drink, before resuming our journey to the big house.' Bamboo and crinoline, however fashionable for the upper class, were not suitable wear for stormy weather on the beautiful but windswept road of Saint Finan's Bay.

My sister, Mary Kirby, became a seamstress and earned her living in Ireland and in the United States. During her apprenticeship the first thing she was taught was how to make buttonholes. The teacher inspected the work at intervals, and while looking at a sample of Mary's work exclaimed in front of the class, 'Mary, my girl, you'll have to do better! I often saw a better buttonhole under a pig's tail.' Later on, Mary became very successful at her trade, designing and making ballgowns for wealthy people in the United States.

I grieve to think that the era of the village tailor is past. Computers, not people, are in charge of tailoring now. One more landmark, the tailor's shop, has disappeared forever from country life. If our grandmothers could only see a modern girl going to church on a Sabbath morning dressed in her mini, smelling salts or medical aid would surely need to be administered. I believe that air, water and sunshine are necessary for a healthy body, and that the soul does not need clothing or fashion. In the last analysis, grace is the clothing of the soul. Are naked people banned from heaven? As the old man said, blind people are a great pity.

> The long loose stitch for the fool,
> The short stitch for the wise.

THE VILLAGE COBBLER
Skelligside

The shoemaker, too, is gone from the countryside around Ballinskelligs. Only a short while ago, the cobbler was a very busy man. At least ten shoemakers worked in our parish before and after the 1914 war. An old rhyme has it as follows:

> Find four cobblers who can't tell lies,
> Find four Frenchmen who are not sallow,
> Find four Churchmen who do not covet;
> In this Island they are not found.

The lying shoemaker has vanished. Frenchmen are yellow-skinned as ever. Clergymen are no more covetous than lay people: an old saying goes, 'Monks can't survive on vespers alone.' But the era of the bristle tip, the waxed thread and awl, the iron last and lapstone is no more.

The village cobbler was a most interesting person. People came to him at all times of day and late at night. Sometimes he would teach a young apprentice – perhaps the son of a neighbour – how to fix patches on torn uppers and to sew

The Village Cobbler

neatly with the bristled waxed thread. He knew all the local gossip: people confided in him, while coming with their many foot complaints, their corns, bunions and ingrowing toenails. Some cobblers were known to make tight-fitting shoes. One old man swore that the shoes the cobbler made for him would put corns on the hooves of a donkey. The shoemaker sold leather thongs which he cut neatly from the tanned hide, leather belts and leather muzzles for dogs who were known to attack people. I found great pleasure in visiting the cobbler's shop. He was always asking questions which to my mind were amusing and harmless: 'Does your mother keep hens?' 'Are they laying well?' 'Did the cow calve?' 'What colour is the calf?' 'What bull did she get?' 'Are you finished school yet?'

I remember a pair of boots being made for me: size 10, they weighed ten pounds each and were hand-sewn, copper-nailed and wooden-pegged. The soles, three-quarters of an inch thick, were covered with metal hobnails, and the heels were raised with heavy iron tips. They were watertight, warm and durable, and their total cost in 1935 was thirty shillings.

America Calling

FAMINE AND AMERICA
Skelligside

I heard many gruesome Famine tales at the fireside, terrible but true, of corpses lying by the roadside in South Iveragh, their lips stained green from chewing nettle leaves and other herbs. Thousands left the countryside even up to the eighteen-fifties. Two 'side-wheelers' which had sail and steam were sent as a humane gesture by the American government of the time, to help the remaining destitute families by offering them free passage to the 'Promised Land'. Two great liners sailed up the Shannon to Limerick for this purpose only, one being the steamship S.S. *Jane Black*. Entire families left Ballinskelligs and the area from Cahersiveen to Bolus, Valentia Island, Saint Finan's Glen and Portmagee. Most of them settled on the east coast, between Boston and New Jersey. As people fled their smallholdings, the few fields where they had never experienced security of tenure, the English masters set up soup-distributing centres in some of the more stricken areas – alas! too little, too late. A large iron pot which contained one hundred gallons of beef soup, with a glowing fire beneath, was set up in the village square, and a starving populace queued up to avail of the life-giving broth. Two warm blankets, plenty of soup, and a farm cut from the best estates was offered to any Irish families who would renounce allegiance to Rome and turn to the Church of England or any of the non-Catholic persuasions.

A story is told about an old woman nicknamed 'Kate the Souper'. Kate was missing from Sunday Mass for several weeks. Rumour had it that she had forsaken her Church. One

Sunday morning when the parish priest arrived to celebrate Mass, he noticed a dejected, forlorn figure sitting outside the church, with a shawl pulled over her face and head, shunned by all her friends, the pariah of the community. The priest approached her, saying, 'Welcome back, Kate! I knew you would return. Did you get the blankets, Kate?'

'I did, Father.'

'And why not, Kate! I suppose you drank as much soup as would float the *Jane Black*?'

'I did, Father, and I am sorry.'

'Come, Kate, let us offer the sacrifice of the Mass. And I will have material for a nice sermon this morning, and you will be the prodigal daughter.'

Some Irish families turned Protestant to regain lands they were deprived of by Queen Elizabeth. Others turned for the sake of wealth and rank – those who would sell their souls for a cap and a stripe. Some of the Irish 'soupers' became high-ranking officers in the king's army, and some studied medicine in Trinity College, Dublin. I remember a verse from a poem I read in my schooldays. I do not know who the author was, but it refers to the hunger of the Famine years.

> It has gnawed like a wolf at my heart, Mother,
> A wolf that is fierce for blood;
> All the livelong day, and the night beside,
> Gnawing for lack of food.
> I dreamed of bread in my sleep, Mother,
> And the sight was Heaven to see;
> I awoke with an eager, famishing lip,
> But you had no bread for me.
>
> [A.M. Edmond]

Emigration was the ultimate legacy of the poor. I remember the American wakes, which were sad and tearful occasions.

Famine and America

The neighbours got together in the house of the intending emigrant, where tea and light refreshments might be provided and the accordion played for set dancing and singing. The emigrant might be given little gifts of money to help him on his way. The friends would all stay until it was time for departing, usually for the early morning train from Cahersiveen. People who lived twelve or fifteen miles away had to travel by horse-cart or sidecar, and therefore make an early start. For a lot of them it was the last sad farewell, only some being fortunate enough to see their parents again. Many made good, but many others fell by the wayside.

***

My grand-uncles Jerry and John Kirby along with Michael Geoffrey O'Connell emigrated to the United States during the Famine year of 1847. Michael O'Connell was the husband of Ellen Kirby and a stonemason by trade. Ellen Kirby stayed at home in Ballinskelligs with her three young children. After working for three years, Michael paid for their passage to join him in America. Ellen left Cobh in the year 1850 with her three children, Mary, Daniel and John, the youngest, who was only four years old. By all accounts, the voyage was prolonged and stormy: in those days the normal voyage required six weeks or more. The ship was overcrowded with thousands fleeing from hunger. The O'Connell children became very seasick and one day Ellen Kirby was thrown violently to the deck suffering fracture to several of her ribs. Worst of all, little John did not survive the ordeal and when he died the great ocean received his body.

Finally, the ship reached the Gulf of Saint Laurence where the passengers disembarked at Quebec. Michael Geoffrey O'Connell met his depleted little flock. They proceeded down the Saint Laurence to Montreal. A short time later they moved to Albany, staying for a while until work became scarce, whereupon they moved to Boston. Work was scarce in Boston also, and O'Connell was advised to travel south where stonemasons were in demand for building walls and milking-houses for farmers. They started to travel once more and on reaching Virginia lived some time at a place called Farmville in Prince Edward County. They moved again to Kingsport in Sullivan County, Tennessee, together with the Kirby brothers, Jerry and John. Very soon after, the American Civil War began. John Kirby enlisted with the Northern and Jerry Kirby with the Southern side, taking a horse valued at twenty-four dollars with him into the cavalry: two brothers from Ballinskelligs fighting to uphold their opposing ideals in the land of their adoption. John Kirby was killed in action at the battle of Vicksburg in May 1863. Jerry survived the war and came to live with his sister Ellen Kirby O'Connell until his death a few years later. The brothers are buried in Tennessee, as the poet has written:

> Under the sod and the dew,
> Awaiting the judgment day;
> Under the laurel, the Blue,
> Under the willow, the Grey.
>
> (Francis Miles Finch)

Many thousands fell on both sides, all honourable men in their own right, all warriors, victims of unpredictable circumstance. The story ends as Michael O'Connell and Ellen Kirby purchase a piece of land at Cropper, in Shelby County, Kentucky. They had eleven children. Ellen Kirby died in the year 1899, and her husband in 1910 at the grand old age of ninety-seven. Ellen was laid to rest in Shelbyville, and Michael in Louisville. Their many descendants still live in Kentucky, proud of their Irish ancestry, and come back occasionally to visit Ballinskelligs, whence their forebears fled. I dedicate the following verse to Ellen Kirby's great granddaughter, Nancy O'Connell Kirby, and her husband Howard Maxfield.

> This night I'm in exile
> Far over the foam,
> Away from my friends
> And my dear ones at home;
> How quickly I'd come
> My joy to reveal,
> To see once again
> Dear old Sceilg Mhichíl.

[These lines are a loose translation of a stanza from a poem entitled 'Sean-Sceilg Mhichíl'. The full poem is reproduced on page 302–3.]

VOYAGE TO AMERICA
Skelligs Calling

The local innkeeper was the owner of two small fishing vessels, manned and skippered by local crews. The hours were from dawn to midnight. No fish meant no pay. The crew supplied their own food: boiled fish, bread and tea. All work, such as scrubbing the hulls, repairing, painting, wintering and mending gear, was not considered by the owners as work to be paid for. You took what you got and asked no questions. The work was hard and backbreaking for the lack of power winches, only a crude windlass for lifting a heavy trawl full of fish from thirty-five to forty fathoms of water. Landing facilities were bad and hours unlimited, men often working a whole week of eighty hours for a pittance of fifty shillings. Conditions which smacked of the 'Georgia Chain Gang' left within me a feeling of being caught in a vicious poverty trap, or rather being owned, body and soul, by some set of unknown economic circumstances for the sake of my daily bread.

It was because of conditions such as I have described that I wished earnestly to escape. I wrote to my brother Timothy, who worked in Connecticut, asking him if he would help me to get to the United States. He kindly sent me the passage boat fare, for which I was extremely grateful. I felt like the bird in the poem:

> I'm free, I'm free, I'll return no more,
> My weary time in this cage is over.

If only I had knowledge of what lay in store for me, I would also have a cure for all ills. This I take from an old saying in Irish, which I often heard from my mother, how true:

> *Dá mbeadh fhios agam, bheadh leigheas agam.*

I was virtually jumping from my unhappy position in Ireland into the middle of a great depression – the Wall Street Crash. Having collected all the necessary documents required from Church and State by the US Department of Immigration, I was called to Cobh for a medical and mental scrutiny. I stayed at a hotel with other aspiring immigrants.

The morning was bitterly cold, with a light snow on the ground. Ten of us were ushered into a hall fitted with cubicles, and told to remove all our clothing. I was in the cubicle nearest the door, protected only by a flimsy screen. Being stark naked, I felt miserably cold. We had waited some time for the American doctor to arrive. I remember him dressed in white, jovial, smiling with dark, horn-rimmed spectacles. Glancing into my cubicle as he passed, he must have observed goose pimples, or perhaps a shiver. He stopped suddenly and asked if I felt cold. I answered, 'Yes Sir.' He checked all the other cubicles and ordered heaters to be brought in, saying, 'These men are cold.' I was the first to be called. He made a quick check of my body, observing once more that I should put some clothing on in case of being chilled. After a quick reading and memory test, some mental arithmetic and inspection of personal underwear, he gave me a full okay on all grounds. When dressed, I waited my turn to appear before the American consul and staff, who stamped my passport and scrutinized my other documents. They asked me why I wished to emigrate. I replied that I had the intention of bettering myself and finding employment. They asked if I had a job waiting for me, to which I answered in the negative. After noticing the addresses of my relatives in the USA and that of my sister with whom I was to reside, I was given a visa and an immigration quota number, enabling me the legal right to enter, seek work and stay indefinitely in the USA.

I booked passage with the North German line, Hamburg American. It was an old liner, the S.S. *Dresden*, which took seven days to cross the Atlantic and which was taken out of service soon after. At this period, newer more luxurious and faster ships were contending for the blue riband of the Atlantic: mighty ships such as the S.S. *Rex*, *QE2*, S.S. *Bremen*, S.S. *Europa*, S.S. *Queen Mary*, S.S. *America*, and the S.S. *Andrea Doria*, which tragically sank in a collision in the North Atlantic, with loss of life.

Tearfully and reluctantly I said goodbye to my parents, who were now ageing. I was the last of seven to leave the little thatched cottage and the postage stamp-sized farm of cutaway bog. The farm was divided into six one-acre lots among the rural and unsettled peasantry of South Iveragh. The resident landlord and his agent levelled an exorbitant rent on each holding, payable in half-yearly gales. Woe betide the tenant who was found in arrears; he could expect the sky for a roof and the roadside his garden.

Humble though our lot in life, the thatched cottage was our castle. Even in poverty we were proudly poor. Like our many good neighbours we had plenty of potatoes, cabbage, turnips, onions, eggs, milk and fish and also the love of a closely knit family who accepted and shared fortune or tribulation.

That evening, as dusk was enveloping the receding shoreline behind the Fastnet Rock, the great ship seemed to gather speed, scattering the white-capped waves into spray and ploughing a giant furrow through the back of each approaching Atlantic billow. The last streak of cold winter sunlight illuminated the western horizon. A stiff westerly breeze was building up, carrying with it a sniff of approaching rain. I could enjoy each moment, each pulsating movement of the ship whose deck was vibrant beneath my feet, her great, white superstructure and bridge. I could visualize a wise and competent captain, nursing and gently guiding his beloved ship, bringing her safely through the awful fury of an Atlantic hurricane. Somehow, I felt a void in my heart that night. I was lonely; the mercury of ambition had plummeted. My old father was lonely. I could see it in his countenance, bereft of any emotion when I said goodbye. Mothers, too, suffer in loneliness and love for their offspring. The deck steward ordered us below. Just as well, I felt I had betrayed my parents in the selfish interest of self-betterment. I refused to feel sorry for myself.

Mike Moran, my school companion, and David Fitzgerald also travelled on the *Dresden*. We were all in the same boat, trying to adjust to whatever lay in store. The majority of the passengers were continental, Germans, Austrians and some Jews. We soon made friends with different people, some who were returning to the States.

On the second day the weather grew steadily worse, blowing a full gale. We were confined to the salons of the lower decks. Many passengers suffered from severe *mal de mer*. Some were confined to their bunks. It was pitiful to see healthy folk vomiting all over the place. They showed a film for the passengers' entertainment in a small theatre. The theatre was almost empty, owing to seasickness. The breakfast table had many empty chairs. We got fillet of raw, salted herring rolled into a ball, and held with a wooden pin. Mike Moran tasted one, making a wry grimace in disgust. Paddy Browne observed, 'They must think we're cats, serving us raw fish.' One American-born German returning from Hamburg to the USA on hearing Paddy's remark exploded into a convulsive fit of laughter, nearly choking and set us all into a laughing gag. One of the waiters asked, 'Vot is so vunny, zat you not like vish?'

We passed near a four-masted barque beating her way westward under shortened sail: a large ship, laden deeply. A sailing ship was becoming a rare sight on Atlantic routes, 'A tall ship and a star to steer her by' becoming a ghost ship in the memory of seafarers.

The third day, the weather cleared; the face of the ocean appeared more placid and we were allowed on deck. Myriads of Manx and greater shearwaters, with undulating flight, were forever rising and falling in unison with the movement of the sea. Storm petrels like little black chicks with short, webbed, flat feet seemed to stand momentarily on the lip of a billow, scooping a microscopic droplet of rich plankton oil floating in the ocean. Nature provided a perfect spoon-recess on the lower bill for this purpose. Deep-sea sailors are highly superstitious regarding this beautiful, bat-like creature, the harbinger of storms and foul weather when the birds are seen to congregate in wisps. A wisp of petrels is three or more birds. From a fisherman's point of view, I could stand by the rail for long periods, being rewarded

Skelligs Haul

for my patience by observing a small school of flying fish scatter by, leaping into the wind with fins outstretched, awakened by the bow wave of the rushing, leaping bulk of an ocean liner. I often observed dolphins expose their blue-grey arching backs, and once a pod of small, black, spouting whale calves.

The voyage westward became more pleasant as the passengers found their sea legs. It was obvious that some German females and some young Irish Paddies became more and more interested in each other's companionship. Language didn't seem to create an insurmountable barrier to friendship. Three things that can be found anywhere in the world: an Irishman, a German woman and a Swedish matchstick.

High on the main mast, the crow's nest was manned night and day. There were also port and starboard lookout posts. Paddy Browne from Clare had ginger hair, was five foot six inches tall, had blue eyes and was well built. He was always neat, clean and well groomed, a young, well spoken, well behaved man who nevertheless would call a spade a spade. A German girl, much his senior, took a liking to Paddy. She dressed in an untidy fashion, or so it seemed to him. Her dress hung wide and voluminous from beneath her arms to the floor, thus concealing entirely whatever footwear she wore. Her sleeves were filled at the wrists, her upper deck showed bulging breasts below a thick neck and square head, with a mop of flaxen, flowing hair. She haunted Paddy, hung on his shoulder and suggested she give him singing lessons. With a song that she had translated from German, called 'Apple Blossom Time', she would demonstrate her ability by placing one hand on Paddy's shoulder and using the other as if conducting a choir. She sang in a sweet voice:

I vill be wit you in apfel bloomen time,
I vill be wit you to change your name to mine.

Turning, she would say to Paddy, 'Now I teach you love song.' Paddy decided she was cuckoo, saying, 'If only I could say coo coo in German, I'd tell her so.' The boys would retort, 'Can't you give her an Irish cuckoo?' Whereupon Paddy would tell us all, in modern jargon, to 'piss off'.

As we got to know each other, we enjoyed the crack. One young man from another province was dubbed 'Sly Britches'. John Rodgers from Dundalk was an engineer and believed hydraulic power would play a great role in future industry. He was a kindly and serious person and an asset to the country of his adoption.

Another mysterious young man – whose name except that of William, I can't remember. His hometown was Maynooth. He bore the hallmark of the academy or perhaps the boarding school. He was very fond of a dark, unclouded night, when the stars were blazing. His knowledge of astronomy was amazing. He educated both John Rodgers and myself, one starlit night, while we were walking the deck. He believed strongly, while expounding the Darwinian theory, in the possibility of a non-existing supreme being, and that Galileo would be proven right. He lived, he said, in this agnostic and atheistic void and was perfectly happy. His love of poetry became evident, how beautifully he quoted lines to prove a point. Whether a spoiled priest or a professor, looking back, it was nice knowing him. It takes all kinds to make a world.

Maybe it was because we had lived together in the same 'house' for a whole seven days, that we became curious of our different traits and outlook on life. Although we were birds of a feather, we all seemed different. No doubt each individual became an object lesson to the other. One middle-aged man called 'Mack' was returning to the USA to live with his sole surviving daughter. He had been in the States in his youth and didn't relish the thought of ending his days there. He cherished the idea of coming back to a small holding that he still owned in Tipperary. He was convinced that there was no place like Tipp. A sad kindly man who recited the rosary and exhorted us to do the same, undoubtedly he had a great devotion to the Virgin. I only pray that he realized his wish and returned to the vales of Tipp.

Notices written in several languages were placed on the walls of all the salons and recreation rooms: 'Beware of Professional Gamblers, Pickpockets and Prostitutes'. Someone asked Paddy Browne what the difference was between a gambler, a pickpocket and a prostitute, to which he replied, 'No difference at all, men – don't you know they're all hoors.'

Time went by quickly. The laugh and the crack were great, like all fleeting moments of happiness which seem to pass so quickly. As the S.S. *Dresden* moved under reduced speed into the narrows, the great towering skyscrapers of Manhattan stood like giant monuments along the waterfront. It was a calm morning. There was an oily sheen on the face of the great port. Merchant ships with sirens blaring, entered and left, all observing the law required by the port authority. There were city council tugs towing a string of barges, full of litter to be dumped off the coast, fruit ships from the south, cruise liners with holiday makers bound for the sun, coastguard cutters, port police boats, luxurious yachts, fishing vessels, buoys and markers with port traffic lights for the mariners' benefit. A pilot boat scurried alongside, a ladder-like gangway was lowered. An agile figure in blue uniform with gold braid jumped like a cat onto the ship's ladder. Making his way to the bridge, this man's job was the safe berthing of the ship. He was a professional port pilot. Two tugboats, which seemed so tiny, one at the bow and one at the stern, they mothered, pushed and puffed until the great ship lay safely berthed beside the pier allotted to her. All Irish passengers were assembled in a large office-like room on the liner, where an immigration official checked our passports, which seemed to be a formality. The medical examination was quick and efficient. This was carried out in case of an outbreak of disease during the voyage. We said goodbye on the dockside. I only met Mike Moran on two other occasions, once in New York and once when he visited Ireland. We were school companions and neighbours.

A returning Irish woman from Cavan joined me in sharing a taxi from the dockside to the vast Central Station. Here we took a train, which served all the shoreline stations from New York to Boston. The landscape was still gaunt and barren, recovering from the sub-zero temperatures of the New England winter. I noticed only small parcels of open countryside. The built-up areas with many great chimneystacks suggested a highly industrialized country with a large population. I parted with Mrs Whelan at New Haven railroad station, which I was to know so well in the very near future. With brown suitcase in hand I walked through the station to the taxi rank outside. As I approached a uniformed driver, he immediately swung the door open for me. I said, '33 Wilson Street', which was my sister's and her husband Paddy Reardon's address. The taxi driver informed me of how difficult it might be to get work, owing to factories laying off staff and closing down. He painted a dismal picture of the approaching depression, saying, 'I guess you hit this country the wrong year, Irish!' How prophetic his words!

My sister Mary must have heard my footsteps on the raised veranda, with its rocking chair. Mary must have mistaken me for a distant relation of the prodigal son, so embracingly emotional was her welcome. Having reached destination, 'Hope and Glory', I confessed I felt rather tired. Only at this juncture did I realize how misinformed I was in relation to the work problem in the USA. My sister Sheila, who lived nearby, came immediately to bestow on me her version of 'the prodigal welcome'. Thank God they didn't have a fattened calf, as the creature would surely have been sacrificed on the altar of ignorance, especially in regard to the Wall Street Crash.

Paddy Reardon came home from work at the storeroom of the New York–New Haven and Hartford railroad. After greeting me, he asked me a question, which in the first place caused me surprise, and at the same time, required a sudden decision. 'Mike, do you think you could turn out to work on the railroad at half-six tomorrow morning? The section boss asked me this evening if I knew of anyone who could fill a vacancy. It's hard work and only two dollars fifty a day. I said you were arriving this evening, so he told me to contact him on the phone. What do you say Mike, will you take the job?' I replied, 'Okay, I'll take what's offered.' Paddy contacted Mr Bernhardt, a German who had been working for the Canadian Pacific Rail Road. He was curt in his reply: 'Okay Pat, bring in the harp in the morning.' After a warm bath, I got to bed early, and Morpheus, that beautiful God of slumber, folded his gossamer wings across my tired eyes.

I must have slept like a log. I thought I heard Paddy's voice in the distance saying, 'Will you go to work Mike, or are you too tired?' 'Oh! Of course, of course,' I said jumping up and rubbing my eyes, at five-thirty. Paddy had some porridge, coffee and rye bread ready for my breakfast. Mary had prepared some meat sandwiches for my lunch. It was as yet early morning and I remember we walked into Lambarton Street by the intersection of Howard Avenue. We passed the seamless rubber factory, through the watchman's gate of Yard Four Freight and Passenger Complex, which was the station house.

Paddy left me at a wooden hut-cum-office and tool house, situated on the waterfront. A rough, boarded floor with a large coal stove set in the centre with seating all

Voyage to America

around. Mr Bernhardt's roll-top writing desk with swivel chair occupied one corner. A burly figure, weighing at least two hundred and eighty pounds, dressed in a blue boiler suit, jacket and peaked hat, stood by the stove, cursing and muttering in broken sentences. I was left in his care by Paddy, who seemed to be an old friend of this huge, good-natured native of the Italian Tyrol. He poked and fussed with the coal stove, which seemed to lack a draught. Going outside, he returned with a long iron rod with which he riddled the grate violently. Suddenly, the flame sprung to life, the big man uttered an expression of satisfaction – 'Ah! I make you pull, you son of a bitch.' He then sat down and asked if Pat Reardon was married to my sister. 'Pat is a nice man.' He went on to say, 'This was good country, Mike, but Hoover ruin it. You only come from old country yesterday and get job today.' He chuckled with a suppressed half-laugh, half-cough, 'I'll be a son of a bitch, luck of the Irish.'

Mr Bernhardt, our boss, arrived in company with two other men who were permanent members of what was known in railroad terms as 'Section 4'. One was Frederick Breault, a French-speaking Canadian; another was Samuel Marks, son of an English father and an Irish mother, who to my astonishment was from our neighbourhood in Ireland. John de Maio, the big Italian, was our trackwalker. He was nicknamed 'Jumbo'; Frederick was called 'Frog'; Sam was 'Bottle Arse'; and I was 'Green Harp'. We were responsible for the upkeep of the rails in the freight yard. Mr Bernhardt recruited me to the permanent gang, asked me to sign my name and gave me a brass cheque with my register number. Shaking hands, he said, 'Mike, I hope you become president of the railroad!'

The first day passed quickly. I got every assistance from my fellow workers on how to use the heavy tools: the heavy jack for lifting track, spike pullers, tamping irons, gauges, spiking mauls, Jim Crowes, etc. I walked back to 33 Wilson

Street without losing my way. My sister viewed it as an intelligent achievement for a greenhorn.

The summer turned into a real scorcher with high temperatures and many violent thunderstorms. We never laid tools flat on the ground, as in a short time a bar would become too hot to handle.

Freddie Breault and myself decided we would discard our shirts for a few minutes each day, until our skins became accustomed to the heat. We finally turned a dark yellowish-brown, which didn't harm us. We walked in public with only our trousers and hats. Some dubbed us as the Mutt and Jeff Indians.

New Haven city was relatively free from crime. The relationship between the different ethnic communities seemed very good. Sex was discussed by men on the job. Peddlers selling ice cream also sold condoms on the side. Some said brothels existed in New Haven. In American slang they were called 'Cat Houses'. I never had evidence such was the case. Some Americans had a superstition that if you were down on your luck, you should make love to a coloured woman.

Work on the railroad was reduced to three days a week. Lay-offs became the order of the day. As the depression grew worse, the real recession started to take effect. The workers had no protection, no social welfare benefit. The factories simply shut down. The mill owners took to their yachts and sailed south. The Salvation Army and city charities opened soup kitchens. During a short stay in New York, I witnessed people huddle side-by-side, sleeping under store awnings and in the under-street levels of steam-heated Grand Central Station. To board a train I picked my way through rows of sleeping men, lying on sheets of newspapers on the tiled platform.

All private banking firms folded. People lost their complete life savings. I knew of Irish emigrants who were

Voyage to America

committed to mental institutions on hearing that they had become destitute in one telling blow. I was present when a young, newly married man tried to end his misery because he could no longer support his wife. Luckily, he survived in hospital. Only deposits in the Federal Reserve banks were safe. Twenty-eight million were unemployed, from Florida to the state of Maine, and from New York to San Francisco. The richest and most powerful country in the world, which held the world's greatest gold reserve, was now burning a surplus of unwanted grain – enough to feed millions – all because of a stupid trade war concerning protective tariffs on both sides of the Atlantic.

The Prohibition Act, concerning the sale of intoxicating liquor, made matters worse. The great brewing industries had to close down. Federal agents discovered several casks of Canadian beer, in with other merchandise, in our section of the freight yard. They ordered the casks to be rolled to the waterfront and borrowed our spiking hammers to burst the cask heads, before departing. Our gang salvaged several water pails of a rich golden beer. The 'noble experiment' proved to be a most ignoble piece of legislation. It bred a new breed of criminal: bootleggers, beer barons and gangsters of all vile description.

The three-days-per-week pay cheque I received, I gladly surrendered to my sister, so that I might compensate her for keeping a roof over my head, thus avoiding the bread lines, which in New York could extend for blocks. The navy recruiting office in New Haven carried the advertisement: 'Join the Navy and see the world.' Many a time I stood at the bottom of the stairs, undecided as to whether I should take the plunge or not. I consulted Paddy Reardon, my brother-in-law, on the matter. 'Take it easy Mike,' he cautioned. 'You made one mistake by coming here in hard times, don't make a hasty decision.' As the old Irish saying goes: *Léim chaorach i nduibheagán* – 'the leap of a sheep into the abyss'.

Then came a turning point in my life, which leads me to believe that our lives are governed by some force other than our own wish. Some call it destiny, kismet or whatever. One evening when I arrived back from work, a letter from Ireland awaited me. To my surprise it contained a cheque for a considerable sum of money, from my mother, saying I could use it to take a trip home to see my father, who was not feeling well, or use the money as I pleased. I immediately took passage on the S.S. *Saint Louis* of the Hamburg American Line – the ship about which Gordon Thomas and Max Morgan-Witts wrote the true story, *Voyage of the Damned*, concerning a thousand Jews fleeing the concentration camps of Hitler, only to be refused entry to Cuba or the USA on 13 May 1939.

The S.S. *Saint Louis* was a new luxury liner. The swastika and the Hamburg American line pennants flying proudly from her masthead. Many German passengers wearing swastika emblems made no secret that Germany was gearing itself for war, and that the Third Reich would emerge victorious and become a global power under Hitler. The Irish passengers disembarked at Galway, and I made my way back to Ballinskelligs. I must admit to feeling a little crestfallen. Shattered were my grandiose dreams of starting a better life in the New World. There was a sudden realization that my mother had rescued me from the scrap heap of a jobless democracy. My whole life's ambition for betterment seemed futile, like shovelling muck against the wind. There was no use in feeling sorry for myself – why didn't I join the navy?

My father was glad to see me and I was compensated by the fact that I was with my parents in their greatest hour of need. Dad was losing ground day by day and died happily in the spring of the year. My mother implored me to leave her by herself and return to the United States. This my conscience would not allow. I would feel as if I had deserted her. Economic conditions in Ireland were at their worst, with the economic war of penal tariffs against the Irish Free State, to compensate absentee British estate owners because of arrears in rent annuities. Britain refused beef trade with Ireland. I sold two very fine bullocks for two pounds each. Calves were slaughtered at birth. If ever a case could be made for jumping out of the frying pan into the fire and back again, it could be applied to my next move. I went back to the fishing trawler and long hours of slavery.

World War Two broke out as predicted and half a million fools went flogging through hell. I was the 'kid of the drum'. 'Buddy, can you spare a dime?' was America's marching song of the surviving heroes of Roosevelt's New Deal. I was offered eighty pounds for my six acres. I declined. This was the last straw. The forces of destiny seemed pitted against my people – the Kirbys of Munster.

My mother went to her reward in 1941. She was expecting her death, and told me the day she would pass away, saying; 'I will die tomorrow with the help of God.' My parents were secure in an unquestioning faith and accepted being poor as part of their social status. I continued scraping the seabed for fish, late and early, until 1943. A local farmer's daughter, Peggy O'Sullivan, agreed with my suggestion that it is bad for man to live alone. It required a certain amount of courage, visiting her parents to ask her hand in marriage. I will always remember her father's answer: 'You're as welcome as the flowers in May.'

In those days marriage was a serious business. A letter of freedom, signed by the local canon who resided in Cahersiveen, was necessary. This freedom was given after he had scrutinized a sealed letter given to me by my pastor. Having signed the forms giving the consent of the church to the forthcoming marriage, and before sealing the envelope, he asked me how I earned my living. I answered, 'from the sea, Father – I'm a sailor.' Before I had time to explain that I was a trawler man, the good canon threw up his hands, as if in despair. 'A sailor, oh my God, go off and marry her at once and don't stay away from her too long. God bless you both, boy. God bless you.' The saintly old man probably visualized Peggy standing forlorn on some South Kerry beach, singing 'Red Sails in the Sunset'. Jack-of-all-trades and master of none, I had increased my acreage from six to twenty-six acres.

I carried out maintenance and repair work for the Board of Public Works, small farming, fishing, building a new house, storm repair on roofs, rearing a family, cutting our own peat, keeping pigs, fowl, cows and calves. In 1951 I decided I would say, 'Goodbye old ship of mine.' I divested myself of my oilskins on Ballinskelligs pier and vowed I'd be my own boss from then onwards. There is an old saying in Irish: '*Is olc an chearc ná scríobann dí féin*' – 'It is a bad hen that can't scratch for herself.'

Peggy and myself have celebrated over sixty years of married bliss. Our family are all married and around us. We have great satisfaction in the knowledge that we can never go broke. We have our own potatoes, milk and vegetables in the garden, pork and beef in the barrel, our own hens, turkeys, and our own fuel. Perhaps I owe it all to a partner who has lived her Christian faith to the full – for better or for worse, for richer or for poorer.

The Running Tide

EARLY SEA MEMORIES
Skelligs Calling

My father, John Kirby, kept a small boat down near the old ruined castle, which to this day stands on the beach in the townland of Ballinskelligs. The boat was built locally, of carvel design, from native timber, only twenty feet long overall, and five feet ten inches beam, propelled by oars and a small sail of old rough linen resembling sackcloth. The local builder swore by the Book that each and every boat built by his hands would contain three special qualities, which he described in Irish as *siúl, iompar agus cosaint*, meaning 'speed, cargo capacity and resistance to a rough sea'. Old Johnny Morty Galvin from *Brácathrach* was proud of his skill; his was the *modus operandi*, the knack and the know-how of his time. Therefore my father's boat became our family's most sacrosanct item of property, and small wonder, for it provided a goodly supply of prime fish, which helped us to survive within a lean and meagre period in our economy. It is neither my intention nor my wish to write a history bewailing the lot of those who survived the Great Famine, and who were yet only one step away from the coffin ships or morsels from a landlord's table.

Now, up until my eighth birthday, I had not yet seen the boat. I was prohibited from straying too far from the scene of my delivery. It never occurred to me that I was being a good boy, and I had heard that the boy Jesus went down to Nazareth and was subject to his parents, to grow in wisdom and understanding, traits I confess I have never fully achieved. I had heard of the word 'curfew', which for me at any rate meant that I stay indoors, say my bedtime prayers and go to bed.

Then one day something utterly surprising happened. The curfew was lifted. A milestone, which to this day stands out clearly in my mind, my father saying, 'We're going fishing – tell Mam get your boots and jacket.'

I had only one pair of boots, rough boots, complete with heavy iron tips and hobnails. I was allowed to wear them once a week to attend Sunday Mass, and maybe some special occasion like the 'Pattern' day – the remainder of the week it was God's leather to God's weather. Oh, but this was a special occasion; my dad had lifted the curfew, he had invited me into his workplace, that vast kingdom below high-water mark where: 'They don't plant taters / And don't plant cotton'.

That evening perhaps my father knew he was about to foster in me a lasting permanent love for my native surroundings, which in so many ways would influence my development and behaviour for years to come. This coupled with my eager drive to know more about the strange and fascinating secrets of nature, some of which are beyond our capacity to understand. This is the workplace that my dad introduced me to, that of a small-time fisherman. This is the kingdom I would feign have the temerity to understand, much less to write about. That fishing trip was the commencement of a way of life, which culminated in thirty years' involvement with the sea.

I will only vouch for what I have observed from my own personal experience. The picture which I try to lay before you is only an attempt at describing an immense, beautiful world of water and wave, towering cliff, crag and cave, sand and seashore, green islands, barren rock, pebble beaches and silver strands.

This is Neptune's territory, Mannanan's Kingdom, containing fin, fur and feather. Its many gardens show a manifold array of marine plants, each with diverse mineral content, most having curative healing powers beneficial to man and beast. A rock pool can become an Aladdin's Cave, teeming with multi-species of life, from the microscopic organism to the pearl oyster.

It is my intention to describe as far as possible the habits and lifestyles of some different bird families, those beautiful creatures I became familiar with during my life as a fisherman.

Weather signs of other days, which clash with modern technology, make interesting reading; shellfish, marine plants and animals, are all part and parcel of

> A life on the ocean wave,
> A home on the rolling deep
> Where the scattered waters rave
> And winds their revels keep.
>
> (Epes Sargent)

I am not familiar with the Latin names of my marine species – my Latin happens to be Irish. To all you good people, both ornithologists and scientists, I crave your pardon. If I have become a fly in your ointment, please let me off the hook.

THE SEA IN HIS BLOOD
Skelligs Calling

Together with other boys from the neighbourhood, we sailed little boats, assembled from green *feileastram* fronds, held together by prickly furze thorns. What fun it was to watch our little green ships steer an erratic course across the placid face of the duck-pond at the foot of the meadow, while frolicsome summer zephyrs determined the course of each unpredictable voyage.

I also looked longingly towards the harbour beneath our townland. Often in wondrous awe did I watch the towering blue-green billows between Horse Island Sound and the mainland rise up, up and ever upwards, like a performing circus stallion, until the white frothing lip of the mighty breaker came boiling over, slowly curling downwards with a mighty thunderous boom, filling and spilling a crazy volume of tormented water into the harbour's mouth.

'He had the sea in his blood.' Every so often do I hear a father or mother give utterance to these words speaking of a sailor son who'd answered the call of the sea. It was put beautifully by John Masefield in his poem 'Sea Fever' from *Salt-Water Ballads* (1902):

I must go down to the seas again, for the call of the running tide,
Is a wild call and a clear call that may not be denied.

True words: that mysterious inexplicable force which arouses curiosity and suspense, calling for a journey into the unknown. Such is the powerful attraction the poet so aptly describes.

This could also be attributable to my own people. My brother John joined the navy at the age of sixteen; another two brothers went steamboating to foreign parts, as able seamen. Men who follow the sea are often found to be quaint, having unusual and perhaps odd beliefs. I knew one such gentle seaman who had spent most of his life afloat. He always kept the crown of his head tonsured, then a ring of hair plaited into little pigtails hanging over a lower shaven ring, which he called a double tonsure. He completed the effect with large gold or ivory earrings. This hairdo was in vogue during the pirate period.

To most deep-water sailors the sea is regarded as a fickle mysterious sorceress, a mistress both bountiful and unfaithful, with ever-changing whims and vagaries. Therefore, despite new technology, sailor men still harbour within themselves a certain superstitious respect for the mighty ocean.

Deep-water men are superstitious, believing in signs and omens that seem to fill the vacancy left by the awesome nature of the great ocean. Long voyages are now very rare, as present-day ships have power, speed and all modern comforts. Despite all, the call of the sea remains, a longing to visit strange lands, to be out there alone, far from the madding crowd, with only the dark canopy of the sky studded with myriad fiery constellations.

The terrible feeling of complete aloneness is experienced by the lone voyager. Noises come in the darkness from the heaving hills of a seemingly boundless ocean. On a calm night can be heard the sudden explosive crash of disturbed water dislodged by the ponderous bulk of some huge denizen of the deep, or maybe a once-off, sickening, human-like cough in the vicinity of the boat. Phenomena such as these serve only to add to the mystique of the ocean. Some men have sailed alone across the several oceans having endured privation, both mental and physical. Still, after only a short stay on shore they are already plotting the course of other such voyages.

The sailor's love is the sea; her breaking billows his serenading song of love, her heaving bosom his pillow, the careening deck and dancing prow his pride. He knows his boat as a lover knows his bride. She becomes all things to him, he knows her every whimsical movement in a seaway, be it fair or foul. He will guide her with steady hand among the furious frothing white-maned stallions of the storm that come charging down from the green-bellied mountains, shaking their hoary heads, rearing and snarling without

The Sea in His Blood

rein or rider, derisively spitting white-raged froth at the man-child who has dared to lay claim to their territory

When the going gets tough he has one, or perhaps two, more aces up his sleeve. He will trim his bride down to storm wear, only little kerchiefs on bare poles; turn tail and run. Then the white steeds give chase once more, crashing, chasing and charging, trying in their fury to overwhelm. 'Run like the devil or do not run at all.'

Then comes the time when the last card must be played. The running is all over; to survive he must heave-to. He awaits his chance for a gap between the breaking billows. When he finds it, he must be quick. Helm hard over, he brings her head to wind and casts the sea anchor, paying out the line, fathom after fathom, while the little boat slips astern. The can of oil with its tiny puncture is hung overboard. She hangs well on the canvas cone. The big waves are not crashing aboard any more. The oil is doing its job, drip by drip marvellously calming the lip of each seething breaker.

The sailor brings out a night storm lamp, also a red and green navigational light. He will slip below for a quick warm drink before coming on deck again to look the storm in the eye and share his vigil with his sturdy boat. The wind has shifted a few points, making a witch's cauldron of a jumping cross-sea, causing the sea-anchor rope to whip dangerously. The moon shows momentarily through the broken cloud scud. My God! It scurries like a rat across a screen of torn cloud, appearing again and again at intervals. The cloud layer is not so dense. Later, a sudden burst of moonlight shows on the turbulent, tormented horizon. It is only a game of waiting; the wind comes in fitful gusts. The heavy seas are losing their surface speed. The line to the sea anchor does not whip so much. The little craft hangs easier now. Two hours more of weary vigil. A cold dawn breaks. The sea is much smoother. He has slept in a sitting position, feeling cold and cramped. He hauls and stows the sea anchor, takes the can of oil on board, waits for sunrise to plot his position, shakes out his sails, rigs the tiller, hauls home the sheet, away again, pulling across a favourable breeze, perhaps to a land full of swallow wings.

Why does he do it? Why suffer another trip across this boundless waste? Maybe because he has the sea in his blood!

> From Neptune's cup
> He quaffs
> A draught of dreams
> Of lands beyond the bay,
> Where ocean streams
> Run swift,
> And gambolling dolphins play;
> Where nymph sprites strum
> The sailor's lyre of love,
> Within the shrouds
> He must not stay.
> So heave the halyard,
> And away!
> The sea is in his blood.
>
> [Michael Kirby]

A FISHERMAN LOVES HIS BOAT

Skelligs Calling

If I write about birds, rocks, sea, sharks and seaweed, I feel I must also write about boats. Great ships have foundered and small boats have remained afloat. A fisherman loves his boat; he knows exactly what she is capable of in a rough seaway. Jim, our skipper, was like that. I would often hear him speak in low tones when taking her through a high breaking sea where green water could be seen towering at a level with her lifting bow. He would miraculously avoid the menacing hillock of water that seemed poised to crash aboard. A sudden flick of the helm would 'knock her away' to let the breaking sea pass harmlessly by starboard or port quarter. This 'trick' might be repeated again and again until we entered sheltered waters.

On occasions such as this I often heard him give instructions to the helmsman. If he saw an extra-dangerous sea he would say, 'Watch out for that one!' 'Turn her away quickly, beautiful!' 'Bring her up again!' 'Split the weather in the eye!' He would praise the boat that would climb and pull steadily in a heavy seaway: 'Over it, old girl'. On the other hand, he would call a sluggish boat a 'dirty bitch'. The boat is always feminine. Another type of boat would be referred to as 'a giddy little whore without enough gut', 'gut' meaning width or beam. The jargon of a fisherman can be excessively salty at its best and, at its worst, unsuitable for the cloister or the early Victorian drawing-room.

Boats broad on the transom, and feminine-breasted lobster boats from Brest and Saint Malo, fished for crayfish off the Kerry coast. On board, wooden-clogged Breton sailors drank caskfuls of dark, sour claret wine with every meal.

An old schooner from Brest called *Sea Thrift* came monthly to the South Kerry coast to buy and collect lobsters and crayfish for the French market. I loved to go on board, if only to smell the Stockholm tar and the rich perfume of the ships that pass in the night. We called her captain *Mataí na Leathchoise*. He wore a yellow, wooden peg-leg stump from the knee, complete with the ferrule and leather pad for use on deck. It was fascinating to watch this big middle-aged man stomp all over a slippery, rolling deck, as agile as a cat without ever a slip. He used a more modern artificial limb for special occasions when going ashore. A neighbour of mine, Michael

Skelligs Haul

Curran, 'Old Curran' as we called him, came of old fishing stock and always sold his lobsters to Mataí Peg-Leg. Michael often arrived late only to be berated by Captain Mataí, who would say, 'Why are you always coming aboard when I'm just about to turn in? I will be heaving my anchor at dawn. I'm an ordinary human who needs eight hours' sleep.' Old Curran never made excuses or answered back, only hung his head and remained silent, whereupon the Frenchman would feel a little sorry and proffer him a jigger of cognac when paying him. His parting remark was, 'Do try and come a little earlier next time, Michael.' Curran would sing the praises of Captain *Mataí na Leathchoise* as a gentleman, *duine galánta*.

Michael's punt was only twelve feet long, carvel built having only one seat amidships and one stern seat. It was known as the *Tar Pot*, because of annual applications of boiling tar over the years. Old Curran was an expert swimmer. In his declining years he never ventured far from the harbour reefs owing to his frail craft. He carried his lobster pots, eight at a time, and always had a bucket for bailing. He would say, 'I'm always ready to abandon my ship.' One day his words were put to the test. The *Tar Pot* sprang a leak close to Horse Island. Michael stuffed his jacket into the gaping hole, jettisoning all his lobster gear, and rowing as he never rowed in his life, pausing only momentarily to ply the bucket. He succeeded in staying afloat until finally he beached his stricken vessel on the shingle of Horse Island, where he was well received by the Fitzgerald family, who instantly set to and repaired the damaged plank.

The great craft was once more declared seaworthy and in the words of the poet [William Cowper], 'Her timbers yet are sound, and she shall float again.' Old Curran put to sea once more on the evening tide, bringing to mind Tennyson's beautiful poem:

> Sunset and the evening star,
> And one clear call for me!

A Fisherman Loves His Boat

And may there be no moaning of the bar
When I put out to sea.
...
Twilight and evening bell
And after that the dark!
And may there be no sadness of farewell,
When I embark.

Many British steam trawlers found anchorage in Ballinskelligs Bay. It was a very convenient base for shelter owing to its close proximity to the rich fishing grounds on the Atlantic shelf off south-west Ireland, from Bantry Bay to Galway and south-westward to the Porcupine Bank. The sea in this area teamed with fish which were of great commercial value. Big iron-hulled steamships replaced the wooden boats. They could work in very severe weather. The 'Castle Boats' worked out of Milford Haven and Swansea. Others came from as far apart as Aberdeen and Hull. Large Dutch trawlers, manned by English crews, enjoyed the rich pickings and rape of the Irish coast. Poaching was blatantly indulged in. The British authorities who were responsible for the conservation of Irish fish stocks and the fostering of the fishing industry in Ireland, turned a blind eye on fishing within the imaginary three mile limit, which in terms of legality was only a cruel joke. The fishing vessel used for the protection of the entire Irish coast, was an old tin can version of a gunboat, carrying a two-pounder gun mounted on the forecastle. This ship, called the *Helga*, was seldom at sea, and was used later in defence of the realm, being ordered to sail up the Liffey and quell the disorderly but successful Irish 'rabble' who dared challenge the might of the British Empire. History tells us that the two-pounder was kept busy that morning, not adding greatly to the glory of a mighty empire.

I can remember names of ships like the *Thomas Booth, Isaac Walton, Cleopatra, Dunraven Castle, Tenby Castle,*

Cardigan Castle, Princess Maria Jose, Princess Alexandria, Labore et Honore, and a host of ships too numerous to mention here. Their skippers were tough old sea dogs who had only one motto in mind: keep the net in the water, and get the fish in the hold and, when ice and coal were low, run for the market, replenish the ship's stores and it's back to the fishing grounds once more.

The crews were a mixture of different nationalities, all badly paid for the strenuous work and long hours they endured, but at least provided with good food and bunks, plus three pounds ten shillings per week. The fishing trip was usually for a fourteen-day period. This hard work was better perhaps than loafing around dockland in a crowded port on the Welsh coast. The trawler skippers knew the Irish coast like the back of their hands, every bay and inlet where they would foray illegally for special fish on moonlit nights. They knew all the village taverns on the south coast and kept on courteous terms with the proprietors. They loved to take a trip ashore to ease the constant, wearisome routine of a seaman's life. The ultimate aim was to slake a thirst or perhaps in more modern jargon, to have a good 'piss up'. The skippers would bring a full basket of fish as a gift for the tavern landlord, who would reciprocate in suitable fashion. Sometimes an affinity might develop between a salt-seasoned old codger of the deep and the maid behind the bar, who might perchance entice him to return once more, just to admire – even from a distance – a creature so elusive as the landlord's daughter.

Seamen are known to be good-natured and affable creatures who yearn for female companionship, maybe to break the monotony of the long trip. When stepping ashore they become boyish, boisterous and sometimes naughty towards the opposite sex. When free from the confines of ship life, the safety valve of pent up energy is suddenly released, be it in the bright lights of some American port, or the red light district of Marseilles, Mumbai (Bombay)

A Fisherman Loves His Boat

or Hong Kong, where a man's life can be as cheap as a kiss in a brothel. Yet the aura, power and mystery of the sea belong to the sailor alone. This rollicking machismo is a being from another kingdom, a realm far removed from the term 'landlubber', which he will never understand. This is Eros and Cupid of the wave, vagabond lover and ravisher of virginity. Many and various are the ballads relating to his amorous exploits. The sailor seems to be forever saying farewell to his lover, as in this old ballad:

> Fare you well lovely Mollie, I'm now going to leave you,
> To the western Indies, my course for to steer,
> Though the big ship be sailing, and the wild waves be raging,
> I'll come back, lovely Mollie, in the spring of the year.
>
> I'll dress like a sailor, true love, I'll go with you,
> Through the midst of all danger, I'll go without fear,
> When the big ship is sailing, and the wild waves are raging,
> I'll be with you, lovely Johnny, to reef your topsail.
>
> Your delicate hands, love, stout cables cannot handle,
> And your pretty little feet, love, in the rigging can't go,
> Your delicate body wild waves can't endure, love,
> Be advised, lovely Mollie, to the seas do not go.
>
> The big ship set sail, and left Mollie bewailing,
> Till her cheeks grew pale as the lily that grows.
> Her gay golden locks, she kept constantly tearing
> Saying, I'll sigh till I die, love, will I e'er see you more?

Many beautiful sea shanties were sung by sailors in chorus when turning the windlass, heaving the anchor, raising the great sails or heaving the ropes. For instance, 'The Leaving

Skelligs Haul

of Liverpool' and 'The Holy Ground' were known and sung by sailor men the world over.

> Oh the sun is on the harbour love,
> And I wish I could remain,
> For I know it will be some long time,
> Before I see you again,
>
> So fare thee well, my own true love,
> And when I return, united we will be,
> It's not the leaving of Liverpool that grieves me,
> But, my darling, when I think of thee.

Before embarking for America on the S.S. *Dresden* of the Hamburg American Line in January 1929 [Michael misremembers: he actually left on 22 March 1930 – ed.], I walked along the famous trysting-place called the Holy Ground. This pathway, which is situated beside the sea at the eastern brink of Cobh Harbour, was frequented by sailors and their lovers.

> Fare thee well my lovely Dinah,
> A thousand times adieu!
> For we're going away from the Holy Ground,
> And the girls we all love true.
>
> We will sail the salt seas over
> And we'll return for shore,
> And see again the girls we loved
> And the Holy Ground once more.
>
> Fine girl you are!
> You're the girl I do adore,
> And still I live in hope to see,
> The Holy Ground once more.

The Wreck of The Hercules

The sailing yacht is now the expensive toy of the rich. Modern steamships are oil fuelled or diesel driven, with mod cons for officer and crew alike. Gone are the heady days of the Nelsonian swashbuckling, cutlass wielding, yo, ho, and a bottle of rum. Pirate and smuggler, with the Jolly Roger floating gaily from the cross trees, make past history. Despite all, tradition and custom die hard. The sea is still the sailor man's benign or cruel mistress, and ambition for a night ashore his besetting sin. I saw American navy ships pay a courtesy visit to a port on the New England coast. The crew were billed for shore leave on a certain night. It was fascinating to watch bevies of beautiful American girls await the sailors as they stepped ashore. Females of all colours, shapes and size, were perched on every vantage point. It was truly evident the fleet was in. There seemed to be only one Lily of the Lamplight, my own Lily Marlene, waiting at the barrack gate, in contrast with the many lovely girls who have succumbed totally to the advances of this most amorous of creatures, this playboy Casanova of the deep.

THE WRECK OF *THE HERCULES*
Skelligside

The last day and hour of December at the end of the year 1808, the sky over Ballinskelligs Bay took on a strange and frightening appearance. A great ink-black wall seemed to rise on the horizon, some parts resembling frowning fortress-like castles. There were other signs, like giant pot hooks and fingers that reached high into the heavens. The old people shook their heads and spoke in hushed voices. (This was how I heard the tale as it was handed down from knee to knee.) The wind was coming alive in the south-east, with white horses kicking their heels skyward and tossing their silver-crested manes as they careered across the bay towards the towering cliffs of Bolus. All the signs foretold a formidable hurricane. The lion was already baring its incisors, snarling and spitting pieces of iron snow into the wind, as the proud frigate *Hercules* sailed into Ballinskelligs Bay, unaware of her fate. A three-masted ship, well found and equipped with cannon on both port and starboard, *The Hercules* was a privateer licensed by the British Crown to prey on ships of the Spanish Main in the western approaches to the British Isles. Spanish ships blown off course on their way home from the West Indies were attacked and plundered by these legalized pirates, who relieved them of their rich cargoes and then destroyed them. Three sailing boats from Brittany sheltered in Ballinskelligs Bay on the same evening. These were poor French fishermen, who netted for mackerel on the south coast of Ireland. When they saw the ugly apparition enter the bay displaying the skull and cross-bones they immediately put to sea under shortened sail, rather than share harbour with the dark pirate. *The Hercules* sailed across the bay into *Lúb an Rinnín*, the Loop of Rinneen, casting two anchors near *Pointe na mBiorraí*, where she lay steady under the shelter of the hills for the night. But things do not always happen as man supposes; God had not yet given consent.

The night fell under the light of a full moon, which seemed to scurry across the sky, as if playing hide-and-seek between the rushing clouds. The wind now steadily increased to a full gale, and as the tide turned to flow inward from the Atlantic it attained hurricane force. From that moment on, the pirate *Hercules* was forced astern inch by inch, her anchors losing hold as she was driven across the bay. The inches became feet and the feet became fathoms. The

The Wreck of The Hercules

dark pennant depicting the skull and cross-bones, the 'Jolly Roger', now began to symbolize *The Hercules'* impending doom.

After two tortured hours, she had found holding ground once more, south-east of Hector's Point, where her heavy anchors gripped again the rough rock-strewn bottom. *The Hercules* lay there until dawn broke at low water, unable to escape. The wind suddenly changed to a less favourable point, forcing her towards *Cuas an Mhadra Uisce*, the Water Dog's Cave. The mighty backwash from the breakers hurled itself against the low cliffs, creating a mountainous mass of disturbed water. Within this churning vortex lay the helpless ship, pounded unmercifully as each towering breaker with curling frothy lip bore down on her. Her once swashbuckling crew could be seen clinging to the rigging in terror. A raging laugh from the billows seemed to scream louder than the storm, saying, 'Ho! Ho! Mighty *Hercules*, why has your strength forsaken you?' The drama was not yet over. A large crowd on the shore watched a desperate attempt to leave the stricken vessel, as seven seamen lowered a boat that was dashed to matchwood on the cliff and its occupants drowned. Later that morning the fury of the storm abated, and *The Hercules* lay on her beam-ends, across the Water Dog's Cave.

An old pirate seized a heavy axe and chopped the main mast at deck level. Fortunately, it fell onto the low cliff with its yard-arms and shrouds, creating a temporary bridge which gave the crew enough time to scramble ashore. Some time later the remains of three drowned pirates were found, and buried near the cliff face. The graves were still visible in my youth, but the sea has since claimed them back again, to rest forever within its tumultuous bosom. I do not know why they were not buried in consecrated ground. One of the pirates made a gift of his waistcoat to a local labouring man who had saved his life when he fell onto a rock as he tried to scramble ashore. It is said that the waistcoat had gold coins hidden in its fabric. The local man went missing at once, and it transpired later that he had reached America, where his progeny thrived. It surely is an ill wind that blows no good for somebody.

Some years later, the rocks at the Water Dog's Cave were exposed at low water during one of the spring tides. It happened that Mary Hoare, Francis Sigerson's maidservant, a woman both muscular and strong, usually fetched a large wooden pail of spring water from the well nearby. On this particular morning, she noticed some glittering objects strewn among the rocks, and going down the rugged cliff face, she collected many pieces of gold and silver. She filled her apron and the wooden bucket, proceeded homeward and emptied her valuable cargo on to the kitchen's flagged floor. The master of the house, who was upstairs, heard the clang of metal against the floor, and came rushing down saying, 'Good girl, Mary! You have found riches. It makes a musical, pure sound!'

Several other pieces were found during other great tides which followed. Francis Sigerson and Maurice 'Hunting Cap' O'Connell, uncle of the Liberator, put the hoard up for public auction. The proceeds of the sale were used to buy food for the Famine survivors in the immediate area. Perhaps some of the loot still lies buried beneath the sand near the mouth of the cave, which was known from then on as *Cuas an Airgid*, the Cave of the Silver. Let it disintegrate beneath the mud of timelessness, because as the old saying goes, wealth is not wed to happiness, nor is all gold that glitters.

This is the story of the pirate *Hercules*, registered out of London, as I heard it by my father's fireside. I neither add nor subtract.

THE NIGHT HAUL AT BOLUS
Skelligs Sunset

Seán and myself were busy preparing our lobster pots for the night haul, a slow business requiring time and patience. Some pots needed repair after being savaged by some huge conger eels, who, finding themselves trapped, had bulldozed their way to freedom, leaving behind torn ends and wrecked lathing. And of course it was most important that all torn and missing baits were replaced. Lobster pots fall prey to many predators on the scrounge for the bait that was only intended to attract lobster and crayfish. Yet man has failed to devise an effective plan to deal with these freeloading, uninvited guests.

When the gear was ready, we set the pots carefully in selected places, sometimes near a sunken reef or the dark, deep side of a sheltered cave. Then we cast our mooring stone in the shelter of *Faill an Reithe*, the Cliff of the Ram. We carried a large iron pot three-quarters filled with gravel, on which we built our fire of peat. I got ready nice cross-chunks of fat red bream, first removing the heavy silvery scale. This I cooked in a gallon can made of gleaming white tin that had formerly held boiled sweets called bullseyes. The cans were readily available when empty at any grocery store and were very good value for sixpence. We kept two tins, one for boiling fresh water and the other for cooking meat or fish. The water container was an oval oak keg, which wouldn't roll with the movement of the boat as a barrel would. Seán brewed some excellent tea, half a gallon in all. We ate several slices of buttered, homemade griddle bread. The butter was also home-churned with little droplets of fresh buttermilk still trapped in its body. With the boiled portions of bream, salted and peppered, washed down with Seán's delicious tea, it was feast enough to set before a king.

The evening sun settled gently behind the heathery hill of Bolus, its last rays like little rivers of gold cascading over the steep steps of the darkening cliff face, growing thinner and thinner by the second, until only faint golden threads remained before vanishing entirely. We sat there in the peaceful solitude of the eve, waiting until the first hour of darkness would elapse before hauling our pots. The only sound emerging from the muted silence was the soft murmuring ripple of water flowing gently among rock crannies within the caves. We carried a paraffin lamp with globe and wick called a hurricane lantern. This provided enough dim light to enable us to see what the pots contained when we hauled.

I sat near the bow sheeting where we stowed fishing gear of a light kind. Seán, who could not contain himself sitting idly, asked me to hand him a fishing line, which we kept coiled on square wooden frames. He could not resist the adventure of testing the unknown with a fishing line and would say: 'One never knows what's down there! You'll catch something, if it's only trouble.' He used soft crabmeat bait, which he wrapped carefully around the bright steel hook with some soft cotton yarn that he kept for that purpose. Before casting the line I saw Seán gazing upwards towards the cliff top, his countenance wearing a tense, fixed expression. He exclaimed in Gaelic: *'Dalladh is caochadh ortsa go háirithe. An bhfeiceann tú an striapach ag féachaint anuas orainn?'* ('Blinded and sightless be you without a doubt. Can you see the red whore looking down on us?') Looking upwards, I observed a large, red fox sitting on its haunches on a little knoll overlooking the cave. The fox was taboo where fishing was concerned; totally disapproved of and unmentionable. Seán felt very strongly in favour of the

The Night Haul at Bolus

old superstition that a fox, a red-haired woman and fishing were a bad mix. 'Never mind,' I assured him, 'give the bait a try, at any rate!' Seán reluctantly played the line overboard until it reached the bottom. While waiting patiently for a nibble, some time passed ere Seán said: 'I feel some miserable creature down there tearing at my bait.' Suddenly he started to haul what seemed to be a very small fish, which proved to be a species of mini-wrasse, called in Gaelic *moirín*, meaning the mother of the gunner wrasse. A more abject specimen of fish is hard to imagine. It wouldn't provide a dinner for a mouse. Seán flung it back in disgust, saying: 'It will soon be time to haul our lobster pots.' Clewing up the line on its frame, he wished affliction on the baleful villain fox, which he blamed for such a poor evening's fishing.

Night having fallen, we pulled on our yellow oilskins, which protected us from the water that came aboard with the rope. We lit the lantern, which showed only its dim light. The haul was good for fifty pots. We got twenty-five lobsters of good size. At least we had thirty shillings' worth, at fifteen shillings a dozen, if the price did not slump. We were happy, but we would never be rich. The savage black conger were few and any that we caught on a wrecking rampage we lulled to sleep with the charms of the goddess Nemesis. Having replaced missing bait and reset the pots, we rowed back to the pier and stored the fish in a floating crate. We would meet again for the morning haul after a good night's rest.

The grey Atlantic seal is a very intelligent animal. Where and when a fisherman may set a net, the seal will surely find it, if it is anywhere within its territory. It has a very keen sense of hearing and of observation and is perceptive of the fisherman's movements. It can propel itself rocket-like through the water at an astonishing speed, following the fisherman far out to sea and gorging itself with the fish from his nets. Miles from land in the darkness of night, it will cram itself until it can eat no more, and always at the fisherman's expense. I have watched the herd bask on flat rocks under the midday sun. Some of the great bulls attain a ponderous weight, presenting a very unwieldy appearance on land that is so different from the acrobatic agility they display in water. We are told that the seal possesses a large brain, hence its intelligence, and it is easily trained from infancy. The seal is also very curious, becoming fascinated with music, especially that of the button accordion.

Seán believed the folklore story that seals were part of the human world at one time. One day Seán and myself were waiting at Little Skellig for our skipper, John Fitzgerald, to bring us food supplies from the mainland. We were in the rowing boat, anchored in a cave at the south side of the rock. Seán responded to a common but rather urgent call of nature. Unzipping his trousers, he eased his tail clear of the stern transom, enjoying with relief and satisfaction the smooth flow of events, when suddenly out of the blue ocean came a great, splattering splash, sprinkling and dousing Seán's back porch with water, accompanied by a loud exploding 'poofh!' of exhaling air. Seán jumped in terror into the stern sheeting, struggling with his trousers, which had fallen about his ankles. Looking behind him, he saw that a large grey seal was staring at us, his head and shoulders exposed within a half a metre of the transom. Giving another loud 'poofh!' he dived beneath the surface, and Seán exclaimed in Gaelic: *'Gurab é do tharrach deirneach é, a bhastaird!'* ('That it may be your last breath, you bastard!') Later on we both laughed heartily at what seemed like a human prank.

Seán has now passed on. He was a good neighbour, with a knowledge of Gaelic from his cradle days, and a great conversationalist with a broad sense of humour who loved the art of storytelling. Not one word of English did he ever use while in conversation with me, but the purest of Gaelic.

If there is one tribute I can pay to my comrade fisherman and complete Gael, it will be in the words of Shakespeare: 'Good night, sweet prince: / And flights of angels sing thee to thy rest.'

THE RICHES OF THE SEA
Skelligside

When I had grown a little older and my bones were stretching, the Great War broke out. What a change it brought into being! The old adage says that Death is seen on the face of the old man and on the back of the youth. Destruction and shipwreck were visited on the south coast during that time. Sudden death lurked beneath those once peaceful waters, now a hiding-place for powerful submarines of the warring nations. Many a proud merchant ship was sent without warning to the bottom of the sea, the crew unable to take to the boats before the deafening roar of the exploding torpedo. Within minutes, nothing was left but little pieces of torn wood and the corpse of a sailor being borne away on the ocean stream.

All kinds of wreckage came ashore on Ballinskelligs beaches then, including empty lifeboats and dead bodies from the *Lusitania*. A substantial reward was offered to the person who discovered the body of Mr Vanderbilt, the American banker and millionaire who perished in the sinking of that great ship. Police and coast-watchers scoured the beaches of Cork, Kerry and Clare in search of his remains. It was rumoured that these were found on the Clare coast in an advanced stage of decomposition

On New Year's Eve 1916 four hundred wooden casks of white paraffin came ashore at the little beach in the creek

Skelligs Haul

of Boolakeel. The entire population of the little hamlet converged on the beach and rolled the casks to a place of safety above the breakers. Some took barrels home, but to no avail. Members of the Royal Irish Constabulary came and searched every house, every field and dyke, even the manure heaps. My neighbour had a few gallons stored in a tub in the cowhouse, where they were found by the sergeant. He took the tub to the doorway and spilled its contents into the drain. I do not wonder why the people rebelled against British rule in Ireland.

Fish was plentiful during those years. My father bought a small rowing boat, specially ordered to his own dimensions, for line and lobster fishing. The first I took on board myself was a pollack about eight pounds in weight, but I imagined it was as big as a horse. My father praised me on how well I handled it. I was eight years old then. By the age of ten, with constant practice, I had mastered the art of rowing with short paddles. We filled large casks with white fish, mostly pollack and cod, cured in brine and dried, and my father sold it for three pence per pound. Many a day we would row westward under the great cliffs of Bolus to the most likely places, which my father would pinpoint by getting certain landmarks on shore into line. When he reached the desired position he would order me to cast the mooring-stone and make fast. As soon as we had our hooks baited with glistening cubes of fresh mackerel or mussel and set for bottom fishing, we were kept busy hauling until the little boat was heavy with a varied catch of codling, red sea bream, large whiting, grey and red gurnard, ling and ray. Those were halcyon days of my youth, which time will never erode from the living cells of my memory.

One day while we were westward in the bay, my father took what seemed to be a heavy fish on his line. After a long struggle, he caught sight of the great creature for a fleeting moment. He knew immediately it was a large halibut. No sooner had the fish surfaced than it plunged again to the depths of the sea, taking all of thirty-five fathoms of line singing over the gunwale in its wake. My father paid out line when necessary, and also took up the slack. At one time, the fish leaped clear out of the water and fell over on its back, sending a shower of white spray heavenward. But it failed to dislodge the small whiting hook stuck firmly in its jaw muscle. This exciting struggle continued for some time, with the fish slicing the water like a broad spear. It was lovely to watch the seasoned old fisherman deftly handling the pressure on the line. Only one golden rule had to be followed: not to let the fish break you when your gear was too light for the burden. After some time my father spoke urgently to me: 'Get the gaff and look out for him!' I knew then that the great tussle was nearly over. The noble heart of the fish had weakened, and its pulse was a mere fluttering. My father eased it gently toward the side of the boat into my reach, and I sank the barb of the gaff deeply in its side. I helped my father take the fish on board. 'Ó, a Mhuire!' exclaimed my father, 'Oh, Virgin, what a beautiful fish!' It was a little short of ninety pounds, and it took only a small whiting hook and a cube of fresh mackerel to do the job.

I often listened to the old people tell of the Great Famine and how many of Ireland's poor fled to the coast for survival. A million people are thought to have died in Munster during the Famine period. Thousands came to the rocky beaches and sandy inlets searching for shellfish – limpets, winkles, mussels, cockles, crabs, sand eels and rockling. Edible seaweed – sea dulse, *miabhán*, carrageen, green *sleaidí* – was boiled and eaten. Ballan wrasse and gunnar wrasse were very plentiful. People were seen to fish from every vantage point, even on the rocks of the most dangerous headlands. All that was needed were some small hooks, a piece of line made from home-grown flax, some lugworms for bait and a stone for a sinker. This crude

Skelligs Haul

fishing tackle could mean the difference between survival and death. Large hake were plentiful in the inshore waters of the south and west coast. The trawl had not yet been invented and the large foreign steam trawlers did not arrive for many a year to come. Local fishermen also brought gannets from the Great Skellig, which they salted and used as food. I heard of how the English agent who collected the land rent saw many large fish in my grandfather's house. He warned that the rent would be increased if the landlord became aware of how well off we were.

Because of fishing, the death rate from hunger was not so high on the coast. One old woman, called the Fishing Hag, was well known in the area during the Famine. Many tales were told about her powers of attracting fish wherever she cast a hook. She always kept a supply of salted fish strapped to her back to prevent it being stolen, as hordes of people roamed the roads of Munster in quest of food. This poor old woman did not have a name and never told anyone who she was. The Fishing Hag died in the house where I was born. The neighbours and my people made her coffin, and as night was falling it was brought across the fields and buried in the old graveyard by the sea that was once Saint Michael's Abbey. It was by the light of bog deal torches that the last sod was laid on her grave.

There was a place near the old graveyard which was called *Bearna na gCorp* or the Gap of the Corpses. So many people died each day during the Famine that it was impossible to bury them all, and some were left near the opening in the wall until the next day.

* * *

'Today is *Rabharta Rua na hInide*, the Red Tide of Lent,' said my father. '*Carraig an Eascú* will be exposed, so bring the long holly rod from the rafters of the cow byre.'

'But, Dad,' I said, 'the holly rod has neither line nor sinker this many a long day.'

'That makes no difference, son. On certain days, you can get fish with a rod without a line or sinker.'

I did as I was bidden. I took the seasoned holly rod from the rafters and brought it along. It was all of eight feet in length and tapered to a point. 'I'll bring the gaff, a sack, and my knife too,' said Dad. 'There's an old saying: a fisherman without a knife, a greyhound without a tail, a ship without a rudder. Come! Let's go. You never know where lurks a lobster.'

My young heart fluttered with wings of joy as I went to search the exposed harbour reefs with a master fisherman. Standing on the shingle beach which overlooked the strand, we could see that the *Rinn Dubh*, the Black Reef, was entirely exposed, the Lough of the Dulse without a drop of ocean.

The sweet edible sea dulce lay in great fallen swathes like a field of ripe corn after heavy rain, losing some of its iodine content in the bleaching of the noonday sun. Because I was barefoot, Dad told me to be careful when wading in the pools lest I tread on a sea urchin. It was my first time seeing the marine anemones with their beautiful coloured fringes. I thought it odd to see things like cows' teats growing on rounded boulders beneath the sea. I questioned Dad about what form of life they were, so very strange did they appear to me. 'Nothing new, my boy! Nothing new,' he replied. 'Scientists call them *metridium dianthus*. Take to the books, boy, take to the books.' Ah! but Dad was droll.

The colours of the different anemones fascinated me. Some were ruby, some were pink and blood-red, others a mixture of green and greyish blue, their delicate feathery fringes forever opening and closing, capturing the plankton they relied on for their existence. Dad explained that many microscopic forms of life exist on both land and sea whose time has not yet arrived to be of benefit to mankind. Years later, I read some more about lesser forms of life, but I have come to the conclusion that my greatest problem is trying to understand myself.

My father showed me a narrow gravel bed between the rocks, where the cockles are found. Burrowing beneath the loose gravel, he found smooth and tiger-tooth cockles, and very soon I was able to find them on my own. We put a quantity of the choicest ones in the bag. 'It is not so much in quest of cockles that we're here,' said my father, 'so give me the holly rod, and we'll search for lobster. Perhaps it's yet early, after winter, but an old "Jack" may be hibernating.'

My father started to search, thoroughly and methodically, all the flat slabs of rock in the pools. He poked the slender end of the rod underneath, and explained to me what signs to look for. 'The lobster is a hermit by nature,' said he, 'and will stay under a flat rock or boulder for long periods. He has usually two doors to his dwelling, an entrance and an exit. If the rock is on sand or gravel bottom, the front door will be like a rabbit burrow.'

I noticed a rock in the middle of a pool, which had about twelve inches of water around it, and because I did not have boots, Dad gave me the rod, telling me to poke underneath in the place which he indicated. When I inserted that rod I felt as if something caught hold of its tip. 'He's in there,' said Dad, 'Deal roughly with him: push the rod quickly!' No sooner said than done: the lobster came rushing out tail first, making a clapping noise through the shallow water. I was about to grasp it, but it reached both its claws upwards menacingly. 'I'll show you how to lift a lobster,' said the master. 'Slip your open hand under his armpits from the back, and grasp it firmly; a lobster can inflict serious wounds, especially with the scissors claw.'

The Riches of the Sea

My father reached into the water and lifted out a nice two-pound lobster. He then sat on a rock, placed the lobster between his knees, and deftly cut the nerves of both claws with his knife, before putting him into a bag which we had for lobsters only. We found two more at the western corner of *Rinn Dubh* before arriving at the reef underneath the old monastery. The large boulder called *Carraig an Eascú* lay naked. As we approached it my father said, 'This rock was never without a tenant underneath,' and how right he was! He inserted the steel gaff, and hooked a large black conger eel, which he released onto the strand nearby. I watched it squirm and writhe its way snake-like towards the water after receiving only a minor wound from the gaff.

The Eel Rock yielded only two large, red edible crabs, which my father put on a string. John Shea's house stood near the beach, so Dad asked him for the loan of his spade to dig for green-shelled razor clams, which were to be had in abundance. He dug many hundreds of them, some as thick as thole-pins. When mixed with great oval clams, these make a mouth-watering chowder. The rock pools teemed with marine life: red rock ling, speckled blennies and many shrimps could be seen sheltering under the fronds of the sea kelp; rowing crabs, velvet-backs, and green soft crabs swam about in all directions. There were purple sea urchins, whose internal segments are nice to eat. I saw several blue and yellow flat-headed dragonettes in the pools. I have found them in very deep water also. The fish is not edible and their spines can be very poisonous. The sea-mouse and the little scorpion crabs were to be found beneath the sand, when we dug for the clams. [...] Sea cucumbers are found within the ponds and in the dense kelp as well, some brownish-black, soft and boneless, with many hundred sucking discs. Being blind, they have a compensatory sensory intelligence, and exude a white thread-like membrane as a defence. The great spider crab, with its long crooked claws and pear-shaped body, I was introduced to for the first time at the edge of low water, although I became more familiar with its freeloading habits inside my lobster pots in later life.

Queen escallops are found within the harbour on a calm day when shadow is on the water. We used to take them out with a hoop and net mounted on a long pole, and sometimes with a pitchfork. Their flesh is delicious, the orange part having a very savoury taste. Horse whelks were in plentiful supply, but only the black winkle had a commercial value. Yellow winkles, pearl winkles, striped cone winkles and miniature ear-shells shared pools with hermit crabs, showing one great claw and antenna from within an old whelk shell – a curiosity in the vast order of marine life.

The tide had now turned. As we turned our faces homewards, I heard Dad murmur to himself, 'The lower the ebb, the sooner the harbour will fill.' I was fortunate in my tutor, who knew his environment so well, though he was hardly aware of the precious gift he was handing down to his son.

* * *

Lobsters and crayfish were very plentiful, and wherever along the rocky coast you set a pot with good fresh bait you would not look forward in vain to a black haul. The big ones could be found in the deep dark caves which were fished but seldom.

It would depend on the weather being fair and calm to go by rowboat beyond Bolus Head and westward to the cliff of *Dúchealla*. After two or three days' fishing in that area you would return home not empty or poor, but with several dozen lobsters for sale. They were cheap then – five shillings a dozen and often much less. I loved to go west with my father and Michael Curran hauling the pots on moonlit nights. Nothing was more beautiful than to look westward to where the sea and sky met. The planets were like fiery jewels climbing the peaks of heaven, while *Dubh Inis* and Scariff lay sleeping on the margin of Ballinskelligs Bay. The hills of Iveragh and the great Reeks of Kerry stood in the eastern sky, like giant sentinels guarding the harbours. Over it all the full moon shone, leaving a silver pathway on the waves, as if bright ghosts were dancing on a crystal mirror. You could hear the yawning of seals in their breeding caves. Long wailing cries came to a climax, then slowly died to a last bitter sob. It was like the cry of some lost soul echoing from the dungeon of the damned. On the other hand, it was music to our ears to hear the loud clattering of a lobster when a pot broke the surface, or the rasping of crayfish when they moved their antennae.

Red crab and large marauders of conger eel all went into the pots in pursuit of the free meals put up by the fisherman, and intended for lobsters only. Many different kinds of crab were to be found: the red and green, the rowing crab, the velvet-back, the large spider crabs and the hermit crabs. The fisherman had to deal with all the uninvited guests, replacing all eaten and torn bait before resetting the traps. Unwelcome visitors included the blind sea-leech, the pipefish, the speckled hagfish, the grey nurse, the horned bullhead, the yellow blenny, the pink and purple sea urchin, and the octopus.

Red bream was found in every bay and estuary on the Kerry coast, a delicious fish to eat, with its sweet savoury taste. We had large wooden casks full of pickled bream, which had a ready local market. Far from hunger was the kitchen that could serve potatoes, milk, butter and fresh bream. Whiting and gurnard were also abundant. The red gurnard was called the piper because he has a double air sac resembling bagpipes, while the grey gurnard has only a single one. The old people had great faith in the healing power of gurnard broth, which was good for swollen tonsils

Skelligs Haul

and digestive ailments. The broth was very rich, full of a peculiar fat, sweet and invigorating to drink. In my early adolescence I was anxious to find out how I happened into this world. It was unthinkable that I should be told the dire secret that I had come from my mother's womb, so I was fobbed off with the story that my father had found me in the belly of a gurnard. Much as I had liked gurnard broth, I developed a revulsion to it from that time on.

Seine boats were numerous on the south-west coast during my teenage years. Two open boats were used to operate the seine purse net. Each boat was thirty to thirty-five feet long with only a seven-foot beam, and was propelled by six seventeen-foot oars. The seine boat carried the large net and two men operated each oar. The second boat, called the follower, had six single-man oars. This boat took the towline from the end of the net when it first entered the water, while the other sped swiftly away, casting the net overboard as it encircled the fish school and joined up with the follower. The two boats took eighteen crew members, two skippers and an experienced fisherman who stood upright in the bow. He was the lookout, and director of the haul. His orders were given in a loud clear voice and always in Irish.

Great mackerel and herring schools were to be found in the harvest season, when the phosphorescent light was at its peak during August. The movement of schools of fish in the water looked like light on a dark screen, which was at once detected and appraised by the experienced eye of the lookout navigator. It was he who could tell whether the school was dense or near to the surface, whether it was mackerel or herring or other fish, and what direction and speed it was travelling. The crew would keep the oars out of the water and remain completely silent as he watched his prey from the bow. Some seine boats made good harvest, bringing in large catches of fish night after night. The old castle seine was called Kirbys' seine. My father was well versed in the mounting and sewing together of the great purse net, which in order to operate successfully had to be correct in all dimensions. He was sent to Donegal for a term to instruct the fishermen of that area in its use. This instruction was sponsored by the old British Congested Districts Board.

My father, John Kirby, took the greatest school of fish ever recorded in Ballinskelligs Bay one night in August 1908 west of Bolus Head at a place called *Lúb na Leacach* or the Loop of the Flagstones. The night was calm, and near the cliff face he saw a small circle of phosphorescence which turned out to be fair and deep. He studied the school for a while and told his crew he intended setting the net between the school and the cliff, as close as possible. When he gave orders for the cliff-face oars to be lifted he wanted no panic, as by then the boat would be at full speed. Now was the time of truth – every man at his sharpest. These are some of the orders you might have heard on that night: 'Straighten the boat for me!' 'Cast net on it!' 'Take her forward!' 'All oars together!' 'Give me speed!' 'Easy! The net-side oars!' 'Keep away a little!' 'Back water the second oar!' 'Pull hard on the bow oar!' 'Easy! Steady!' 'Keep coming!' 'Close the circle. Easy!' 'Take her forward together!' 'Give her speed!' 'More speed!' 'Back water!' 'Lift the oars!' 'Take the holding rope!' 'Pull us up against the current!'

Those last instructions were given to the follower boat, whose job it was to keep the seine boat from drifting into the circle of net while the haul was in progress. This involved hauling the heavy running-rope which ran through a set of metal eye-rings mounted to the bottom of the net. When this was done there was no escape and the purse was considered closed. The work was always carried out through the medium of Irish. It was unheard of for a member of the crew to use English – laughable, like hearing a fart breaking the silence of solemnity. The night that I refer to, the net was set carefully and the great school was trapped. God's blessing seemed to shine on the fishermen of Ballinskelligs. Some of the crew were sent ashore and scaled the cliff face to the roadway above. Their mission was to reach Ballinskelligs, three miles away, to alert the neighbours and bring back as many empty boats as possible. They brought ashore seventy-five thousand prime mackerel that morning, and because of a shortage of empty boats had to release several thousand more. Five seine boats operated from Ballinskelligs harbour, employing more than one hundred fishermen, in those days long gone.

* * *

To hear my father say we'd go trammel fishing always filled me with joyful expectation – the joy of a young boy included in men's work. Fishing had a certain call for me. Michael P. Sugrue of Ballinskelligs West was my father's fishing companion for as long as I can remember. They were both masters of hook, line and sinker, having developed a traditional skill through the practical experience of years. Our fishing boat was carvel-built, twenty-one feet long, and we used it for sea angling, net fishing and lobster pots. We prepared the fishing gear the evening before, carefully boarding the nets into the boat in such a way as to avoid any snagging or entanglement of the meshes when the nets were set into the sea. Trammel nets were mounted to a specially weighted foot-rope, and the top rope was fitted with floats which kept the net standing upright on the bottom of the sea. The nets would be carefully mounted according to a certain formula that served to keep each mesh open in the water (the net could become 'blind' if not properly mounted) and set twenty or more fathoms deep.

It was now nearing the end of August, and time to lay by some casks of cured fish for the winter. The early morning dawned bright and clear. Mike Sugrue, never known to be late, arrived just as the sun was peeping over the Kerry Reeks. My mother waved us goodbye from the door of our cottage and wished us luck with her usual blessing. We quickly walked the few hundred yards to the beach. Mike Sugrue brought the oars which were stored in the castle ruins. I found the bailing bucket and thole-pins which were kept in a hideaway known only to the boatmen. My father had numerous fishing lines coiled on frames ready for use, and several types of fresh bait prepared the day before – fresh mackerel, mussels, lug sandworms and red crab, whose meat is an excellent bait for bottom fishing. Mike Sugrue found a suitable stone to which he attached the long mooring rope for anchoring the little boat in rough or weedy ground. He also attached the heel stones to each net. All ready at last, we pushed the boat into the water, from the pebbly beach in front of the MacCarthy Castle. In no time we had our oars in the water and were leaving Carraig on our stern on our way to the Bay Rock, a sunken reef which lies a mile and a half directly east of Horse Island point. There we set the nets carefully.

I was given the task of keeping the boat moving slowly ahead with the short oars. When the nets were set and the buoy lines cast overboard, my father decided we would go westward to a part of the bay known to be a rich ground for bottom fishing. Our boat sped away from each thrust of the oar blades as if eager for angling. We passed by the *Bealach*, known in English as Horse Island Sound, and the Cave of Elinore, by *Cuas na Móna*, the Cave of the Turf. We passed by Boolakeel creek and the Gownach Rock, under the cliffs of Kilreelig, whose whitewashed thatched cottages stood out under the heather-clad hill in the morning sun, the small green paddocks with their dry stone enclosures beautiful to behold. We sped by *Carraig an Scéalaí*, the Storyteller's Rock. The Cormorants' Cave came into view,

Skelligs Haul

and we reached a point where the landmarks my father had in mind came into line. One was the Great Skellig, showing itself just clear of Bolus Head, the other the old fortified observation point on the headland on the shoulder of Canuig Mountain.

My father ordered the boat to be brought to a halt. We stopped rowing, and when the boat had lost all momentum, he dropped the mooring-stone overboard with thirty-five fathoms of slack rope. The little craft immediately settled head to wind, which was only a faint breeze from the southwest. The oars were stowed and we all got busy getting the hand-lines ready. My father operated two of these, with different baits, each line having two hooks. Michael Sugrue had already paid out his hand-line baited with mackerel. I was the last to pay out. Being over-anxious to be first, I tangled my line, and my father helped me to unravel it, smiling as he remarked that a peaceful mind helps to undo the tangled skein. Finally, I got my line to the bottom. Mike Sugrue said, 'Let's see who will catch the first fish,' and immediately started to haul in two whiting. My father said in Irish, 'Good man! You've broken the spell of the sea witch.' Soon afterwards, I felt several faint tugs on my line. I started to haul, and to my surprise brought on board two grey gurnard. When I took them off the hooks they escaped on to the bottom of the boat where they made little croaking noises like frogs in a pond. My father said that the fish were trying to sing but suffered from sore throats because of the wet. Mike Sugrue got busy once more taking on board a very nice codling.

My father was becoming anxious because he was not getting any fish on his lines, and examined his baits carefully. He smelled them in case he had contaminated them with the scent of tobacco from his fingers. Fish are sensitive to smell, and even great sharks are known to swim away from polluted water. Having satisfied himself that all was well, he sent his lines humming over the gunwale once more and soon hauled in several whiting and some white Atlantic pollack. For my part, the fish seemed to have deserted me completely. I was the fool sitting at one end, with a piece of mackerel dangling from the other. Michael Sugrue's customers were also slow to buy his line, and he was getting worried because there were no red sea bream to be had. He suggested we move to *Ceann an Aonaigh*, the Headland of the Fair, nearer to the rough ground, where we might find a school of sea bream. My father consented and proceeded to haul the anchor. We put out the oars once more, going farther to sea for about a half-mile, and cast anchor for the second time in much deeper water, my father remarking, 'If it's not for the better, let's hope it's not going to be for the worse.' Again we sent our lines to the bottom and to our delight, great red sea bream began to come in pairs over the side.

The fisherman must be careful to lift sea bream carefully out of the water and clear of the side of the boat. The lips of a sea bream are brittle and easily torn if the line is worked too vigorously as the fish pulls in the opposite direction. We were kept busy with the many bream and a mixed bag of other species. The unwelcome spiked dogfish would be dealt with in a brutal manner because of his dangerous fighting attitude, and kept within the boat while fishing was in progress. Another unwelcome guest was the speckled dogfish, infamous for its snake-like wriggling and its attempts to sandpaper the skin off your wrists when being taken from the hook. A small baton of hardwood was kept to render dogfish or small sharks unconscious: a few well-aimed blows of this baton across the navel of the fish was all that was needed. The baton was called the 'priest', and salmon fishermen also kept it to hand to administer the last rites, as salmon were known to leap into the sea after being brought on board. Some fishermen called it the 'clergyman' or the 'reverend parson'.

Michael Sugrue took the prize fish of the day, a small turbot of about eleven pounds. Using a small hook and light gear, Michael played the fish with unusual dexterity, while my father watched, gaff in hand, ready to bring it on board. My father would murmur, 'Easy, easy, Michael! Give him a bit of his own way; don't let him break you.' I enjoyed myself thoroughly and did not feel the time slipping by.

The last fish I brought on board was the middle species of red gurnard called the 'tub', whose flesh is not as tasty as that of the grey or red piper. I noticed my father furtively glancing towards the far horizon. Michael Sugrue exclaimed, 'What's troubling you, John?'

'Do you see that black wall appearing on the skyline? It seems to be approaching rapidly; maybe it is some kind of a sudden storm. However, we'll continue fishing while the going is good, and in the meantime we'll be ready in case we have to run for it,' my father answered.

He decided we would move closer to the land in case a sudden wind came up. We hove anchor once more and moved to within a quarter-mile of the shore. Three moves, they say, are as bad as a fire. This time my father got a huge conger eel on his line. He succeeded in bringing it up, but it was pull devil, pull baker, all the way from the bottom, until the fish finally broke the weaker snood on arriving at the surface. Watching the fish disappear, my father exclaimed, 'I hope you never come back – you are not a great loss to us.' The day was changing and the weather deteriorating rapidly. Large droplets fell plop into the sea once in a while. Small white clouds like balls of cotton wool came scurrying low from the direction of the Bull Rock, and we heard a rumble on the horizon ending in an ominous growl. It was the first bark of the coming storm.

We hauled anchor immediately, and put all our fish into a rod basket near the bow sheeting. The basket was overflowing with bream, whiting and codling. I bailed the boat free of surplus water and we clewed up our lines on their frames and made everything shipshape before pulling on our yellow home-made oilskin trousers. We put our cloth jackets into a sack in a dry place under the bow breasthook, laid our oilskin jackets near at hand in case we might need them, got the oars into the water and swung the boat before the south-west breeze, into a running position.

The storm was fascinating to watch, with the cloud layer becoming lower and more disturbed by the minute. I heard my father mutter, 'The wind will increase. We must hurry.' Shafts of lightning, like rivers of red liquid, stabbed the sea in front of the nearing storm. We kept up a steady long light stroke – easy work so far, running before the weather, but we had yet two miles and a half to cover, with the explosion of thunder and continuous rumbling as if from some fiery volcano in Hades. We were now approaching the *Scéalaí* Rock. The sky suddenly took fire above our heads, as a great bolt of light grounded on the hillside only yards above the cliff face, setting fire to the heather; the gulls screamed and scattered, while cormorants standing on the ledges disappeared beneath the water. Bolt after bolt entered the bay about a mile to our right. One blue streak of flame danced temporarily in front of our eyes, leaving us stupefied. My father stopped rowing, rubbed his eyes with the back of his knuckles and said, 'Oh Virgin! That was a near one!', though his face kept its usual placid expression. 'We'll make the Sign of the Cross,' he added, and, reaching into the bows, he produced a little bottle of Holy Water which he sprinkled on us in the name of the Holy Spirit. We continued to row eastward.

The force of the wind now made a worsening short-breaking sea. I saw a large plank of wood some distance off our beam, which I prayed God my father would not see, because he would risk life and limb to salvage it. But his gannet eye caught sight of it, and he ordered Michael

Sugrue to swing the boat in its direction. We were now running in a following sea and brought the boat head to wind. My father lifted a fifteen-foot beam of pine from the water, pushed it gently under the thwarts, leaving some four feet protruding over the stern transom, remarking, 'Some more of those planks are in the currents, if only the weather was suitable to search for them.'

The white-caps were now like 'charging steeds' racing free and high; the lip of one caught us on the stern quarter and splashed harmlessly aboard. Soon my father made another change. He ordered me to stow my oar and Michael Sugrue rowed in the bow position with my father in the second berth. I was told to sit in the middle of the fourth seat with the bailing bucket on my lap, to keep the boat clear of any heavy water. The old master knew how to handle his small craft in a tormented sea. 'Row her long, light and steady! Let her rise, and only one way to run, run like the devil, from the break of a following sea, keep her perfectly straight on course, and above all don't let her fall across when she is planing on the crest of a wave.'

We were now running by the little headland of *Cráiteach*, which the seine fishermen nicknamed 'Greenland', because of its acre of tossed water. We avoided the worst by staying close to the cliff face where there is a deep channel. One heavy white-cap came half smashing over the side, spilling in about fifty gallons of water. I plied the bailing bucket furiously, in a continuous, looping movement, so busy I didn't have time for butterflies in the gut. At last we ran through Horse Island Sound and into the shelter of the harbour, continued by the *Rinn Dubh* or Black Reef round by the head of *Carraig*, beaching the boat where we had started that morning. We sheltered under the ruined castle wall, for the storm had not yet lost its intensity and was spreading inland. My father forbade me to enter the castle, saying it was less dangerous standing in the shelter of the great outside wall, as lightning was known to follow air currents.

Some forked lightning streaked dangerously near into the waters of the beach, one flash in particular leaving a sulphurous stench like burning rubber. The wind continued to pull landwards, now blowing a full gale. Michael said, 'John! If we were out there now, we would surely be lost!'

My father replied, nonchalantly, 'Well, maybe! But Michael, you must always keep that "weather eye" open, and that is exactly what we did today: we were running away before the storm really got to us.'

Heavy squalls hit the length of the harbour, spiralling spray high into the air. We made the boat and gear secure, waiting for the weather to improve before hauling our nets, and my father and Michael divided a fine catch of fish between them. We were welcomed home by my mother, who was getting anxious about our safety. Our intention of making several trammel hauls in the course of the day had been thwarted by the spectacular thunderstorm. Mike promised he would come at dawn to haul the nets.

Next morning dawned bright and fair. The bay looked like a sheet of opal, streaked with azure. Hog's Head and Scariff Island still wore collars of frilly surf, the residue of yesterday's angry tempest. My mother was first out of bed and had the turf fire blazing on the hearth. The old iron kettle gave occasional coughs of steam, assuring us that it was about to boil over. She had cooked half a dozen fresh hen eggs, the produce of her prized Rhode Island Reds, the shells of which were a rich pink brown. My father had prepared thick cutlets of sea bream, which tasted delicious with a sprinkle of salt and pepper and a knob of butter. Mike Sugrue arrived and again we made our way to the beach, eager to salvage our nets. We lost no time in getting the boat afloat, taking a direct course to the Bay Rock. The

Skelligs Haul

marking buoys were in the same position as we had set them the morning before. I took small paddles to keep the boat clear of the nets while they began hauling. The nets were, as old fishermen would say in Irish, 'dirty' with fish, meaning that more fish than net were visible. Michael and my father decided that the nets must be stored carefully on the boat floor, to distribute the weight more evenly. The catch included white and black pollack, many species of crab from the great edible red crab to the velvet-back wader, who is very handy at snipping meshes, and of course, the notorious spiked dogfish.

The last fish to be taken on board was a large conger eel, who reacted violently to captivity and succeeded in tearing several meshes and escaping onto the stern sheeting. My father had to resort to the baton, administering the last rites and dropping the eel into the sea. The hauling of the nets being finished with, we headed back for the old castle beach.

It was good to watch my father and Michael produce their tobacco pipes and light up, looking so happy after a job well done. My father had a brown beard with whorls like Moses, now streaked with grey. He was a tall man, a little over six feet, with long Roman features. Michael Sugrue was tall, dark and good-looking, with a moustache. They both spoke soft musical Irish, in which they had a large vocabulary – many thousands of words each with its own distinct meaning. No word of English passed between those grand men of the past, who were proud of their Gaelic culture.

I was detailed to fetch the ass and cart with several home-made osier baskets while they stayed to clean the nets of fish. Our task done, we went homeward once more, and the fish were again divided.

Episodes such as this were part of my everyday life, and it was only much later that I became conscious of the debt

I owed to these men who shared with me their knowledge and love of the sea, especially to my father.

SEA KELP, ROCK POOLS, BEACHES AND STRANDS
Skelligs Calling

The ebbing and flowing of the tide – called the ebb and the flood, and caused by the gravitational pull of the sun and the moon – has two high tides and two low tides in each lunar day, perpetually ebbing and flowing, leaving two tide marks, one high-water and one low-water mark. Within the tidemark can be found an array of marine life and a feeding ground for many of the seabirds I mention. The exposed rocks of *Rinn Dubh*, the Black Reef, could at low tide be described as an undersea garden full of different sea plants and rock pools of clear green seawater, where rockling and bull-horned blennies dart for cover beneath the seagrass, the bladderwrack and 'the drowning man's seastrings'. One part in particular was my favourite, where the sweet, edible sea dulse grew in profusion. The red fronds would turn a bluish-green in July – then it had less iodine content. When dried to become crisp in the sun it had an appetizing salty flavour. It is widely used as something to whet the appetite. The long searods, each with its clump of red-brown kelp for a crown, were exposed in thousands like a forest of miniature tropical plants, each searod rooted firmly to the rock. Other species of brown kelp are called ribbon and stripe, having a shorter leg than the searod.

The dark bladderwrack, with short root, is branched like a fuchsia bush, containing numerous air blisters like modern 'bubble foam', which perhaps were provided by nature to help it stand upright in the water – clever fellow, this nature. How he seals the air into all those little sacs is beyond me.

Several other sea plants grow on the *Rinn Dubh*. Carrageen moss is to be found in large quantities; having a rich mineral and medicinal content, jellies and beverages are made from it. Another interesting seaweed we call 'Mermaid's Hair', or 'Tresses'. In Irish we knew it as *Triopall na Muirmhná*. It grows in separate skeins from one root, having long, thin, hair-like strings.

One pond in the shelter of the reef had a dense growth of sea laces, or drowning strings, we called *rachacha*, making it impossible to row a boat or swim in that section. Some strings would measure eight feet long, thin and tough as shoelaces and firmly anchored to the seabed, making a dense carpet of hundreds of thousands of drowning strings.

The reddish-purple coloured minor dulse, which sprouts in little bunches – each little plant with a tiny blue mussel clinging to its root – grows best in shelter and among the baby mussels. When dried in the sun it is sweet and tangy and is sold commercially, especially to beer drinkers.

Among the other salt-water rock plants is the dark, glossy *sleaidí* and also the shiny brown *sliúcán* (which if boiled and eaten with butter makes a tasty and wholesome dish). Both marine plants are tidal and need exposure to air and light between tides. *Sleaidí* and *sliúcán* are both Irish names, the English and Latin versions are 'sea-lettuce', *ulva lactuca*, and 'laver', *porphyra*.

One small plant, which grows only about two inches high, and is brown, branched and brittle, we called *Seán te*, or 'hot John', because of a hot sweet taste. Others say it is a species of agar-agar. There are many other forms of kelp: two-tufted short searods, serrated yellow ribbon kelp, broad stripe whipleg kelp. All these forms we used to

Sea Kelp, Rock Pools, Beaches and Strands

manure our potato and vegetable plots. When mixed with farmyard manure they made excellent fertilizer.

The seabirds came in flocks to search for food in the strand by the *Rinn Dubh*, and still do. The grey heron would stand as still as a statue of slate-grey stone gazing into that part of the rock pool it had chosen, waiting for an elver to appear.

A large flock of sand larks called dunlins, and several tide waders called sandpipers, little strand hens, greenshanks and turnstones, curlews and whimbrel, feed on the table of the tides, when there is a scarcity elsewhere. The exposed sand banks and mudflats offer a variety of food – small crabs, sand eel fry, sand-hoppers, sea mice, sandworms and green lugworms. The curlew and the sandpiper can insert their sharp, pointed bills to a depth of three or more inches into soft sand to drag out sandworms. Many of the smaller waders are migratory to north or south, and numerous in name and size, varying also in colour: redshanks, greenshanks, little stints, turnstones, that work on shingle beaches at night, feeding on sand-hoppers and sand fleas. Equipped with strong stubby beaks, they flip over flat stones of considerable size.

Hidden beneath the fronds of kelp in the rock pools there dwells a variety of marine life; green edible shrimp will jerk-swim for cover, leaving only their long hair-like antennae barely visible in the sea growth. I loved to grab a large one, and after mercifully disjointing it I would eat the tail section. Raw shrimp is nutritious and excellent to eat, so is escallop and razor clam. Boiling, I think, destroys the taste. I recommend we go back a little. After all, the man who ate the first blackberry took a chance. Pardon my digression: back to the pool.

We might see a large pink sea-urchin, cunningly hidden beneath a rock shelf, while several smaller edible purple urchins are in various stages of growth, some baby button size, some large as and the same shape as spinning tops, some as big as goose eggs. In the pool also we find three or four different species of crab – the green-backed or *portán glas*, 'the velvet back', and the *luthóg*, the 'rowing' or 'swimming' crab which has flat hinged toes it can use as oars, like the 'freshwater boatman'. The hermit crab is seen to scramble along taking its house on its back, usually an empty whelk shell. The large spider crab will keep to the deeper pools, so also the large red edible. Periwinkles and whelk winkles, also small bright yellow winkles, and striped mother-of-pearl, abound in the pools. In the gravel-bottomed rock pools can be found the smooth-shelled oval cockle, also the round, rough, serrated cockle which make delicious chowder.

The *circín trá*, or 'little hen of the strand', is Irish for the sanderling, sand-lark or the dunlin. I often wonder if the little bird takes time to rest or sleep. Night and day I have watched it run nearly as fast as it can fly along by the lip of the wave where the sea joins the sand, running in short fast spurts and uttering its clear sweet short pleasant stuttering whistle, as notes played on a dulcimer. An old Irish proverb says, 'The sandpiper can only feed on one beach at a time.' *Ní féidir leis an ngobadán an dá thrá a fhreastal*. The *gobadán* in this case is the sandpiper, seapie, oystercatcher or redshank; in stormy weather they move inland to get earthworms. [...]

Common limpets – *bairneach* in Irish – are plentiful on the *Rinn Dubh*. Pyramid limpets and flat limpets called 'Chinese hats' are both edible – when boiled in a stew, limpets make an excellent soup. Shells of limpets, mussels, cockles and winkles are still being uncovered by the bulldozer in the excavation of building sites close to the shore wherever the midden heaps of old dwellings existed, providing proof that the poor Irish peasantry during the Famine years availed of this shellfish for survival.

Sea Kelp, Rock Pools, Beaches and Strands

What other life forms do we find in the rock pool? Sea anemones, very much like cow teats attached to the submerged rocks, some very beautiful and varied colours, red, blue, pink, with an array of pastel colours on the hair-like fringes and tentacles with which they capture the micro-organisms of plankton. I do not know what science has discovered regarding this form of life. The Irish term that was used in reference to it was *bod lice*, meaning 'the rock phallus'.

Starfish are so numerous – they are found on the floor of the ocean, at great depths, on the sands of the shallow seashore, in the rock pools of *Rinn Dubh* and, may I say, almost everywhere. Too many starfish clinging to a lobster pot or a net will immediately give warning to a fisherman that he is operating on what is termed 'hungry ground'. The old fishermen called it *talamh gan beatha*, meaning 'a place devoid of the fruits of life'. The most common starfish is the five-pointed (echinoderm), five flat pointed legs radiating from a central disc. Only on two occasions did I find the sun starfish in the trawl. The central body is a round flat disc, bright yellow, and twelve flat legs of paler yellow. Starfish are very brittle: when dry they become like pieces of dried lime. The species are so plentiful and multicoloured, they contribute to the sedimentation of the oceans. One species of rough, spiny, grey-blue five-tentacled starfish, have legs which are sometimes ten inches long, tapering to a point. The creature will wrap itself, octopus-like, around a piece of fish bait in a lobster pot. It is also known to smother escallops, depriving them of oxygen. It is a denizen of the kelp floor of the sea. It has thousands of light, pink-coloured, pimple suckers on each arm. I often examined it to find evidence of eyes but on finding no evidence, the eyes must be, I presume, a television screen in its brain, which shows a clear picture of a lobster pot and juicy bait hanging therein.

One rock near *Rinn Dubh* deserves special mention. It is called *Carraig an Eascú* – 'Rock of the Eel'. The eel in question is the conger. During Famine years a conger eel would be considered manna from heaven. Only on a very low watermark would the rock be exposed. I always found it to have one tenant, or more, in residence, sometimes a lobster or red edible crabs. Conger is not eaten locally, and is not regarded as having a very high commercial value; it is also considered the bane of the lobsterman, wrecking, devouring and wreaking havoc on his gear. Only on very rare occasions did we take the electric eel in our trawl. A near cousin to the conger, it wears a necklace of raised red lumps around the base of the gills and later, in the City Aquarium, New York, I read an information display panel that said the electric eel could emit a static electric shock powerful enough to immobilize a horse. The eel we captured had its storage batteries weakened from being dragged with the trawl net along the sea floor for a considerable period of time. It still gave shock enough to sting.

ROCK CLAMS AT *TRÁIGH FRAISCE*
Skelligs Calling

The beach at Boolakeel is wide open to the south-western ocean, which stretches to the Gulf of Mexico and thence to Pine Head, Maine, the pristine, unpolluted water, cleansing and purifying the old bed of razor clams and piddock which have grown in the area during the memory of man. Each year we would await the great 'red strand of Easter', when the sand banks were exposed.

I would go to the strand of *Tráigh Fraisce* with my father and my sister Sheila, who was two years my senior. As

Rock Clams at Tráigh Fraisce

teenagers we loved to accompany him – he was the expert and when arriving at the strand, he would study the oval eye-shape signs on the sand left there by the razor clams underneath, telling us in Irish not to trample the sand where the signs were showing plentiful. The razor clam is very sensitive to vibrations overhead and will quickly pull itself down deeply into the soft sand and disappear. Dad was adept with the spade; he would open a trench by the side of the clam bed, exposing the clams as he dug gently along a wall of falling sand. Sheila and myself kept collecting until our rod basket was full of beautiful green-yellow razor clams and fat blue *brilliocáin*, 'piddocks'. Then Dad would lay his spade on his shoulders, as we turned homeward. Mom always bade us welcome with the words in Irish saying, 'Ye are home from the strand and ye have something good' – '*Sibh slán ón dtráigh agus rud maith agaibh.*' We also knew that Mom's clam chowder was the best in the world.

May I come back to the *Rinn Dubh* and *Loch an Duilisc*, the pool or little pond, among the rocks where the dulse still grows. Many other marine creatures lurk beneath the shelter of the dulse frond; such as a dark, sausage-like, squirming thing we called a *súire*. Marine biologists tell us this species is blind. From my experience, it can get in and out of lobster pots at ease, and like the spider can exude from its body a white milky sticky thread-like filament. It has many hundreds of yellow pimple suckers underneath and has no bone structure. All things fair, the black *súire* is a harmless fellow – to me, a fisherman, at any rate. I feel I have a lot to learn. Another inhabitant of the rock pool is the 'sea needle', known in Irish as *an snáthaid mhara*, a slender amber-coloured serpent-like fish, sometimes twelve to fourteen inches long, with a body no thicker than a pencil. It has a transparent bugle-end beak, tiny yellow eye-beads, and a wavy dorsal fin. Why it will enter lobster pots I do not know, as it can only feed on minute forms of plankton.

Skelligs Haul

The colourful dragonet can be found in the depths of the Atlantic shelf at one hundred fathoms, and also in the rock pool on the sea shore; adorned in bright blue blending with buttercup yellow, pastel green and grey stripes, with an underbelly of faded white, it presents a very beautiful array of complementary colour.

The dragon-fish has a pyramid-shaped head, with nasty needle spines growing from its forehead and from the side of its gills; its dorsal fin is a feathery growth, concealing several needle-pointed spines. Two ferocious glaring green eyes add to its formidable appearance. It is not edible and its sting is poisonous. Usually it measures not more than nine inches in length. Another comrade in the pool is the horn-headed lumpsucker, in Irish called *an deilgín deamhain*, 'the spiny or thorny demon'. But though nature did not endow poor old lumpsucker with handsome features, I'd much rather shake hands with him than his colourful neighbour the dragonet. The lumpsucker has a round disc on its undercarriage which it adheres to its prey.

DIGGING SAND SPRAT

Skelligs Calling

I will go back some four score years ... I was a raw-boned *garsún*, talking, walking, sleeping, eating ... twelve years for my coming birthday. My Dad loved the strand and what better place in the full of the moon, when the tide was low, than *Boig a' Chaisleáin*, the sand bank below the old ruined castle on Ballinskelligs Strand. It was there the *scadán gainí*, the sprat-like sand elvers or sand herring, were plentiful. The little silver fish were no more than two and a half inches long. When washed and dried, sprinkled with flour, pepper and salt, fried to a crisp in butter they make a tasty meal. Dad brought a short shovel – he didn't have to use it much. We just danced on the soft sand and this brought the sprats to the surface. I carried a wooden bucket; when this was about half-full of the silver minnows my father said in Irish, '*Tá do dhóthain díobh agat*', meaning, 'You have enough [of them].' Nights such as these have a marked chapter in the book of my memory, with moon rays glancing on the soughing wavelets on the strand beneath the old castle, and mingling with the laughing cackle of the sand lark – simple events of beauty that are so hard to erase from the mind.

A small bed of blue mussels grew on the side of the *Carraig* where the fresh water from the mountain entered the sea. Mussels were allowed to grow undisturbed when I was a teenager. We did not buy mussels in tins, or in frozen packs. The only occasion my Dad would ask us to get a bucket of mussels was when he ran short of bait for bottom fishing. He would parboil them, making them easy for impaling on the hook. It was good bait for whiting and cod.

SEA GRASS

Skelligs Calling

Banks of rough shelly sand, where the plain piddock clams grow in abundance, are found in the shallow reaches of Ballinskelligs Harbour. Most of this area is covered with a growth of green-blue sea grass, called in Irish *muirleog*, not unlike our rye grass the roots are sweet and edible. At least we as youngsters chewed them and the experiment only whetted our appetites for more.

Where the *muirleog* is found growing in profusion on the sea floor, there too will be found the many species of fish that inhabit this healthy environment. The ballan wrasse and gunner, also called connor fish – in Irish *ballaigh* – live and breed in the sea grass floor. Some take on a bright blue-green shade, others remain a light brown, while still others are bright and speckled.

Plaice love to hide beneath the cover of the *muirleog*, where they grow fat on succulent lugworms, and browse on young clam tips. The plaice, sand dab and black sole will dig in and lie completely covered; except for tip of nose and two beady eyes barely visible, black sole will cover itself with an inch or more of sand. Codling love the sea grass floor, because of the small green crabs they find among the stalks, in addition to the rays and skate, especially the thorny-backed species.

Lobsters are hermits by nature and like plenty of cover. I have set lobster pots and have found many in the sea grass. Of course escallops shelter and breed there as well. A most likely place to set a trammel net is in the shallow sea grass in the shelter of a point near the shore.

Fin and Feather

SHARKS AND OTHER SPECIES
Skelligs Calling

The angler, fishing frog or monkfish, called *anafláig* in the old tongue, has a likeness to a frog because of its great curved semicircular jaws, which are adorned with rows of sharp needle-point teeth on the upper and lower lips. The teeth will grow long in accordance with the size of the fish. The monk is equipped with two great flabby wide cheeks, back of its gills. Sometimes it may not be possible for the fishing frog to consume all it may catch, especially on a day, or perhaps a night, when fishing was good. I often found some uneaten fish stored in the pouches of its great cheeks, for, believe it or not, this ugly disciple of the art is a fish that fishes for a living. Bountiful nature provides the young angler with a new fishing-rod, complete with a pastel grey-blue bait, on its first birthday, and by the time it has attained a length of thirty inches or more, it will be operating three or four fishing-rods. The rods grow from the centre of the backbone in a direct line between head and tail, about six inches apart. They are almost transparent, like nylon, flexible aerials coming to a slender downward loop from which the grey-blue butterfly bait dangles only inches away from the treacherous teeth.

The monkfish can set itself into the sand, or on a rough kelp-grown bottom, with only its eyes exposed and its fishing rods in operation. Only its round stout tail is nowadays much sought after as an expensive fish dish. The creature is not endowed with good looks – in fact, it has a most formidable appearance – yet the bountiful Creator did not leave it destitute, equipping it with an everlasting supply of free fishing tackle. The fishing frog can be found from the depths of the ocean to the shoals of the harbour.

Many species of shark frequent the South Atlantic coast of Ireland, especially in warm weather conditions. One day while trolling for pollack in a small sixteen-foot punt off Bolus Headland, in company with my father, we had occasion to stop while partaking of some lunch. Previously we had disposed of some fresh mackerel entrails over the side. The sea was calm and suddenly we became aware of something solid rubbing against the keel of the boat. My father glanced over the side – he was in the stern seat – and motioned to me to take a look, saying two words only in Irish: *'míol draide'*, 'grimacing shark', which to me meant only one thing: a man-eating shark. I will describe the shark as best I can. It was a cobalt blue on top, with a great wedge-shaped, blunt nose, and large, round, bright eyes. The underbelly seemed to be a dirty, whitish grey. The most frightening feature was its great semicircular mouth widening beneath its gills like a giant horseshoe, with serrated rows of glistening white saw-teeth adorning what must be its gums, and, as a matter of interest, I noticed some grey marine shell-like growths on its wide back.

Although we were lying in thirty-five fathoms of water, the great fish lay perfectly quiet less than two fathoms beneath our frail craft, frail in comparison to our unwelcome monster visitor whose dorsal fin nearly reached the keel of the punt. As our punt drifted in the current, so too did our visitor with perfect timing. My father said, 'The mackerel guts we threw overboard attracted it.' I said to Dad, 'I'll get the oar and strike the water to scare it off,' to which he replied, 'Don't dream of it, we will row towards the headland, near the cliff where we won't have the current to shift us while we're eating.' We put out our oars and rowed gently at slow speed towards Bolus Head. When we reached a place called *Leac an Chinn*, 'the Flagstone of the Headland', and where the water was still as a duck pond, we shipped our oars once more and proceeded to have our delayed snack in peace. 'He was a big fellow, Dad,' I said. 'He was, and a nasty customer to deal with,' replied Dad. 'He had jaws wide enough to swallow a man.'

We had finished our snack and while Dad was fixing his pipe I got the bailer to empty the well under the stern sheeting; we would then resume our pollack fishing. I stood upright in the boat, preparing to get my short paddles into position. Just then I got the shock of a lifetime to see the blunt nose of the ugly shark within inches of our stern. This time I could peer into the gaping circle of its great maw, and look more closely at its glistening rows of sharp band-saw teeth. On the side nearest the boat, the round, bright eye was but mere inches below the water surface. I beckoned to my father, who on surveying the situation, said something like, 'The so-and-so is taking a right look at us this time.' My Dad was by nature very stoic – I could depend on his self-control in the event of a sudden decision. But when Dad asked me to hand him the boat-hook, I thought he had really blown his head gasket. I countered by asking, 'Dad, what in the name of all that is holy do you want the boat-hook for?' Dad replied quietly, 'I'll give it a bang in the eye.' 'Dad, one swish of its great tail will surely swamp us.' Dad answered, 'That is true, but while its tail is well clear of our stern and the body of the punt is in shelter of the *Leac*, it can't sink us.' I felt little flutterings of some winged creatures in the pit of my food basket. Without any more useless arguments, I handed over the boat-hook. Now, our boat-hook was a solid instrument. It consisted of a nine-foot shaft of ash, with a nine-inch heavy iron spike on top, with a curved hook on one side. This was the time of truth. I can picture my dad standing upright in the stern sheeting and taking careful aim.

Sharks and Other Species

I do not know to what warrior, saint or hero I should compare my father, who has departed from life's screen many, many years ago. May he rest in peace. Perhaps he looked like Saint George and the Dragon, or maybe a Wexford pikeman at Vinegar Hill, or Captain Ahab in pursuit of Moby Dick. As he thrust the pointed boat-hook with unerring aim at the shark's eyeball, I remember vividly a great curved wide tail lift high in the air behind the boat – the wide wedge-shaped body of the shark exposed for a second – and come crashing down only yards away from our gunwale. Our little punt lurched while salt water rained from the sky in torrents, drenching us to the skin. 'That was a near one, Dad,' I ventured. 'It was,' Dad retorted, 'but I think that shark must go to see an eye doctor.'

The boat was bailed free of water once again but this time the sea was tossed around like surf on a stormy day. We removed our inside shirts and put on our dry jackets which fortunately we had stored in the bow, it being a warm day in June. There will be some who, no doubt, will be sceptical as to the veracity of my story, but I can honestly assure you I would much rather deal with ghost stories than with rogue sharks. We continued our trolling for pollack undisturbed for the rest of the evening.

On another occasion I heard my father tell how old Patrick Barry of Horse Island, together with a helper fisherman and a little boy, were chased by a thresher or killer shark which kept continually leaping out of the water within feet of their rowing boat. They were shipping water disturbed by the shark's continual broaching. It was only when they collected some foul-smelling bilge water that was lodged in the bottom of the boat, and fed it into the wake of the boat, did the shark desist from worrying them. Sharks do not like foul-smelling water.

Another immense inhabitant of the deep is the great basking shark, which can be found in our south and

Skelligs Haul

west inshore waters in early spring and summer. Among the many names in Irish for the basking shark, one finds *liamhán gréine, ainmhí na seolta, cearbhán, seoltóir* and *liopadaileap*. The authorities differ on the exact location of their breeding ground, somewhere in the depths of the South Atlantic. All the information I have gathered from observation of their annual movement is that they seem to approach the Irish coast from the south-west and swim north, entering the shallow bays and estuaries.

I had experience of one basking shark that became entangled in a fishing net. We had to tow it ashore to recover some part of our gear, which turned out a total loss. It was a creature of huge dimensions. It measured thirty-seven feet in length and seventeen feet in girth. I remember having taken pains to measure it accurately. The basking shark is not a dangerous shark – in fact its gullet is very narrow and is equipped with a series of vertical plates on each side that act as filters through which plankton is strained. Fishmeal manufacturers have bought the huge carcasses of red beef-like meat. The shark is most prized for its huge liver. One liver produces seventeen casks of oil when rendered. The sharks usually swim in pairs close to the surface at very slow speed, following the warm sea currents, some of which have a rich mixture of several species of plankton. This shark is not aggressive and does not pose a threat to fisher folk or swimmers.

There exist many leviathan denizens of the deep oceans that have never been exposed to the gaze of man. Hundreds of different species of shark live in the tropics, also many hundred species of turtle, and in some Australian and Oriental waters live large and poisonous sea snakes.

Very few fishermen ever get close enough to the round, leather-tan grampus to get a detailed picture of this enormous sea monster which some call 'the herring hog'. Only on two occasions in my life have I witnessed it broaching the surface, and then only exposing a long, looping coil rolling downwards into the depths, a brown leathery gloss on its skin and not showing any fins. All I could say – its body was round like an earthworm and of immense girth. It must have weighed tons, judging from the amount of water it displaced when it surfaced.

The blue porbeagle shark, which in Irish is called *an preabaire gorm,* is much sought after by rod and reel sportsmen. It requires very high-breaking strain lines, powerful reels and heavy fibreglass rods to bring a porbeagle to the gaff. Shark-fin soup is supposedly supped in chic eating-houses and, as I have never tasted the delicacy, I must not be critical in matters of appetizing taste.

The common dogfish, or *madra glas,* spike dogfish, is a near cousin of the shark family, and as a fisherman it did not help me commercially, domestically or otherwise to become involved with spur dogs. Only one time, when fish became very scarce in the last World War, was there a demand for flake dogfish. Then, the export price did not justify the labour in skinning, icing and boxing.

I remember a night when a train of herring nets got badly torn by a school of spur dog. Not content in gorging with live herring, they can tear an expensive net to tatters while doing so. Spike dogfish are a voracious species. I have seen them drag little guillemot chicks beneath the water and devour them. The spur female can give birth to six fully developed pups, complete with spikes and fins, all ready to do for themselves, each with a transparent sac attached to its navel containing a yellow yolk exactly comparable to that of a hen egg. In this sac, I have been informed, nature has provided enough vitamins via an umbilical cord to its stomach, until the young dog is able to fend for itself.

Dogfish are equipped with two sharp spikes near the back and dorsal fins. I have special reason to remember a day when a dog spike was driven deep into the flesh near my shinbone. I remember my father washed out the wound with seawater, and encouraged the puncture to bleed more by enlarging the entrance to the cut with the point of a small penknife. After several more washings in the brine, although it was painful and stiff, it cured from the word go. My dad was a great believer in plenty of air and sunlight for wounds. Being only a *garsún* of twelve tender years, and unable to control the muscular swishing tail of a twelve-pound spur dog, the encounter I speak of only served to infuse in me a healthy respect for the species that lasted the duration of my career as a fisherman.

An chailleach bhreac, the grey hag, and the great spotted dogfish are related in blood and bone, except for one redeeming feature: the grey hag does not have the formidable spike. The grey hag has a serpent-like appearance, is an ugly-looking fish and not commercially profitable in the fish food chain; inshore waters can become totally infested with it and become a nightmare for trammel-net fishermen when there is one in every mesh.

The female hag will lay an elongated, opaque, cigar-shaped purse some months after copulation; attached to the purse are four sensitive tendrils which twine and curl around the kelp stems, anchoring them until the purse will open and young dogfish will emerge, with a yolk for sustenance. I do not know how many purse eggs are laid by one female. Skate and ray also lay large flat purses in the shape of the letter H.

Some fishermen call another large-type species 'the white hound'. The old Irish name was *fámaire*, meaning of course 'the robust, overgrown, muscular fellow'. This species is called a tope. It is more shark than dogfish. I happened to take one some years ago, when sea angling. I had quite a struggle to get it into the small boat. It kept rolling over and over and weighed in excess of sixty pounds. The maw and open jaws are like the blue shark, except that the tope is a greyish white. They are also voracious eaters. In one tope's stomach I found three large mackerel, one large black sole and one medium pollack. Why I performed this gory, gutty operation was to retrieve my steel hook, trace and swivel the white hound had swallowed into the nethermost region of its stomach. It is also interesting to note that each mackerel had its tail severed, as if by a sharp knife; thus the name *gearrthóir*, 'cutter'.

Having nothing more interesting to occupy my time in the Depression of the early thirties in the great USA – in which country I was allowed to stay under a valid immigration quota – I sat on the end of a wooden pier at a place called Savin Rock, outside New Haven, on the shore of Long Island Sound. With some sand lugs for bait, I often got some flounders and blue fish when they were running. But not tonight. Poor Irish Yorik immigrant, I could only land one solitary wriggling sandpaper-skin, eye-blinking son of a spotted dogfish, *cailleach bhreac*, which must have chased the liner all the way from Skelligs Rock to the tip of Sandyhook. I rubbed my eyes to examine my contorting catch more closely. Yes, there was no difference between the Old Hag of Beara and the grey hag of Long Island Sound.

Dolphins and porpoise are seen to congregate in great schools as they approach the coast at the end of May. Some fisher folk regard this as a prediction of a fine summer to come. The porpoise will hunt the early salmon schools, and also the sturgeon. They can pursue their quarry for days without end, until finally encircling and closing in for the kill. Porpoise and dolphins are not dangerous to swimmers, are highly intelligent creatures, and have shown a certain curious affinity towards humans. Sometimes they stray from their herd when they come into shallow waters and can be trapped. The natives of the Polynesian Islands in the far Pacific had a chant, which they called 'porpoise calling'. They would stand on the reefs when the wind was favourable to carry the sound of their voices far offshore. In perhaps a matter of days the porpoise schools would follow the music of the chant into a narrow channel where they were harvested for their meat, liver and skins.

SQUID, CUTTLEFISH AND OCTOPUS
Skelligs Calling

Squid, cuttlefish and octopus can be found in almost all seas of the world. The lobsterman is well acquainted with the octopus, who will avail of a free meal from the lobster pot whenever possible. Thankfully, the octopus will not grow to a large size in North Atlantic waters and does not pose a threat to swimmers or divers. Only in warm tropical waters are they known to endanger life. We know it by names such as 'the devil's hook' – *crúcaí an diabhail*. Even a small one with eight tentacles, ten inches long, equipped with hundreds of razor-sharp cutting discs, can become an ugly customer to deal with. Drastic measures have to be used to make it relax its tentacles. It can change the colour of its skin to suit that of its surroundings. It has two evil-looking, small, blue-green eyes, and is capable of changing shape as well as colour.

All squid are equipped with an ink sac which they use to squirt into the face of an attacking adversary. The torpedo-shaped squid, with side vanes, is a milky grey opaque colour, with soft streamer tentacles, without the disc teeth of its cousin, the octopus, and is used as a speciality in the table menu of many restaurants. In Mediterranean countries the octopus is used widely for its food value. It is processed, cured, sometimes dried in the intense heat of the sun. Octopus soup can be very palatable.

The only bone in the squid is its backbone structure, which is not bone as is common to other marine species. The back of the squid is a structure of brittle white gritty lime-like substance, very lightweight, and will float buoyantly on water. It is oval-shaped, and in early spring it can be found washed ashore on beaches of the world. The pre-Christian Irish called it the *teanga bó bailbhe*, 'dumb cow's tongue', connecting it to the mythology of the Fianna, and 'the Land of Youth', *Tír na nÓg*. The 'dumb cow's tongue' is sold commercially to aviaries and bird-fanciers, as an important form of mineral grit for the life of all cage birds.

Another squid is the deep-water cuttlefish with a beak-like bottlenose; this species can grow several metres long and is not known to frequent shallow water. I have often witnessed large schools of cuttlefish come to the surface, leaping and cavorting. They will also take artificial bait, like red rubber, or feather.

THE GANNET
Skelligs Calling

When asked too many questions regarding bird life, a Gaelic poet, becoming annoyed, answered: '*Ní bod gaoithe mé, ná sciathán leathair, go bhfaighinn duit cúntas ar éanaibh reatha*,' meaning, 'I'm not a kestrel nor a bat (wing of leather), that I can give knowledge about birds of feather.' Be that as it may, I will try to bestow on you, my lay brothers and sisters, the little I know about out feathered friends of the sea. Few fishermen are without some knowledge of seabirds. Each day they are seen in company with them trying to eke out an existence, sometimes frugal and difficult in stormy weather.

Skelligs Haul

Fishermen are keen to observe the movement of different seabirds and how they congregate in numbers in a certain area. More often than not, they are the telltale token that vast schools of fish move beneath the surface, especially schools of herring, mackerel, pilchards, sprat, etc. The trained eye of the fisherman will also judge the direction in which the fish is moving. Despite new technology, we should not ignore our feathered friends who live beside us in the same vineyard, 'the Kingdom of the Wave'.

The first of our many seabirds that I wish to present to you is the gannet, or solan goose, of which at least 30,000 make their home on Little Skellig, a rock situated nine nautical miles west of Bolus Headland, County Kerry. The great bird is visible to the eye, when the sky is clear, at a distance of two or three miles, usually hovering over the schools of fish, high above the waves when the fish swim deep, and flying low when the fish are near the surface. Cruising at an altitude of more than two hundred feet, it will suddenly close its wings and plummet from the blue, entering the ocean depths like a spear cast from the heavens. Nature provides the gannet with a system of air sacs around the base of the neck that fill automatically, acting as shock absorbers to take the energy from the impact of the dive. The solan goose – its name is Scandinavian – is a ferocious, daring bird, full of muscle and staying power. It can cruise above the water for hours, wheeling high above its prey, gliding on outstretched, rigid pinions. The white of its plumage stands out when seen against a background of blue sky or the green of the ocean, becoming like some astral white light glinting in the sunshine.

In early spring the gannet will prepare for nest building. It will forage far into shoreline estuaries to collect sea-laces and floating strings of bladder wrack, to line its nest with. The nest can best be described as having only the semblance of a place to hatch out their young. The goose gannet will produce one egg in March, of bluish grey-green colour, speckled with little black and brown dots, the dots sparsely arranged at intervals, forming a beautiful, ornate design. The parent birds sit on the egg for a period of six weeks, relieving each other at intervals, faithfully covering the egg with their wide, webbed paws, something not peculiar to any other seabird. The newly hatched chick is black as coal and is continuously fed by both birds for a period of not less than three months; by such time the chick will resemble a fluffy ball of fat. The method of feeding is by regurgitation – the parent bird will insert its beak into the gullet of the young chick, leaving it some partly digested food (usually fish). The feeding continues incessantly during daylight hours.

Scientists tell us that the chicken will take five years to become fully grown, and that the adult life span can be as much as fifteen years. Judging from my own experience it will take the chick three years to lose its black plumage, except for the extreme wing tips, which remain black for life. When the fat chick is more than three months old and can waddle unsteadily on its webbed feet, it will be coaxed and nudged over slabs and ledges until it finally reaches the sea. Sometimes it may float off on a retiring wave, or fall flop into the sea from an overhanging cliff-face.

Once in the water, the parent birds in some mysterious way will spirit their offspring clear of the surf-bound shore, out into the free ocean currents. From now on it will be starvation diet. It is not known whether the chick is entirely left on its own, to live off its own fat, until lean enough to become airborne, or perhaps fed occasionally. I have seen chicks that appeared lean and scraggy make several attempts at take-off before finally soaring into the blue.

Before the couple starts nest building, they enjoy a long courting season, and can be seen like human lovers with necks and wings entwined. This is like a long honeymoon period before they mate, and long after their offspring is reared, this amorous display of lovemaking continues.

It was a very special day in my life, when I climbed the dangerous, lofty cliff-face of Small Skellig. Looking back, I have reason to believe how foolish I had been, since I had no experience or training in climbing, but was only imbued with a burning desire to view the habitat of the great gannetry at close quarters. Nor was I disappointed in an adventure that gave me excitement, pleasure and overwhelming wonder. The raucous din of thousands of birdcalls filled the air, shutting out even the noise of the surf in the caves below. The overwhelming smell of guano, lime and calcium through the salt air, seemed to permeate the gentle sea breeze. This was the effect caused by the accumulation of bird droppings over the centuries. Fragments of rotting fish, eggshells, dead birds and feathers also filled many deep veins in the slatey rock structure of the island.

Some parts of the nesting colony were very dense, and here I observed the birds constantly pecking at each other, but never in actual combat; others squabbled over nesting material. Every square foot of one flat area seemed to contain a parent bird and chick. The most amazing feature was how each gannet found its own square foot of space within what seemed to me a maze of confusion.

The birds will not attack a human if one stands still and completely ignores their presence. I had received this piece of good advice from a qualified bird woman – I found it worked perfectly.

Gannets swallow their fish head first, and consume many times their own weight. When diving, the bird will utter a hoarse warning cry – 'krake, krake, krake'. Scientists tell us the gannet once had a tongue and can no longer taste. All I can say is I have examined dead birds and find that a part of the tongue is still there, the front part not pointed, it is very short and straight across – perhaps it is the root. It also has nostril apertures. It probably is speaking from its stomach. The bird has many different sounds. No doubt the bird may be equipped with taste buds and all faculties for survival. I have found drowned gannets entangled in fishing nets, their length 34–37 inches, wing span 19–20 inches. My father referred to the gannet in Irish as *an súlaire*. Today it is called *gainéad* or *ogastún*. The great beak is likened to a sharp, pointed dagger, and is slate blue in colour, as are its webbed feet.

In summer gannets are found from Iceland to Canada, from the Faeroes to Rockall, from Skellig Michael to Land's End, and the Azores.

[...]

THE PUFFIN

Skelligs Calling

Puffin Island is situated close to the headland of Moyrisk, or *Maothroisc*, on the northern arm of Saint Finan's Bay, near Ballinskelligs. It is now a bird sanctuary.

The puffin, a member of the auk family, measures about twelve inches in length and seven inches wingspan outstretched. The bird has many names: 'sea parrot', 'clown pope', and *canán dearg* and *puifín* in Irish. Its ponderous beak seems out of proportion to the rest of its face, giving it a clown-like appearance. The beak will increase in size during a long spring mating season, the varied and beautiful colours becoming more pronounced and vivid, bright orange mixed with red and blue stripes; this is more apparent in the male, who seems to show off his gaudy finery, while his wife's plumage is drab in comparison. The colours remain until winter, when a portion of the heavy beak is shed in October, a process repeated by Mother Nature at the advent of the next mating season.

The body of the bird is rotund and plump; its little webbed feet and shanks are of a red flesh-colour hue, and its back feathers are a grey mouse colour with a neck-collar of the same above; white breast. A puffin will assume to the beholder a pose of authority, like that of an admiral; it will stand on a ledge for long periods, gazing out to sea, seemingly indifferent to its immediate surroundings.

Late in spring the hen will produce one large white egg to be hatched underground, safe from the prying eyes of the arch marauder, the great black-backed gull. The underground nest site is usually a narrow tunnel expertly constructed beneath a mound of peat-like soil, the residue of many centuries of decaying sea pinks, also the yellow and white sea samphire. With only its great strong beak, short muscular wings, short legs and little sharp-toed, webbed feet as tunnelling tools, the little bird must be commended for its engineering skill, so deeply ingrained in its nature. A disused rabbit burrow can also become a ready-made nesting place. The summer is nearly at hand by the time the young chick breaks the shell in the darkness of his underground cradle.

The little infant is not endowed with handsome features at birth. I found young chicks on the Skelligs covered with black hairy fluff, each with an ugly beak, like a crook on a wall. But the old saying in Irish puts it aptly: *Is fada dho ráite gur geal leis an bhfiach dubh a ghearcach fhéin* – 'The raven thinks its own chick is pure white.' In a short time, the black plumage will change to greyish white; by that time the fledgling will be able to waddle towards the daylight near the entrance of the tunnel. There, it will be fed tiny silver sprats and sand eels by both parents.

Puffins do not dive from the sky, but submerge and swim beneath the surface for long periods, searching for sprats and mini-species. I have watched puffins flying towards the Skelligs from far out to sea, their beaks laden with silver sprats. Young puffins are spirited to the sea on moonlit nights; how this is done remains a mystery to me.

Puffin Island is an undisturbed sanctuary where birds can live and breed without much interference from humans. The island has no man-made landing place, with only a few sheep kept by local farmers from the mainland. Rabbit warrens and banks of turf are plenty. Sea-thrift abounds in profusion, making an ideal nesting-place for several species of seabirds, such as auks, shearwaters and petrels.

The north side of the island is home to the guillemot family on the high shelves of the barren rocky cliff-face, where fulmar petrels and soot-coloured skuas patrol the wild and windswept air-space above, while clusters of lesser gulls, screaming terns and complaining kittiwakes dispute their share of mini-sprat and plankton thrown up by the crashing surf beneath.

THE ROCK PIPIT

Skelligs Calling

In Irish the pipit is called *an beagéan carraige*, meaning 'little bird of the rocks'. It is also known as *riabhóg chladaigh*, 'the stripy one on the shore'. The meadow pipit seems to be exactly the same bird as the rock pipit, one of nature's enigmas. I will not even attempt to find myself a suitable answer; both species are so similar, the difference is almost indiscernible. They have the same plumage and flight pattern, and build the same-shaped nest, using the same withered grasses, weaving in some hair and feathers, except that the rock pipit may use a dried sea string occasionally.

Scholars make the suggestion that some millions of years ago the pipit family suffered a severe disagreement, causing the flock to split up. One part took to the seashore, the other part stayed in the meadow. What the disagreement was about the scholars do not tell us. Perhaps it came about at the reading of the will, when bird property was being disposed of. However, they still sing the same ballads. Some say the rock pipit's voice is sweeter. In my youth I heard the meadow pipit being referred to as *Seáinín na lathaí*, meaning 'Johnny of the gutter'. Other names for the meadow pipit are *riabhóg mhóna, banaltra na cuaiche, fuiseog mhóna* and *riabhóg bheag*.

I had found the pipit's nest in the meadow many a time, but later on I was taken aback to observe the little fellow ballet-dancing on the wild spume and spray-soaked rocks of Bolus Head. Of course this was not the meadow pipit I had taken it for: it was the other disgruntled part of the family, the rock pipit. The blithesome creature could be likened to some superactive flying phantom, full of unending energy, constantly running, searching and collecting the minute particles called plankton.

A stormy day is best to enjoy the antics of this elusive feathered artist of the flying trapeze. No matter how high the breakers come combing, tumbling and foaming over his rocky domain, he is never found trapped or injured. The nimble 'water sprite' will always rise higher than the blown sea spray. The little bird will follow the receding wave with perfect confidence and composure, feeding on the micromorsels washed ashore from nature's bountiful larder. One would assume the little mite is only mocking the fury of the elements and the strength of the mighty ocean, and it cannot be compared with other seabirds.

The rock pipit has not the appearance of a fisherman, nor ever will, yet it wins its daily bread between the tidemarks of the wave. It is pitiful to watch a creature so frail, with weak, thin shanks, wading in shallow rock pools in company with other seabirds.

True to their family, agreement or disagreement, the rock pipit will build its nest on the very edge of the cliff top, where the last blades of grass curl down from land overhead. I happened on a nest by mere chance while walking close to the edge of a stony clay cliff. The nest was carefully concealed below the meadow line, yet under the lip of the cliff. It was woven from withered sand-dune grass and some tiny fluffy feathers; it was cosy and cup-shaped, well shielded from the rain and wind by tufts of sea pinks and bunches of white sea-thrift, mingling with other grasses. White sea-thrifts are sometimes referred to as 'dead men's flowers' because of their brittle stems. Climbers must not grasp them for support.

The nest contained four smoky, grey-green, small eggs with a rusty hue at the extreme ends. At the time, I did not recognize the nest – maybe another meadow pipit's nest, so commonplace in the locality? It was a beautiful work of art on the edge of the Atlantic, perfected by nature's insistence that future propagations of the species might survive – the superb cosy home of the undaunted little waif I have the privilege to describe, and may I add, the excellent fisher, who scorns the fury of mighty Mannanan, little fisher of the rocks, *an beagéan carraige.*

THE STORM PETREL

Skelligs Calling

'Little Peter' (*Peadairín*) who walks on the water, phantom of the storm. This is the storm petrel, whose cloak is black as coal, a harmless creature, never welcomed by sailors,

Skelligs Haul

even to see, and unthinkable that the bird should come aboard: harbinger of storm and misfortune – a bad omen. Many superstitious mariners believe that the little black witches revel in the vortex of an Atlantic hurricane; that is because the bird can be seen anywhere on the far reaches of the ocean, a thousand miles from any nesting place. Little Peter seems to virtually walk on the crest of an approaching billow of brine, scooping up minute droplets of rich fish oil and plankton.

The petrel resembles a species of swallow or black butterfly and is called 'Mother Carey's chickens', or 'Laura of the ocean'. In Irish it is called *an guardal* and again *briochtóg na mara*, 'witch of the sea'. Other names include *gearr róide* and *gearr úisc*.

While many other species of petrels exist, the storm bird is the smallest. Years ago, when British steam trawlers fished off the south-west coast of Kerry, and fish was plentiful, the ships would shelter in Ballinskelligs Bay. The captains and crew were generous and would give us baskets of scrap fish with which to bait our lobster pots. I remember finding a dead storm petrel among the debris of fish on deck. Being curious to examine it, I held it in my hand as a member of the ship's crew protested most vehemently, 'Do not touch it, boy, it will bring you bad luck.' I immediately cast the creature's mutilated body overboard and asked the seaman if the storm petrel really brought bad luck. He replied, 'Don't ever handle them, boy, them's bad members!' Despite the seaman's warning, I could not bring myself to entertain any superstitious belief that Little Peter was endowed with any magical power which enabled it to stir up hurricanes in the Gulf of Mexico.

Towards the end of spring, the little dusky seafarers decide to obey the inborn call, which is fixed in the creation of all species (When? I do not know. The answer is blowing in the wind.) The birds will converge upon their natural

The Storm Petrel

habitat, in the local case primarily Skellig Michael, Puffin Island or the Blaskets.

They will faithfully turn homeward, perhaps on a certain date, no matter how far afield, steering an unerring, leisurely course, sleeping, mating and feeding on the broad reaches of the Atlantic. On arriving home they find the old tunnels and retreats, or perhaps will build anew, between fissures in loose stone walls, places difficult to find, and safe from predators. The chick emits a low, hoarse, chirring sound. The nest is that of a sea-dweller, only a few strands of dried grass, a few feathers, a place to keep an egg warm. When June is at hand, one white egg is laid. After that the parent birds are not seen on land in daytime. Under the cloak of night and within the darkness of the burrow the new chick is hatched, fed and made ready to be introduced to the sea. All is prepared under cover of complete darkness, thus avoiding the great black-backed gull, indiscriminate slayer of chicks.

It is not easy to estimate the power of nature, which enables a little bird with matchstick-thin shanks and flat webbed feet to stand momentarily on a hillock of brine, or dance disdainfully in the womb of a storm. At times wisping witches are seen to congregate close to land – a telltale warning for local fishermen of foul weather (a 'wisp' meaning a little cluster of petrels, not more than three or four).

The different species of petrel are rare to the North Atlantic. Only once have I seen the fork-tailed petrel in the Skelligs area. The bird is not known to nest in the South Kerry region. Ornithologists tell us that the dusky little wave-dancer can waltz the ocean ballroom from the Hebrides to Rockall, from Rockall to Skellig Michael, from the Scillies to the Azores, from the Falklands to Tierra del Fuego, to finally revel in the spume of the Horn.

Little Peter who walks on the water, your heritage is the vineyard of the vast ocean – long may you survive.

Skelligs Haul

THE MANX SHEARWATER
Skelligs Calling

A fisherman who is not familiar with following and searching the south-western waters beyond the Skelligs, and from Kerry Head to the Dursey for the dense mackerel schools, will have missed seeing great strings of Manx shearwater or 'mackerel cock'. The bird is referred to in Irish as *púicín gaoithe* or *an chánóg dhubh*. I do not know why the term 'wind fairy' was used, as it is not a bird connected with stormy conditions. I have observed it in most tranquil conditions, in the quiet of eventide in myriads resting on calm waters. It is known to revel in pleasant breezy conditions, but unlike its cousin the storm petrel, it is not a child of the storm.

The flight pattern of the Manx is both a mystery and a beauty to behold; something in its constant undulating movement seems to suggest a bond of rhythmic unison between bird and ocean. It will glide without effort on seemingly rigid motionless wings, up one side of an Atlantic roller, until it reaches the summit of the billow, then balance delicately on the tip of one pinion to slowly roll over to the opposite wing tip, enabling it to glide effortlessly, using the surface air currents which flow between the sea swells to perfect advantage. Without doubt they are the living music of the waves, rising, falling, floating, weaving the self-same tapestry with unerring precision. The mackerel man will welcome flocks of shearwaters near his boat when he is about to cast his nets at twilight, safe in the knowledge that the birds follow the migratory schools of fish.

The mackerel cock comes ashore on Skellig Michael and Puffin Island between March and May. Its beak is narrow and flute-like, ending with a sharp, turn-down hook. I often suffered a tormented sleep while anchored beside the Great Skellig when lobster fishing. The shearwaters would return to their underground tunnels at dusk, all would be peaceful until after midnight; then would start a plaintive persistent clamour, that of a thousand throats, as if mournfully bewailing their lot. English-speaking people defined the cry as a repetition of the expression 'It was your fault, it was your fault,' while Irish speakers interpreted the cry as a repetition of '*Ná dein é, ná dein é,*' meaning, 'Don't do it, don't do it.' The outcry would suddenly cease at the first streak of dawn, making the nocturnal host vanish into the morning mists. Now, in my old age, I am convinced that there is a bird language, and a variety of animal talk which man in his supreme position of superiority has failed to decode. Modern technology and communications stop short at the turnstile to the animal kingdom.

The egg of the Manx is white. The young chick is clothed in a shirt of blue-grey down and, for some reason, is in a few days as fat as a lump of butter. The full-grown bird has a black back and a white underbody. A colourful blue stripe divides the white from the black; beak and legs are black. By August, full-grown birds will be able to fend for themselves and join the main flock in quest of rich micro-organisms in the tide-race of the deep Atlantic. Faithful to their natural instinct, they will return to the coast once again at the approach of winter.

THE HERRING GULL
Skelligs Calling

Several species of gull frequent the rock-bound coast of Kerry. What more beautiful spectacle than to watch a fishing

Skelligs Haul

boat coming to harbour after a successful trip, laden with fish, and the sky around her filled with fluttering white wings of excited seagulls who will faithfully escort in aerial procession until it takes its moorings. The gull family are many, from the grey speckled herring gull to the small black-headed gull, the near all-white, with blue pastel tint on each wing, the grey-brown gull, and the lesser black-backed, a near cousin to the great black-backed, but not as ferocious.

Several of the lesser family fly inland during springtime and autumn, to follow the plough and feed on the rich red earthworms. Gulls have an uncanny way of communication. When a ploughman starts the day, and a sod of soil becomes a furrow, the field may be several miles inland, yet in a short time gulls will converge on the scene, seemingly from nowhere. If a school of sprat or other fish break the surface some miles from land, you will perhaps remember lines from an old poem in our early schoolbooks:

Into the shore the sea-birds fly
On pinions that know no drooping.
(John Locke)

The sky overhead will immediately fill with clusters of fluttering white-winged gulls.

I am of the opinion that most gulls can see equally well in night-time. Very many years ago we fished for herring with cotton-thread nets, always at night. One would often hear the excited call of the herring gull break the silence of the night when it had discovered a fat herring dangling from the surface meshes of our nets. The call sounded like half-laugh, half-cry – 'Ah ha! I have it! I have it!' In those days birds only spoke their bird talk in perfect Irish, saying, '*Tá agam! Tá agam!*' The chicks of today would never qualify for a five-pounds bonus to speak Irish – forgive me if I say they would never be gulled into that.

I often saw a herring gull lift a large hard-shell crab high above flat rocks and let it drop suddenly. This would be repeated several times until the crab burst into fragments, then the bird could make a meal from the crabmeat. Who will say birds can't think?

Gulls nest in secluded areas, places less frequented by man. Their colonies are always crowded, owing to the additional mix of lesser species. Collectors of birds' eggs are known to have suffered serious accidents in pursuit of their hobby. Despite what is said about seabirds and slovenly nest building, the herring gull will work laboriously while building a deep-sheltered nest of mostly damp seaweed, grasses, bits of anything, from withered sea pinks, or bracken. Herring gulls are also scavengers, and will follow the wake of a ship for miles, feeding on titbits cast overboard. They are also easily tamed if fed. I got into the habit of feeding a gull from my hand – it became so friendly it snatched my best knife and dropped it into the Atlantic.

THE GREAT BLACK-BACKED GULL

Skelligs Calling

It is a big bird, king of the gull family, with a beak of bright yellow and a hood, down-turned, with a blood-red stain on the extreme end of the lower bill, giving it the appearance of a bloodthirsty pirate. Only on rare occasions will it nest among other species; even then, it would be considered a most unwelcome neighbour owing to its bellicose temperament.

A bald lump of rough rock separated from the mainland by a gorge-like cleft, wide enough to prevent man's intrusion from the main headland, which is Bolus. The rock which

I mention is called *Oileán na bhFaoileán*, and is situated between the headlands of Bolus and Duchealla on the Iveragh peninsula, some of the most rugged cliff terrain in the south. It is here the 'Royal Gull' can be seen in a small colony, strutting supreme within the rock-bound turrets of its impregnable fortress.

The black-back is an unmerciful predator of young chicks and eggs of all species except the gannet and the hawk family. All other birds are eternally vigilant during nesting season. I have watched the black marauder stand over the remains of a half-devoured chick, swaying its lowered head and neck from side to side, and with blooded beak, scream a loud clarion call as if telling the bird world that might is right.

The ever-watchful eye of the boastful conqueror has great clarity and a wide range of vision. Not a feather will fall from the sky. Not a pebble will fall from the cliff-face. If a lobsterman discards a crab claw it will never go unnoticed. A piece of barnacled wood is most welcome in stormy weather, when other freeloading take-aways are closed, especially if the barnacles are two or more inches in length. Also a dead body of any kind can be a windfall. At twilight one evening in springtime, it being World War Two, as we were about to set our mackerel gear, we heard the cry of the great gull on our starboard bow, and on moving forward in that direction, to our astonishment we saw the great gull standing sedately on top of the lifting ring of a large floating mine, wailing in a high-pitched note as if to say, 'I am king of the gulls.'

The black-back's nest is only a shelter for the eggs, comprising pieces of withered seaweed, feathers and other bits of dry material from the cliff-face. No doubt the parent birds see the construction as a work of art and a labour of love, which also applies to all mere mortals – an attempt at home building.

The Skua

Two or three eggs are produced near the end of May, pale brown in colour, with streaks of a darker brown showing through. The young birds emerge from their shells dressed in shirts of glossy grey down, with spots of black between the shoulders. Very soon, the genes of heredity become apparent in the youngsters who are only some weeks old, yet by now have already turned very rowdy and are given to pecking each other, showing so soon the aggressive characteristics of the parent birds. In their infant stage they are fed from the craw by insertion of the beak where food always awaits them. It will take three to four years for the great gull to become fully developed; by then its legs will be a yellowish red, and its eyes a bright yellow with tiny green flashing pupils.

I have not written in very glowing terms about *an chaobach*. But back in the twenties when herrings were plentiful in Ballinskelligs Bay, hearing the frenzied chuckle of the black pirate in the vicinity of our nets at night – a sure sign that the rogue was having a free serving of fresh herring – was considered a good omen.

THE SKUA

Skelligs Calling

Tomáisín chac na bhFaoileán, or in English, 'Little Tommy Gull-shit', is the pirate robber and tormentor of other birds, devouring all unwanted matter. This is a species of the gull family clad in a sombre coat of sooty dark brown, giving it an ominous appearance. Fishermen call it the dirty seagull. It can manoeuvre in the air like a falcon – chasing, hunting and harrying the other gulls until they drop a piece of fish, regurgitate or discharge excreta – at the same time uttering a wild, terrifying cry, 'Scheer Scheer', frightening the honest bird to abandon its piece of fish. I have often watched the pirate in pursuit of its repulsive occupation.

Not many pairs are found to nest on the Kerry coast. Only a couple of pairs are seen to nest on *Oileán na bhFaoileán* at present, a barren lump of rock between the wild and majestic headlands of Bolus and Duchealla. The legs and webbed feet are also a dirty brown shade, the bill a wicked, turned-down crook. I never had the opportunity to observe its nesting place at close hand. *Oileán na bhFaoileán* was a dangerous rock to get even a foothold on for the person who wanted to scramble ashore. No wonder that the wild skua had chosen it to be his Bluebeard's Castle.

The chicks and eggs are of the same dreary, drab colour. Nature itself must be blamed for clothing you in such dismal attire, and also for condemning you to piracy, poor Little Tommy Gull-shit.

It is interesting to note – according to ongoing Polar research by several countries – that the skua inhabits the South Polar region and can endure and thrive in sub-zero temperatures.

THE KITTIWAKE

Skelligs Calling

The first time I had occasion to stay for a set period of time in the close vicinity of the Great Skellig was the year 1926. I was then twenty years old. Little did I think I would be granted a long and healthy life, time to reflect on what I observed, and a clear memory of the past. Now in my nineties, I will say with the Psalmist: 'Oh Lord! I love the beauty of thy house, and the place where thy glory dwelleth.'

The Kittiwake

That first trip was not intended to be a sight-seeing tour, but a whole week of hard slogging, hauling, baiting and setting our lobster pots while the weather remained favourable and food supplies lasted. We always anchored our boat in front of Blind Man's Cave, at a place called the south landing. Although I had watched kittiwakes pursue banks of sprat during other fishing trips, this time I had a close-up view, a ringside seat, not to witness a pain-inflicting pugilistic sport, but to watch in wonder a flock of beautiful creatures at home in the roost they had chosen. When they made that choice I do not know – perhaps after the last Ice Age. Brrgh! All in all, it was an excellent roost – they had chosen well.

Blind Man's Cave was sheltered from all sides, an oasis within a bowl of blue-grey towering rock and cliff-face. It seemed as if Mother Nature had inspired her offspring to approve of the site plans she presented to them. The cave itself was shaped like an oval amphitheatre, with tiers of narrow natural shelves on the rocky cliff-face, overlooking the placid pool of sheltered ocean beneath. Every square inch of building space had a kittiwake's nest for generations, the birds resembling white blossoms against the dark background of stone, all sitting on saucer-shaped nests, some sitting solemnly, others with beaks hidden beneath the wing shoulder, peacefully oblivious to the incessant clamour of 'Kittiwake! Kittiwake!', the theme song of this feathered choir.

One can't but be impressed by their behaviour and the way they tolerate each other, calling and sharing beakfuls of oily sprat, some standing beside nests full of fledglings, others with necks intertwined, rubbing their heads together and pruning their plumage. The colony is always at different stages of incubation – only when all the young are ready for flight will peace descend.

In the Blind Man's Cave only the parent birds will remain to repair old nests for next year's season. Kittiwakes will nest on the sheltered sides of high Atlantic cliffs where ledges for nesting, free from man's interference, are to be found. Colonies also inhabit isolated islands where sprat, krill and sand eel abound in regions as far north as the White Sea.

In August, when the young are trained to eke out an existence, they are seen to fly south into the temperate waters of the Gulf Stream. I have watched kittiwakes from the deck of the S.S. *Dresden*, in mid-Atlantic – this was in January 1929 – on my way to the United States of America. [In fact, Michael Kirby's passport confirms that he sailed in 1930, not 1929.] It is hard to understand how those weak, gentle birds survive in sometimes severe weather conditions. Perhaps that is how the Creator ordained that little David should be on a par with Goliath. The kittiwake has lost the hind toe or talon, whether through aeons of evolution or not, I do not know. I am also told that I swung by my tail sometime in that murky past – how fortunate I lost that tail.

The kittiwake has not inherited the rough mannerisms of the gull family, its relative. It remains my choice of seabird – a gentle creature, beautiful lark of the ocean, with plaintive yearning call – 'Kittiwake! Kittiwake!'

Spinning Yarns

SEÁN Ó CONAILL: KING OF THE STORYTELLERS

Skelligs Sunset, with some additions from 'Some Poets and a Storyteller', *Skelligside*

Seán Ó Conaill was born in 1853 in the village of *Cill Rialaig*, within view of the *Scéalaí* Rock, as if Nature herself had prepared a monument at the birthplace of the King of the Storytellers, and it was there he died on 21 May 1931. His home was among a cluster of cosy, white-walled, thatched cottages, nestling beneath the shelter of the rugged and majestic crag that looms overhead on the road to Bolus. At one time there were eleven little cottages in all, each house carefully situated with its back to the storm and its face to the rising sun, giving an extended panoramic view to native or tourist, a view such as Brian Merriman portrays for us in his Gaelic composition in verse, *Cúirt an Mheán Oíche (The Midnight Court)*:

> Do ghealadh an croí, a bheadh críonn le cianta.
> It would gladden the heart of the old or weary.

It was into this beautiful setting that Seán Ó Conaill was delivered and it remained his birthright until the day he died. Beneath his feet lay the clear, unpolluted waters of Ballinskelligs Bay. At night he could hear the moaning of the surf in *Cuas na Léime*, the cave where, it is said, a fugitive escaped capture from Cromwell's forces by taking a flying leap across the neck of its narrow span. One could stand on the roadway outside Seán's house and cast a stone into the sea below.

Seán Ó Conaill: King of the Storytellers

Is it any wonder that Seán became king of the storytellers, inspired by the historical Gaelic place names, going back to *Mo Ruth, Árd Rí na nDraoithe*, the high king of the magicians, whose summer residence was in *Béal Inse, Oileán Dairbhre* (Valentia). He had only to look south to feast his eyes on the towering *Teach Uí Dhuinn*, House of Don, son of Milesius, later known as the Bull Rock lighthouse, together with the Calf and the Cow nearby, to which Tomás Rua Ó Súilleabháin makes reference in a little poem where he says in Gaelic:

Tá an Sceilg is an Scairbh Thiar 'na seasamh,
An Bhó's an Tarbh taobh leo,
An Lao go blasta nár ól riamh bainne,
Is ard a's is garbh a ghéimeann.

Skelligs and Scariff are westward standing,
The Cow and Bull lie near them,
And a Calf that never drank of milk,
How loud and rough its bellow.

Seán was a man of dignity who had a huge respect for the oral tradition of our noble ancestry. He valued his culture and his heritage. Professor Seamus Delargy from University College Dublin, visited him in *Cill Rialaig* and, armed only with a small notebook and pencil, transcribed a wealth of stories from the lips of the great *seanchaí*, and published them in *Leabhar Sheáin Uí Chonaill*. Many of these tales were of local origin, but Seán also told stories about Fionn and the Fianna, the Druids, the *Táin*, Diarmuid and Gráinne and Cúchulainn. He was familiar with sagas whose roots were in ancient Greece, tales which seemed to hang between the spirit world and reality. Writers and scholars still marvel at this humble storyteller whose only schooling was two weeks' attendance at the local hedge school.

Skelligs Haul

Dr Delargy wrote of Seán Ó Conaill as having a wide knowledge of natural things: the phases of the moon, the spring tides, herbal medicines and a vocabulary of thousands of words in Gaelic. Weaving his tales, he could hold his listeners spellbound with his soft, gentle voice. He was always in complete command, confidently natural. The professor would say that, like the wayfarer in William Wordsworth's poem 'The Old Cumberland Beggar', he possessed 'a thing more precious far than all that books [... can do]'.

The *Seanchaí* tells of hearing most of his tales from his ancestors by the hearthstones of his neighbours. Only needing to hear a story once, he could retain it, stored in his memory forever. He tells of a time he visited a neighbouring townland where he listened to a storyteller from another parish who told a certain old tale that Seán did not have in his stock. The night rained in torrents and became very stormy, and Seán waited anxiously for the story to finish, owing to the fact of having to cross a swollen stream in the darkness. He relates his ordeal of trying to negotiate the billowing torrent by making a desperate leap and, failing to reach the far bank, he plunged into the water, thereby losing his headgear. On reaching home he stood in the doorway, bareheaded, dishevelled and dripping wet. His good wife Cáit exclaimed in amazement: '*A Thiarna, a Sheáin, a chroí, cad a bhain duit?*' meaning, 'Lord, Seán! What happened to you?' Whereupon Seán replied: '*Chailleas mo chaipín, ach thugas liom mo scéal!*' ('I only lost my cap but I brought home my story!')

The professor visited my father on many occasions when he brought several large maps of the coastline from Kenmare to Dingle Bay, showing the various indentations, caves, islands, reefs, headlands, points, beaches, cliffs, etc. The maps were the property of the Ordnance Survey office. My father supplied the Gaelic place names, while Delargy wrote them into their correct places on the map. Several of those names were in very old Gaelic, beautiful names like *Cuas Elinore*, Elinore's Cave – I never heard the story of Elinore – and *Boilg Anders*, Ander's Rock; names that link us with the Fianna and the Milesians, like *An Carraig Oisín*, Óisín's Rock, *Carraig Éanna*, Eanna's Rock; and names like *Ceann an Aonaigh*, the Headland of the *Aonach*, *Bosca an Pheidhléara*, the Pedlar's Box, *Leac an Loiscreáin*, the Burning Flagstone, and *Leac a' Phriosúin*, the Prison Rock. Many hundreds of place names he identified that the professor himself found difficult to unravel.

Seamus Delargy was a scholar and master linguist, refined, elegant and gentlemanly, who held the chair of *Roinn Bhéaloideas na hÉireann* in University College Dublin. It was during his first visit to Kerry in 1923 that he attended an Irish summer course for national teachers in Caherdaniel. From there he visited Ballinskelligs and met with Fionán Mac Coluim, a founder member of Conradh na Gaeilge, and old John Harty, a man known to all as Seana Sheán. John was a native Irish speaker and a lover of the Irish tongue who was now retired from his job in South America where he was superintendent of a cable station for Western Union.

Fionán and Seana Sheán helped the professor make his first contact with the great mine of folklore that was Seán Ó Conaill. The fine scholar who had visited and lectured in many lands knew immediately he had discovered the untapped mother lode of a great *seanchaí's* mind. A natural storyteller, he loved to relate exploits of a hero or a family; tales of pre-Christian Ireland or long sagas of perhaps Nordic flavour or a mixture of Greek mythology; tales of Fionn and the Fianna, of great feasts and the chase of the wild boar or the fleet-footed fawn; beautiful tales of King Conor Mac Neasa, 'when the stream ran white', and tales of Queen Maeve, the *Táin Bó Cuailnge* and Cúchulainn; tales that astonished the learned professor.

Skelligs Haul

Seán Ó Conaill loved the beauty of his art. It was said of him that as an old man cowherding on the furzy slopes of his native *Cill Rialaig* he could be heard speaking in a loud voice verses from some poem, or speaking lines from one of his many favourite tales of the past. The *seanchaí* admitted to having no approved education, except two weeks in a hedge school, gaining from life his knowledge of nature and how to survive on a few bleak stony acres perched high on the cliff top overlooking Ballinskelligs Bay.

A small farmer and fisherman, he tilled the most fertile strips between the rocks, as did his neighbours, on a patchwork of small fields. The little grey donkey with the pannier baskets, wooden straddle and *srathar fhada* – straw mattress – was the workhorse who transported the kelp and farmyard manure to the field on the hill. The potato beds were prepared with the long iron spade, a slow and arduous task requiring time and patience. The *sciolláns* or split potatoes, each with two eye sprouts, were laid on a bed of farmyard manure and covered with a generous layer of broken clay. What more rewarding sight on a balmy May evening than the lush green potato beds under full blossom, and better still, to dig the flowery shrubs with clusters of ripening potatoes clinging to their roots on Saint John's Eve! [...]

I spoke with the learned master on the telephone a short time before he died. He talked to me about Ballinskelligs and *Cill Rialaig* in loving terms, of the great wealth of folklore he found there and the grand old *Gaeilgeoirí* he met. It was his intention to return to *Cill Rialaig* again. Seán had assured him that the source of the crystal spring had not run dry and that a new set of stories was already taking possession of his mind. Little did Dr Delargy imagine that this would be the last time he was to spend an evening in the company of the man he had learned to admire so much! A man who had no English and did not understand the language of the Sassanach, Seán Ó Conaill never used coarse or vulgar language, and was always gentle in the delivery of his vast wealth of lore. The last meeting with the gentle Gaelic sage was on Sunday evening, 19 April 1931. I quote from Dr Delargy's own words in Gaelic: 'He walked with me to the gable end of his thatched cottage where he bade me goodbye. Little did I realize it was to be our last meeting. He died a month later, on 21 May 1931.'

Seán and his wife Cáit lie together in *Mainistir Mhichíl*, Ballinskelligs. Their home is now in ruins, but a limestone plaque marks the site where the king of storytellers once lived.

SOME POETS AND A STORYTELLER
Skelligside

From 1650 to 1800, poetry and poets flourished in Ireland. Poets were many in Munster alone, often vying with each other, making poetry in beautiful forms. These masters of the language did not speak the ordinary Irish of today. One of their number was Eoghan Rua Ó Súilleabháin (1748–84), who had poetry ever flowing from his lips like a stream in torrent. This is a stanza translated from one of his poems:

> Poems to relate and simulating gentle tones,
> Dancing and disporting with females untimorous,
> Stately maidens swarming by my side in tranquillity,
> Silken and happy, pleasant, kindly and chaste.

Eoghan travelled throughout South Kerry, often teaching in hedge schools. He was a vagabond and a spendthrift who had a way with women. Young girls were attracted to him in companionship and pleasure. Undoubtedly he had a mysterious power which was called the *ball seirce* or love charm, and his flattery could win any woman he liked. It is said that he deflowered as many as one hundred and eighty-nine maidens. Be that as it may. He who is without blame, let him cast the first stone. The oldest game on earth, the game on the mossy sward, is still played and will be forever.

In his youth, Eoghan was courting a young neighbouring girl. He had been her companion for some time and the girl had fallen in love with him. One summer evening, as the lovers strolled by the river-bank, they came to a ford where stepping-stones were placed in the stream to enable people to cross dry-shod. Eoghan and his love were carefully making their way across when she slipped and fell into a deep pool. The water splashed up under her clothes and wet her. On reaching the bank, the story goes, the girl took off her wet clothes, and turning to Eoghan she said, 'Look, Eoghan, the water jumped up on me – the water itself has more nature than you have.' For that occasion the poet composed the fine lullaby 'Seo Leo a Thoil', which I have translated:

> All ye bards in disgrace
> From Cashel to Doon,
> And you of my tribe
> Who may grieve for my kind,
> Come listen henceforth,
> To my teaching give mind,
> And see what misfortune
> Will always be mine.
>
> And hush a bye,
> Do not cry for a while,
> Hush my baby,
> My treasure and store;

Some Poets and a Storyteller

Your eyes are weeping,
And wanting your feed,
Hush my baby,
Do not cry a tear.

When first I met
With this young pretty maid,
Her eyes were green,
And her cheek like the rose;
She did not refuse me
When her I approached:
My grief, I knew not
The trouble in store.

Her troublesome eyes
And scheming also:
A fair one who'd play
The oldest game known;
She left me all loaded
With sorrow and woe,
A-rocking a baby
And weeping alone.

What plans for the future
For a child of this kind?
Not a drop in my organs
For a soft way of life;
Listen, my baby,
Without doubt you will get
All the good things of life
I propose for you yet.

And hush a bye,
Do not cry for a while,
Hush my baby,

My treasure and store;
Your eyes are weeping,
And wanting your feed,
Hush my baby,
Do not cry a tear.

The following story was told far and wide in South Kerry. On one of the many days Eoghan spent there he met a group of schoolchildren. He had reason to believe that since he had sown some of his wild oats in this region several years before, some of the youngsters should show a poetic strain. Rogue that he was, he would put them to the test. So he saluted them. 'Listen a while, boys! Could ye be so kind as to tell me the name of this townland I'm in at present?' All the youths answered with one voice, 'This is the townland of *Abhainn an Gharraí*, the garden river.'

'Indeed,' said the poet, 'the garden river of the fragrant shrubs!' Not a tree or shrub adorned the place except a potato garden in full bloom beside the road. The poet pointed to this and said, 'That's the garden of the fragrant shrubs, and the boy who will complete the rhyme, I'll give him sixpence.' One boy jumped over the ditch and picked a potato stalk with a cluster of young potatoes clinging to the roots, and holding it up facing the poet, said:

This is the garden river
Of the fragrant shrubs so sweet,
These are the fragrant shrubs
That hold their fruit beneath.

The poet gave the boy the sixpence and told him, 'Whenever we meet again I'll give you the same.' Eoghan went on his way, but he hadn't much of the road behind him before the same boy appeared in front of him with his hand out. 'What do you want?' asked the poet. 'The other sixpence,' said the boy. 'You told me if we ever met again you'd give me another one.' Eoghan had no doubt but that he had a boy as clever as himself to contend with.

Another story is told of how Eoghan fell in love with a young widow with one son. Eoghan was teaching him at the local hedge school. By all accounts, the widow had no great time for Eoghan and disdained his advances. She had a beautiful crown of flaxen hair, such as he described in verse:

Her hair a garland,
Crozier-like and kinky skeins,
Like gloss of gold
Without shadow or haze.

One evening as school was ending the poet called the widow's son aside, telling him to cut a lock of his mother's hair while she was sleeping, and bring it to him the next day. He would use the magic of the *ball seirce*, which never failed him: if one lock of a maiden's hair came into his possession she could not but return his affection. What did the boy do but tell his mother the master wanted a lock of her hair. The mother said, 'Well and good, my son. I'll have it ready for you for school tomorrow.'

Now, that widow had a large fierce dog of mongrel breed, with a golden-yellow coat. She cut a shiny yellow tress from the dog's tail, tied it with a silken ribbon and gave it to her son for the poet, along with an invitation for him to come and visit her. Eoghan was delighted. His heart was light with expectation as he neared the widow's house, whistling and singing. Alas! If he had no story coming, he had one going away, for the fierce yellow dog tore the trousers off him, and the poet decided that a good run was better than a bad stand.

Eoghan Rua Ó Súilleabháin stood out among his contemporaries. He wove words in the loom of his mind with never a difficulty, and there was music and rhythm to all he wrote. This gifted poet had no shortage of themes: love, sadness, conviviality, the wrath of war and the tumultuous storm. I feel true humility drinking a sip from the crystal spring of his legacy, and regret not taking more interest in what was said and told: a vast amount of knowledge and story is covered for ever by the great slab and the green sod.

* * *

Diarmuid O'Shea was born near Kenmare between 1750 and 1760. He stayed for some time in Ballinskelligs as boatman to Francis Sigerson, sailing and managing a hooker kept in the little harbour there. Diarmuid was a gifted poet, giving voice to verse like the bubbling swirl of a stream.

The parish priest of that area had joined Diarmuid and a local woman in wedlock. All was bliss until some busybody revealed that Diarmuid had a blood relationship with his new wife: this was frowned upon by the Church of the time. The parish priest decided that the marriage was invalid and forbade any further meeting between the couple. Diarmuid reverted to bachelorhood in his little cottage near the shore. The story is told of how his former spouse would stand on the hillock, waving her love to her separated husband. Diarmuid composed a poem which he called 'An Scur', 'The Untying of the Marriage Bond'. In this poem, he castigates the parish priest in six stanzas, of which I have translated the second:

Oh Mary and Jesus,
Bright King of nature
Without sin,
Who gathered together
In church yard
All my kith and kin;

Who will light the candles,
And lay my bones to rest,
Or who will call the neighbours
When I sink
In the abyss of death?

A local man was heard lamenting over his brother's corpse in Ballinskelligs in the year of the cholera plague in Europe. People said he was composing poetry unknown to himself:

My grief, my brother,
My curse on death,
Seven cursed be the plague.
Why do you sleep so much?
This world cannot rouse you:
The clamour of the fair,
Nor the army of King James.

In 1785, a year after Eoghan's death, another poet was born in Iveragh. Though an Ó Súilleabháin, and a schoolmaster, Tomás Rua was not related to the great Eoghan. He taught at Caherdaniel, Portmagee, Ballinskelligs and Waterville, and worked as a postman plying the roads between Cahersiveen and Derrynane before dying in 1848.

On one occasion, he lost all his books when a hooker grounded on a submerged reef as it left Derrynane harbour. Tomás composed 'Amhrán na Leabhar', 'The Song of the Books', to lament their loss and curse the captain of the hooker, Dermot Rua O'Rahilly, whose people are still living in the townland of Reen, Ballinskelligs. Dermot Rua spent most of his life fishing out of Ballinskelligs Bay and Derrynane harbour. He often sailed his hooker northward beyond Bolus Head and into the Portmagee channel. His sister Ellen O'Rahilly married Jerry Kirby, my great-grandfather, in the year 1814. I heard my father say that

Dermot Rua suffered from failing eyesight in latter years and this affected his skill in handling the vessel under sail.

Tomás declares in his poem that he was asked by the authorities of the day to go to Portmagee and teach for some time. He had all his books and teaching material packed into great sacks which he loaded on board Dermot Rua's hooker to be delivered to Portmagee. It was a fair night as the hooker weighed anchor. She was slipping through the treacherous gap of Derrynane harbour when the wind suddenly failed. The hooker lost way and slewed onto a shallow reef where her planking caved in. Dermot Rua was at the helm and in his panic threw all the books overboard. The poor people of the time were superstitious about poets, whom they regarded as cut off from ordinary mortals. They were considered to have the power of good or evil, and those on whom a poet laid his curse would be unlucky for the rest of their lives. When Tomás Rua composed 'The Song of the Books' he cursed Dermot O'Rahilly:

> It was Dermot Rua O'Rahilly
> Who cast the books into the sea:
> May the red demons hoist him
> Away up into the sky.

When Ellen O'Rahilly heard the verse being sung, with a dire curse on her brother, she vowed to wreak vengeance on the poet. The country roads were mere cattle tracks, and Tomás Rua travelled by pony to and from his native Caherdaniel. The road from Portmagee led across a beautiful, mountainous district through Saint Finan's Glen, over the hill of Coom and down into the valley of Ballinskelligs. This was the place where Ellen O'Rahilly Kirby lived. Having observed the poet's movements, she lay in wait for him on a certain evening. The unfortunate

Tomás ran into a barrage of rocks and stones, together with a venomous tongue-lashing. He tried to escape but the woman was beside herself with fury. Coming down from his saddle he implored her in God's name to cease hostilities. 'Wait! Wait! Be patient, good woman!' said Tomás. 'The poet was full of fury like you are now when he composed that verse, fury and sadness for the loss of his books. When a cask is full, it only spills out what is within.'

Then he raised the curse from Dermot O'Rahilly and transferred it to the rock that caused the disaster:

God's curse and His Church's
Be on that hateful horrid rock,
Which sank the ship
Without fury of the storm,
Without a wind or gale!

It was no wonder that the poet suffered great distress, as on that same night that his books were lost, his clothes were also destroyed by fire. Here he mourns their loss:

My sorrow, grief and weariness:
I'm the relic of great misery,
Forever in lamentation
For my own sad case.

My wearing apparel scattered
Which was made and fashioned for me,
And came from out of Banba,
As a flower that I should wear.

My books are gone into the sea,
Which makes the story sad,
And my clothing consumed within the flames,
While I lay in trance-like sleep.

That morning people pitied me
So sorrowful bewailing,
And the cold I felt had chilled me,
Without shelter from the sky.

Tomás Rua was about ten years younger than Daniel O'Connell, who observed the poet's genius, and had him sent to a college in Dublin. There the atmosphere, cold and anglicized, was so different to that of his kindly Iveragh that he never felt happy. At the end of three years, he was sent to hospital by order of the visiting physician, Mr John O'Riordan. He appealed to God of the Universe to bring him safe from the house of disease, in Irish verse later sung as a hymn called 'A Rí an Domhnaigh', 'King of Sunday':

O King of Sunday, with aid come near me,
Bring succour to each aching pain;
Bright King of Monday, be always constant
And from your keeping may I never stray.
O King of Tuesday, with heart so loving,
Be Thou my shield on Judgement Day;
O King of Wednesday, do not let me languish,
In bondage far from my kith and kin.
O King of Thursday, I crave forgiveness,
All Your righteous rules I have breached in sin;
O King of Friday, do not keep reckoning
Of each wilful act and each foolish whim.
O King of Saturday, I ever plead You
To guide me safe beyond Acheron's shore;
May Your sacrifice be my shield and patron
In Paradise for evermore.

Tomás Rua was a close friend of Father Dermot O'Sullivan, scion of the O'Sullivan chieftains of the Beara peninsula in West Cork. According to local lore, he was also an able poet.

His presbytery, the White House, was in Kinard West where the O'Connell family now lives. This priest was generous, charitable and holy. The poor people of Prior parish called him the Prince because of his work among the sick and destitute who had barely survived the Great Famine, and they loved him so much they would kneel on the open roadway when he approached. It was said that he often healed the sick and had supernatural powers. This rumour spread until it reached the ears of the bishop in Killarney. One day the bishop arrived with two other priests at the presbytery in Kinard West, where they were entertained by Father O'Sullivan to dinner. During the meal, in the ebb and flow of conversation about the Church and other topics, the bishop found an opportunity to mention the rumours. Was it true that the priest had used strange powers of healing? The bishop asked for a drink and Father Dermot filled him a glass of spring water. On taking the glass to his lips the bishop observed that it was a glass of red wine, at which he became amazed and said, 'But Father Dermot! I only asked for a glass of water!'

'Oh yes, Your Lordship!' exclaimed the other. 'See what the glass contains now.' It was clear spring water once again. It is said that the bishop blessed him and, thanking him for his hospitality, went on his way to Killarney.

Father O'Sullivan was also the author of a book on divinity, in which he had a doctorate. Tomás Rua composed a poem of praise to the good priest called 'The Pleasant Prince'. This is a translation of the first verse:

> He is Doctor of Divinity and Holiness,
> The best in cleric coat and deed;
> We are all the better
> Since he came among us,
> And all interested
> In his good counsel;

Skelligs Haul

A branch of light,
A servant of Jesus Christ,
A brave and active soldier,
He is Dermot of the bright heart,
He is the Prince I boast of,
The flower of all good chieftains.

[...]

THE TALE OF THE HAUNTED PIPER
Skelligs Sunset

Stimulating memories fill my mind, bringing a yearning for customs of the past. Winds of change, together with the vehicle called 'mass media', provide push-button entertainment for almost every household and family circle. More than four score years and seventeen have flown since I was born. As a boy of yet tender years, I can remember sitting happily near the cosy glow of a stacked peat fire, full of tremulous, dancing flames, within the wide chimney breast of my parents' kitchen. Each night our neighbours came in their own good time and would sit in their usual places. The long winter seemed all too short. Time flew under the spell of the *seanchaí* and the saga. A discussion would usually start on topics such as farming, turf cutting, fairs, matchmaking, etc., often laced with humorous allusions to the sexual suitability of the couples mentioned. The womenfolk also took part in such discussions and merry banter. Weather formed an important part of the conversation.

My father, John Kirby, whose main occupation was fishing, always came under fire from a barrage of questions

The Tale of the Haunted Piper

from small farmers interested in seasonal crop-raising: 'What do you think of the weather, John?' 'Are we in for a dry spell?' and 'Will tomorrow be fine?' Sleeping or waking, a fisherman was supposed to keep his weather eye open, reading the clouds and the telltale signs of approaching depressions. My father was a tall, well-built man, spare but muscular. His face had distinct Hellenistic features, and he wore a Moses-like auburn beard with natural whorls. In a film he would be a ready-made stand-in portraying some biblical figure. I think that because he was a fisherman he was regarded by some as the village barometer.

The neighbours were no different from any others who lived in the surrounding area, each person possessing individuality in his or her make-up. All were good-natured characters with traits of attractiveness and charm; each would show a different ability when telling a story. Some were gifted narrators, well able to catch the imagination of the listener through the captivating, beguiling power of the telling. Tomáisín Sugrue told tales of great storms, of ships in distress and rooftrees stripped in the violence of a great wind. He seemed very much at ease when relating a story, speaking in a slow, confident manner; a past master knitting detail into the fabric of his weaving. Tales of haunted houses and premonitions of tragic events foretelling disaster were all part of his repertoire. He had a wealth of information regarding the local landlords and the established order of the day. He liked to give a correct and factual account of all historical events of the past, always speaking in a beautiful, easily understood Gaelic. One neighbour in particular told the most fantastic cock-and-bull stories, swearing by all the blessed powers as to the veracity of each word. Tomáisín could not contain himself when listening to such rigmarole, and would object by saying in Gaelic: '*Bail ó Dhia ar an scéal gan dath!*' 'God bless the tale without colour!' or 'I would rather listen to the braying of an ass!'

My mother was the only person who had freedom of movement during the storytelling session. She could put more peat on the fire and provide a drink of water if the need arose, or maybe a firebrand to light someone's pipe. I sometimes heard her give advice in whispering, cautionary terms to younger unmarried women who sat by the fireside, to cover their knees and stop giggling.

Storytelling was a serious business and we did not approve of any emotional distraction that might cause the *seanchaí* to lose his concentration. I listened to my father tell a strange story about a happening that took place in his grandfather's time. It was the 'Tale of the Haunted Piper'. As far as I can recollect, this was how he recounted the story handed down to him by his own father, Timothy Kirby.

'When my father Jerry arrived home from net-fishing accompanied by two other sons one late autumn night, he found not unusually that his wife Eileen O'Rahilly-Kirby had given shelter to a poor displaced person, one of many who were destitute mendicants wandering aimlessly as a result of the Great Hunger. This time it happened to be the figure of a tall, gaunt, middle-aged man, who sat in a hunched position by the dying embers of the kitchen fire. A tattered greatcoat hung loosely across his shoulders, while a set of pipes lay beside him on the long kitchen settle, commonly named the rack, *an raca* in Gaelic. As Jerry Kirby was about to make conversation with the stranger, Eileen Kirby burst into the room with two younger children clinging to her side. All seemed in a very distraught state of mind. "Oh, Jerry! Oh, Jerry! We are so glad you are here," she exclaimed. "We were so frightened. Thank God you have come back."

'Trembling and shaking like a leaf, Eileen clung to her husband. Jerry Kirby stood for a moment in shock and bewilderment before turning towards the huddled figure by the fireplace and declaring in an angry voice: "Tell me,

The Tale of the Haunted Piper

Eileen, tell me quickly, is it this rootless old vagabond who has interfered with you? If he has dared upset you I'll tear him apart!"

'"Oh, no! Jerry, no! It is the fairies or bad spirits! The house is full of them, the *púcaí* [fairy host]."

'A vacuous look of disbelief spread over Jerry's countenance. Putting his arms around Eileen he said soothingly: "Come dear, you are very confused. You must go back to bed. I fear you are developing a fever."

'"I am not sick, Jerry! You must be blind! Can you not see all our seed potatoes for next spring scattered beneath your feet?"

'"But Eileen, the seed potatoes are stored in the loft over the back kitchen."

'No sooner had Jerry uttered those words than the commotion started again. Chairs moved, delph on the dresser danced and the crouched figure by the fireside was being pelted incessantly with what was left of the precious seed potatoes. Two large balls of homemade twisted grass rope, called *súgáns*, which were in hand for securing the thatched roof next autumn, came tumbling down the ladder from the loft above, dancing and bounding precariously close to Jerry and his wife, as if thrown by a team of professional basketball players. Jerry grabbed one of the bouncing balls only, to his amazement, it was swiftly snatched from his grasp by some unseen force, and thrown violently towards the visitor sitting at the fireside. It was at this juncture that Jerry concluded that the figure by the fireside must be jinxed or harassed by some nasty poltergeist. Throwing wide the kitchen door, he decided to take action by ordering the piper to leave at once. "Please! Please! Let me stay until the dawn," said the piper, "All will be quiet then!" Jerry Kirby, being a kind and charitable man, together with his wife Eileen, kept vigil with the tormented wayfarer until morning, when all was peaceful again. They allowed him rest for some time and gave him food and alms before he travelled on. He never divulged his identity or mentioned why he was haunted by the unseen throwing spirits.'

My father also mentioned how the piper stayed the next night in a house at Ballinskelligs West, where the macabre, mysterious manifestations were experienced again. My father was a serious person who would not bother trying to unravel the esoteric. He accepted the evidence that such happenings existed and are still part of human observation.

A Net of Verse

Turas na Sceilge

Chuaigh mé go dtí an Sceilg inniu,
Mise iascaire
Gan bhréide
Gan folt maise
Gan leabhar
Gan sreang púiríní
Idir méara,
Im' bhalbhán
Ag éisteacht
Le clocha
Ag insint
Gur aiséirigh
Nasairéineach,
Mac siúinéara
Ós na mairbh.
Bhí na faireoga
Sa chuas
Ag rá:

'Bhíomar ann rompu,
Táimid anseo fós.
'Cuimhin leat
Oíche an tslada,
Fothram maidí rámha
Ag teacht aduaidh
Ón Ioruaidh?
Is Danair gan trua,
Foghlaí farraige,
Thar toinne anoir;
Na báid mhaola
Gach sciath
Ar shliasta leo.'

A Ancaraigh,
Nach fuar iad
Bhur gcillíní anocht?
Ach táid na clocha
Ag insint fós
Agus na faireoga sa chuas,
A iascaire,
Caith chucu
Giota pollóg.

Barra Taoide

A Fisherman's First Visit to Skellig Michael

I visited Skellig Michael
Today,
A fisherman
Without homespun
Cowl or tonsure,
Book or beads
Between fingers,
Listening dumbfounded
To flagstones
Telling
Of a Nazarene,
The Carpenter's Son,
Who from death
Had risen.
The kittiwakes
In the cave
Saying:

'We were here then!
We are here still!
Do you remember
The dark night

Skelligs Haul

Of plunder,
The clamour
And the boom
Of the Northmen's
Great oars
Coming on the wind?
And the Danes
Without mercy
Raving for loot?
Over the wave
From the East
Came sea robbers,
Their bald prows
And shielded gunwales
Concealing
Battle-axe and spear.'

Humble Anchorites,
Your ravaged cells
Are prayerless tonight,
But flagstones
Whisper yet,
And kittiwakes
In the cave.

Skelligside

Sean-Sceilg Mhichíl

Anocht táim im' dheoraí na mílte i gcéin,
I bhfad ó mo ghaolta is óm' mhuintirse féin,
Ach nach tapaidh a léimfinn is a rithfinn gan mhoill,
Ach radharc d'fháil arís ar shean-Sceilg Mhichíl.

Is cuimhin liom an lá úd cois feorainn na trá
Go rabhas agus tusa ag siúl lámh ar láimh,

A Net of Verse

Gur thugais do bhriathar is do phóigín gan mhoill,
Sinn geallta dá chéile cois Sceilg Mhichíl.

Bhí ciúnas tráthnóna ag titim ar shliabh,
Is cantain na n-éanlaith go binn ar gach craoibh;
Nach álainn bhí failltreacha Bhólais ina suí
Faoi ardbheannaibh naofa shean-Sceilg Mhichíl?

Mo shlán beo anocht chun do ghlaschnoc mór ard,
Is chun bánta Uíbh Ráthaigh faoi luibh is faoi bhláth;
Mo shlán chun mo stóirín atá sínte sa chill,
Is mo shlán beo go deo leat, a shean-Sceilg Mhichíl.

Íochtar Trá

My Lovely Skellig's Shore

This night my heart is heavy,
My eyes are dim with tears.
In memory I'm taken back
To boyhood days of yore,
Where I lived in happy childhood
By my lovely Skellig's shore.

There, in springtime of the year
The young bright flowers, they show.
The lily and the violet blue
And golden primrose blow.
Dakota's hills are beautiful,
The Texan plains and more –
I'd leave them all to walk again
My lovely Skellig's shore.

Kinard and Coom stand side by side
Where the road comes winding down.

Skelligs Haul

In the valley stands supreme and grand
Old Canuig Mountain brown.
The huntsman's pack has waked the morn,
I hear the hillside roar.
Ah, rue the day I went away
From my lovely Skellig's shore!

Kilreelig fair beyond compare,
Its shady dales and dells
Where golden furze and woodbine mix
With purple heather bells.
Oft-times I joined the seine boatmen
And pulled the long clamp oar,
When we hunted shoals of mackerel
By my lovely Skellig's shore.

A mist comes on the islands
And the mountains of my heart.
Your castle and the shining sands
Are tearing me apart.
The crossroad dance
Where lovers glance,
I ne'er will see you more,
The melodeon softly tuning
By my lovely Skellig's shore.

A sadness clouds my heart tonight,
When I know I cannot go
To lay my bones in Ireland
But on a foreign shore.
No neighbours kind will wake me,
No funeral sad and slow
To lay me down in Abbey ground,
By my lovely Skellig's shore.

Farewell to Ballinskelligs!
I may never see you more,
The castle and the Abbey
That stand beside the shore.
Your purple hills so beautiful,
I'll miss you ever more,
Farewell to Ballinskelligs
And my lovely Skellig's shore.

Skelligs Sunset

Mo Bháidín

Bhí tú beo
tamall
fán gcoill,
ceol cleití
id' ghéaga.

Bhí tú beo arís
ar bharr toinne
agus ceol maidí rámha
id' ábhar.

Mo ghraidhin tú,
mo chara dlúth.
Is dona liom
scaradh leat
amárach.

Ceol Maidí Rámha

My Boat

You were no smoke-belching
Rusty hulk
Looming the horizon,

Skelligs Haul

Spilled from the fiery porridge
Of a furnace ladle.

You were the forest-born one
Burst from the womb
Of a seed-spilling acorn,
A sun-glad Spring your midwife,
Trill of the thrush your birthsong,
Reincarnated vibrant planks
Alive beneath my feet. My boat,
Past memories haunt the furrows
Of my mind.

Together we grew old.
Together we watched pale dawns
Replace the dusky canvas
Of many a fisher's night.

You, my faithful ballerina,
Wave-danced with me
Across the stream-foamed headlands.
Together we lie,
Anchor cast and sail furled,
Safe in the harbour of our memories.

Skelligs Calling

Dán dom' Athair

Gluais ort, a Dhaid,
Ardóimid ár seolta sí
Go bhfágfam an cuan seo.
Leagse a thosach le gaoth.
Ciorraigh an siota
Go luífidh a sliasta anonn
Ag tabhairt guala

A Net of Verse

Do shúistí bog cúrach
Thar ríocht na dtonn.

Mise agus tusa, a Dhaid,
Agus Dia inár dteannta,
Réalt eolais an Mhoil
Ag rince os ár gcrann,
Gach leoithne bog ceolmhar
Ag seinm ar théada teann,
Sinn ag bogadh abhaile
Gan bhárthainn
Thar ríocht na dtonn.

Duanaire Mhaidhcí; Barra Taoide

To My Father

Only us both,
You and I,
With God
Up on high,
The wing
Of the gull,
The cloud,
The star
In the sky.
The soft surging
Seas,
The night
And a new dawn
In store.
The beacons
Are lighting us home
To Heaven's bright shore.

Skelligside

Skelligs Haul

Miangas

Do bhagair sleasa na mbeann
Ag cur glaoch orm ón ngleann,
Do chorraigh mo mhoilleacht
Is d'fhág mé faoi mhiangas trom –
Mé a bheith thuas i mease na gcarraig
Ag dreapadh na maolchlochán,
Gan eagla orm go dtitfinn
Ach spleodar im' chroí agus gáir.

Ansiúd is ea a bheinn ag éisteacht
Le crónán na mbeacha rua
Ag siolpadh drúcht na meala
As cupáin fhraoigh gan stua,
Agus géimneach tréada im' chluasa
Thar leabaidh an ghleanna anall
Nuair a chasfaid abhaile chun eadra
Le maolú na gréine ag dul uainn.

Do chífinn arís Dubh Inis
An t-oileán úd amuigh faoin spéir;
Na cuasa faoi sciatháin ghléigheala
'Gus grágarlach na n-éan;
An foirichín go huaigneach
Ag glaoch go hard sa cheo,
Na sulairí á dtumadh féin
Is ag tabhairt a mbeatha leo.

Tógfad scíth ar an gcarraig
Go hard ar spíc an tsléibhe,
Áit go dtiteann drúcht an tsonais
Ó ríocht gheal Flaithis Dé;
Ní bheidh suim agam in ama
I lúib na creige im' shuí,

Ní bheidh miangas ar m'intinn
Ná mairg ar mo chroí.

Íochtar Trá; Skelligs Sunset

Yearning

I was restless.
A yearning had come
To climb the hillside
Of Canuig,
Up where silver mist
Hung curtained
On the crag,
Laced with golden arrows
From a slanting sun.

There I will listen
To red bees,
Murmuring delight,
Sipping sweet nectar
From purple heather pap.
And watch the lowing kine
Wend homeward
Across
The valley's lap.

There I will see
The hermit's rock again,
Skellig Michael
And the blue cave
Where kittiwakes complain,
Scariff Island
And its martyr,

Skelligs Haul

His gushing blood
Not in vain.

Friar Francis,
Stand and shield us
From Hades' lasting pain.
There I will rest
In the crook of the crag,
Where peace of eve
Droops dew
From heaven.
All I ask,
That time be measured
By the looping wing
Of that homeward heron.

Skelligside; Skelligs Sunset

Coinne

Do Bhrian Ó Dochartaigh

Bhí an bóithrín
meirbh le coinne
agus mise corraithe
ag feitheamh,
mo chíocha
teann le tine
i nglasnasc an ghrá.
Cen díobháil satailt
ar bhualtacha feoite,
cearcaillí féarghlasa
ag borradh uathu!
Ba breaca
taobh thall de chlaí

A Net of Verse

ina luí,
ag scéith
le huachtar buí,
Ag brúchtaíl
is ag osnaíl,
ag cogaint a gcíorach
is ag casadh na ngar.
Bhí drisleoga
ina gcrotháin chraobhaing
crochta ar ghuaille,
an t-aiteann bláfar
go caor bheirteach sméarach
nuair a d'éalaigh sé im' dháil.

Sheas sé suas
taobh liom ag féachaint
le hionadh
ar phíosa geal airgid
lánroth na ré;
in ionad na réalt
ag spréacharnaigh
ina shúile
bhí faitíos an neamhchiontais –
b'fhéidir eagla roimh mhná.
B'é seo ár gcéad choinne
fé cheilt
fé chosc
fé thoirmeasc
i ngáirdín an tsóigh.

Bhí gathaí ré ag cleasaíocht
is ag caitheamh
saigheada boga linn.
Chum mé ciorcal le mo bheola
chun é a phógadh.

Skelligs Haul

D'fhéach sé orm go fonnmhar;
Roinneas bláthfhleasc
gathaí gléineach
ar a éadan
le mo mhéara.

Huis, éist
leis an sagart críonna
ag siúl ina aonar
ar an mbóthar iata,
buillí beaga
maide draighne
mar chloigín adhmaid
ag tomhas na hoíche.
Bainig taitneamh
as an solas.
Is leis an útamálaí an dorchadas.
Osnaíl ba breaca
lán sochma
'na luí,
brúchtaíl anála
le clos thar claí,
bóithrín meirbh
le túis chumhra
agus sú dearg
ó sméara dubha.

Cloigín adhmaid
ina thost cois falla,
sagart críonna
síoch ina chodladh.

Skelligs Sunset; Barra Taoide

Tryst

The old lane is sultry.
I am excited
In expectation,
My breasts on fire,
Taut in manacles
Of love.
What matter
If I tread
The withered
Cow turds
That give birth
To green fertility?

Speckled cows
Lie beside the hedge,
Udders swollen
With yellow cream,
Belching and sighing
Chewing and turning
The cud.
Berry-bearing
Briars
Intertwine with
Golden-blossomed
Furze.

Suddenly he stands
Beside me,
Gazing in wonder
At the silver wheel
Of the night.
Instead of stars
In his eyes

Skelligs Haul

I see
Timidity of innocence
Or fear
Of womanhood.

This our first
Meeting,
Concealed,
Forbidden,
Secret.
In the garden
Of desire
Moon shafts
Played
And laid
A silver spell
Of love.

I wove for him
A charm
Of pouted lips.
He glanced
At last
With longing
In his eyes
And with my fingertips
I 'graved
A silver wreath
Of moonbeams
On his brow.

Hush! Listen! it is
The old priest
Who walks alone
The back road,

And like a wooden bell,
The tapping
Of his thorn stick
Proclaims the night
As if to say,
'Enjoy the light,
Darkness is only
For the groping.'

The speckled cows
Lie comfortable
Beside the hedge,
Sighing and belching,
Chewing and turning
The cud.

The old lane
Is sultry.
Flaming fragrant
Furze blossom
Makes incense
With berry-bearing
Briar.

The old priest
Sleeps.
The wooden bell
Is silent.

Skelligside

Skelligs Haul

Deireadh na Buana

Do Mhícheál Ó Siochrú, Lá 'le Pádraig 1985

Nach álainn í gealach na gcoinnleach
Ag doirteadh síoda ar gach gleann,
Gathaí ré i mease na bpunann –
An t-arbhar sínte ina sreatha troma.

Téanam, a ghrá, go gort na stuacán
Mar a bhfuil na stácaí á cur ar bonn,
Agus déanfam ceol am deireadh na buana
I measc sióg ag damhsa ann.

Tá scioból fairsing i Ríocht an Mháistir,
Agus tabhair gach dias den arbhar leat –
Gach sop den dea-bharr, is ná fág aon choinlín,
Mar gurb é an brobh a dheineann beart.

Íochtar Trá

The Harvest Moon

How beautiful
The harvest moon
Spinning silver silk
In every glen;
Moonbeams mingle
While rich swathes
Slumber within
Their stubbled beds.
Come! Let us go,
To where great ricks
Are making,
Where golden sheaves
Are garnered

For the grain;
Tonight we feast
The festival
Of the reaping,
And dance
With elves
Beneath the harvest moon.

Skelligside

The Road to Bolus

The road home to Bolus
Gives me great solace.
There I'll tarry a while
From all worldly care,
Where woodbine and fern,
With honey-sweet heather
All tangle together,
And perfume the air.

An exile returning
And fervently burning
To see the old homestead
I left years ago.
I will rest on the doorstep
In peaceful contentment,
Where the dark cliffs
Of Bolus
Rise up from below.

I see the white gannet
Of dark pinions soaring,
Scanning the ocean
Its prey to pursue.
Then suddenly closing

Skelligs Haul

Its wings as an arrow,
Like a spear
Cast from heaven
It enters the blue.

The hush of the evening
On hillside is stealing,
And high from the shieling
Come notes from a horn,
Across through Duchealla,
A brown fox is leaping,
The huntsman is calling,
His hounds to withdraw.

I see from my window,
The place of my childhood.
The tower on the hillside,
White wings on the sea,
A lobster man hauling,
His pots in the dawning,
Ceann Bólais is calling:
'O come home to me'.

Gone are the old folk,
Who blessed us in Gaelic.
The new ways will follow
In eternity's plan.
The speech of the stranger
Sounds empty and hollow,
But the road home to Bolus,
Let all horsemen pass.

A Net of Verse

Caiple Bána

Bhí caiple bána ag damhsa ar an inbhear aréir –
Na caiple bána d'ardaigh na marcaigh leo siar –
Nach duairc í an chailleach ina seasamh ar charraig na bhfiach?
Ach ní duairce ná an brón dubh atá suite in íochtar mo chléibh.

Nuair a sheasaim ar maidin ag féachaint thar shaoistí na dtonn
Ag súil leanúr bhfilleadh nó comhartha ó Oileán na bhFionn –
Ní bhfuaireas ach seaicéad a bhí smeartha le cúr bán is ruaim,
Is bhí caiple bána ag rince is ag damhsa fán gcuan.

Tá bhur leabaí gan cóiriú anocht is gan bhraillíní glé,
Ach cliabhán an Téitis á luascadh go síor leanúr dtaobh;
Beidh sí-chóir na mara mar shuantraí go deo leanúr suan,
Is na caiple bána ag damhsa amuigh ar an gcuan.

Tá mo chroí-se ina dhobhar is gan stealladh na fola trím' bheoibh,
Is beidh taisteal bhur máithrín tré ghleanntáin an uaignis go deo –
Cé ionadh duit gáire, a Théitis, i gCathair na dTonn,
Is do chaiple bána ag rince is ag damhsa fán gcuan!

Íochtar Trá

Am
A free translation of H. Twells's poem, 'Time's Paces'.

Gol agus suan im' naíonán dom –
Am ró-bhuan.

Skelligs Haul

Garsún gáireach cainteach umhal –
Am ag siúl.

Cuisle an fhir im' chorp ag crith –
Am ag rith.

Fáibrí aois, dronn agus preiceall –
Am ag eiteall.

Is gearr go mbead faoi scáth na lice –
Am imithe.

Íochtar Trá

Storm Petrel

They name you Mother Carey's chick,
Abandoned waif
Of storm.
Why your raucous,
Mocking chuckle,
Web-toed, witching wisp,
Surf-boarding the seething,
Tumbling lip
Of curling, frothing billow?
O happy creature
Who can sleep
Contentedly
In far-flung heaving
Pastures deep
Which make
Your bedtime pillow!
Before Columbus
Ere set sail
You wave-danced storms –
Yes, long before

Flying Dutchman's wraith
Did haunt
Stout mariners who dared
With broken spar
And torn sail
To battle
With the scourging wave
Of mighty Horn.
Mysterious sprite,
Are you the David
Of the deep
Who watched proud
Goliath-galleons
Sink to sleep?
What balance
In wild nature's house
You keep!
New sailors do not
Fear you any more!
Sea witch,
It's cradle time
Once more!
New joy,
New chicks,
New love nests
On the shore.

Skelligs Sunset

Who Scattered the Stars?

Hark! From the abyss
Of darkness
A mighty rumbling roared,
Likened
To a voice-command:

Skelligs Haul

'Roll back, dark night!
My blinding stars
Will fill
The infinite
With light.
I do not toll
A funeral bell
For you!
I give you life,
I fill the seas,
And rock is born,
Where angry wind
Lays battle to a wave.'

Dewdrops glisten
Like diamond glass.
Moonbeams spin
Silk spiders' skeins
Of fairy silk
Among morning stalks
Of grass.

It is time to scatter the stars,
Time to light a thousand
Billion lamps,
To pebble-dash a beach,
Wood a forest,
And flow a river.
Time to banish serpents,
Time to seek the spirit,
Time to be crucified
With love.
Time to wonder,
Time to ponder,
Time to stand in awe,

Trying to understand
Who scattered the stars.

Skelligs Sunset

An Bleachtán Órga

A chréatúirín ghleoite
Ag seasamh go cúthaileach
Gan fothain gan foscadh
I ndoras an Earraigh
Id' ghúna uaithne!

Is drithleog ón ngrian tú
Led' bheolaibh néalta,
Is na beacha ad' phógadh,
Agus ar do chromchinn
Na treisleáin órga.

Ná bí critheaglach –
Tá an geimhreadh imithe thart,
Nóiníní timpeall ort,
Is an samhradh ag gliúcadh
Thar dhroim do ghuaille.

Nach é Críost a dúirt é,
Céad moladh go deo leis,
Ná raibh Solomon riamh
In airde a ghlóire
In éide chomh breá
Le mo bhleachtáinín órga?

Íochtar Trá

Cranna

Sceach gheal na Bealtaine
Faoi bhláth agus finne,
Mar bhrídeach bhán
Ar altóir na cruinne.

Slat chaol fuinseoige
Ag lúbadh le gaoith,
Mar leanbh bliana
Ag tabhairt faoi choiscéim slí.

Crann glas giúise
Ina sheasamh díreach
Mar shaighdiúir cróga
Ar son a tíre.

Sean-chrann daraí
Mar fhear faonlag críon,
Maidí croise a ghéaga gabhlógach,
Bileoga feoite a bhalcaisí.

Crann donn sailí
Mar sheanbhean feasa,
A fallaing leata
De dhroim an easa.

Meathfaidh an phréamh
Agus titfidh an crann,
Ach geamharfaidh an síol
Arís in am.

Sinne na cranna
Óg agus críonna,

Sinne na cranna
Cam agus díreach.

Crann thar chrannaibh
Ar Chnocán Calvair,
Le géaga geala
Nar fhás riamh air.

Crann na Croise
Ár ndídean is Críost,
I gcoilltibh na bhFlaitheas
Go bhfásam arís.

Íochtar Trá

Duan-Phaidir

A Athair na Cruinne,
Go dtagair im' choinnibh
Nuair a bheidh an bás am' thraochadh –
Las coinneal mo bhaiste,
Cuir arís im' ghlaic é,
Is ná leig m'anam ar strae uait.

Óir is tusa a ghlac trua
Dos na mílte slua,
Is tú a mhéadaigh an t-arán
Is an t-iasc dóibh,
Is le grá dom féin
Gur fhulaing tú an phéin
Go hard ar chrois do chéasta.

A aoire na maitheasa,
Bailigh chugat m'anamsa
Agus maith dhom mo ghníomhartha baoise
Go bhfeicfeadsa tusa

Skelligs Haul

Trí shúilibh an linbh
Ar mo shlí chun na cathrach naofa,

Óir is tusa do chneasaigh
Na bacaigh is daill,
Is na céadta aige deamhain
A bhí créachta.
Is le trua dom féin
Gur fhulaing tú an phéin
Go hard ar chrois do chéasta.

Íochtar Trá

Faire go Deo

(*Dom' chara Micheál Ó hAirtnéide. Nuair a bhuaileas leis i Lios Tuathail i ndeireadh Bealtaine '84, dúirt sé liom gur cheap sé go rabhas marbh le tamall anuas.*

For my friend Michael Hartnett. When I met him in Listowel in late May '84, he told me that he thought I had been dead for some time.)

Ta an file faoi throm-ualach –
Carn blianta ina mhála,
A choiscéim ag ciorrú
Le giorra anála –
Faire go deo,
Tusa i dTeampall an Ghleanntáin
Agus mise i mBaile an Sceilg faoi chumha!

Bhí cara dom
Seal gairid liom
Fadó.
Ba ghliondarach
I dteach an leanna sinn

A Net of Verse

Fadó.
Cúr na gcárt
Mar fhéasóga orainn –
Faire go deo,
Tusa i dTeampall an Ghleanntáin
Agus mise i mBaile an Sceilg faoi chumha!

Sinne inár leanaí fásta
Ag raideadh ranna le chéile,
Inár n-ógánaigh doirthe le smaointe
Agus inár seanfhilí,
Ag tórmaigh le dánta –
Faire go deo,
Tusa i dTeampall an Ghleanntáin
Agus mise i mBaile an Sceilg faoi chumha.

Mo bháidín ina chreatlach,
Mo chranna ag gíoscán,
Gan leoithne im' sheolta,
Ag meabhrú cuain sa cheo –
Faire go deo,
Tusa i dTeampall an Ghleanntáin
Agus mise i mBaile an Sceilg faoi chumha.

Glaoim ort, mo chaptaen,
Réalt eolais na taoide,
A stiúrfaidh mo bharc
Thar gach fochais doimhin fíochmhar
Go cuan geal an Pharthais –
Mar a mairfeam go deo
Ins an áit ná beidh choíche
Aon 'fhaire deo'!

Íochtar Trá

Gairdín Gréine

(*Dán do Mhicheál Ó hAirtnéide a bhronn orm an dán 'An Práta'. Freagra é seo ar 'An Práta'.*

A poem for Michael Hartnett, who presented me with the poem, 'The Potato'. This is a response to 'The Potato'.)

Tháinig an dámh
le haoileach, scian, sciollán,
a pheann mar rámhainn
ag déanamh ithir úir
de thalamh lom
ná raibh toirt ann,
is d'fhág agam
gáirdín gréine
na gcrannaíoll cumhra,
is a dtorthaíoll fúthu
go plúrach bán.

An file aigeanta
do bhronn orm 'An Práta'
a thug faoiseamh ocrais
don ainléann im' lár;
is beidh mé aireach
im' gháirdín gréine
ag scagadh cogall
ón dea-bharr;
ath-threabhadh
do dheinis
ar m'intinn saolta,
is ní bheidh mé a thuilleadh
im' shíorbhochtán.

Íochtar Trá

Ollscoil Scairte

(*Nuair a chuala go raibh an tAthair Padraig Ó Fiannachta, ollamh le Nua-Ghaeilge i Maigh Nuad, chun ollscoil scairte do bhunú, chumas aoir dó ag cúirt filíochta i ndaonscoil Uíbh Ráthaigh.*)

When I heard that Father Padraig Ó Fiannachta, Professor of Modern Irish in Maynooth, intended to found a 'hedge university', I composed a satire for him at daonscoil Uíbh Ráthaigh.)

Im' thaisteal dom thar bhántaibh réidhe
Faoin ngealach lán ag fuí geal glé
Is ea a chuala an uaill
Agus an rille-ruaille
Ón liosachán le hais na coille –
Do ghliúcas féin thar claí isteach,
Cé go raibh mo chroí ar lagmhisneach
Le heagla gurb iad na daoine maithe,
An slua sí nó na haingil reatha
A bheadh ag déanamh scléipe
I lár na hoíche
Gan éinne saolta
Dá bhfeiscint choíche . . .
Ach cé a bheadh ann
Ina ranganna dlúth
Ach feirmeoirí an bhaile
Faoi lánchruinniú,
Agus bhíodar ag maíomh
Go gcaithfí feasta
Cosc do chur le hollscoil scairte!
Do labhair sean-chabaire crabanta críonna:
'Cé a bhainfidh móin,
Nó cé a chuirfidh síolta?

Skelligs Haul

Beidh oideachas le fáil
Aige Seán is Séamas,
Is ní measa breis de
Ná bheith dá éagmais!
Beidh oiliúint le fáil
Aige Cáit agus Síle,
Agus an aimid gan chéill
An chléip is an straoille!
Cé a chrúfaidh bó,
Nó cé a dhéanfaidh císte?
Beidh caipín cearnógach
Ar fhia na coille,
Ar chapall is ar mhiúil,
Is ar an bpocán buile!
Agus cé fé ndear é seo go léir
Ach an sagart is oilte dá bhfuil sa chléir!
Cad a dhéanfaimid leis?
B'fhéidir labhairt go dian –
É a ruagairt thar lear go dtí an Bhruiséil!'

Íochtar Trá

Litir do Dháithí

(*Litir i bhfoirm dáin do chuireas go dtí an Dochtúir Dáithí Ó nÓgáin roinnt bliana ó shin nuair a bhí mé tar éis tuairisc a fháil uaidh ar ghinealach mhuintir Chiarmhaic.*

A letter in poetic form that I sent to Dr Dáithí Ó nÓgáin some years ago when I got information from him about the Kirby family genealogy.)

A Dháithí, a chara,
Do dheinis an riabhach orm
Nár fhágais im' shuan mé

A Net of Verse

Cois an Sceilg mhóir ghoirm –
Mo leaba dá luascadh
Le suantraí na mara
Nuair a dhúis fear an phoist mé
Le litir óm' chara.

In aisling aréir dom,
Slán beo mar a n-instear,
Go rabhas thuaidh i gCnoc Áine
I bpalás mo shinsear –
Bhí mil ghréige is beoir ann
Á riar ar na fearaibh,
An mart is an ruaphoc
Á róstadh ar bhearaibh.

Bhí ógbhruinneal teannbhrollaigh
Anteasaí pógach
Ag súgradh le ceithirnigh
Scianbhúclach adharcógach –
Is go deimhin duit, a Dháithí,
A fhíorscoth na léann-mhac,
Is ro-bhreá do shuigh órbhuí
Ar éadan Uí Chiarmhaic.

Bhí an fáidh is an draoi ann,
Ceol téada dá stealladh,
An phíb bheag is mhór ann
Ag baint fuaime is macalla;
Is le hordú Rí Ailill
Thug na laochra trí ngártha
Mar omós do Mhaidhc bocht
Ó íochtar Uíbh Ráthach.

Nuair a d'fhágas Cnoc Áine
Do bhíos ag siúl romham,

Skelligs Haul

Ag taisteal bóithríní
Caol cúnga na Mumhan;
Bhí síolrach Uí Chiarmhaic
Ag brostú ina scuainte
Ag teitheadh ó dheas
Ag lorg foscadh na gcuanta.

Céad gráin ort, a Chromail,
Ná raibh t'anam i bpéin-lic,
A chuir an fán ar mo mhuintir
Fíor-uasal Uí Chiarmhaic –
Ar dhúiseacht arís dom
Nach mé do bhí sásta
Bheith cois Sceilg na Naomh thiar
Mar a bhfuil aoibhneas is grásta!

Íochtar Trá

EDITORIAL NOTE

Micheál Ua Ciarmhaic's / Michael Kirby's distinctive voice, discernible throughout *Skelligs Haul*, conveys his deep, mystical love and acute observation of Skelligside, which he drew from his lifelong experience as fisherman, farmer, artist, observer of humanity and amateur zoologist.

The works included in *Skelligs Haul* are organized around eight themes, together with a section devoted to reproductions of Kirby's paintings and a final section that contains twenty-five poems in Irish and English. Kirby freely translated some of his own poems (as well as one English-language poem entitled 'Time's Paces', by Henry Twells, which he had encountered as a schoolboy). The titles of books in which Kirby's writing was previously published are noted.

The principle governing the editing process has been to allow Kirby's voice to prevail with minimal editorial intrusion. Most of his occasional divergences from the official standard of written Irish, *an caighdeán oifigiúil*, remain unaltered. Exceptions are made to this where there are internal inconsistencies or clear inaccuracies. In one poem, '*Caiple Bána*', for example, twice Kirby writes '*leanúr*', meaning 'to/by/with your' (plural), but elsewhere in the same poem writes '*lenúr*'. The official standard would require '*le bhur*'. Here the decision taken was consistently to adopt Kirby's preferred spelling, '*leanúr*', rather than the standard '*le bhur*'. The standard plural form of '*capall*', a horse, is '*capaill*', not '*caiple*', which is Kirby's preference, but that too remains unaltered. However, in the poem '*Turas na Sceilge*', the inaccurate '*Chuaig*', for example, was emended to read '*Chuaigh*', and the standard imperative form '*Caith*' replaces '*Chaith*'.

The principle of minimal interference is applied to the non-standard spellings of some Irish placenames. For example, the Placenames Database of Ireland of the Placenames Branch of the Department of Culture, Heritage and the Gaeltacht has determined that '*Trá Phraisce*' is the authoritative version of the place name that Kirby terms '*Tráigh Fraisce*'. Nonetheless, Kirby's spelling remains unchanged.

Punctuation has been silently corrected in both Irish and English. Irish-language placenames have been italicized. The occasional misquotations of other writers' verse or titles have been silently rectified, and quoted authors are identified. The full forms of words replace abbreviations: so, for example, 'st' becomes 'saint'. Kirby writes that he emigrated to the United States in 1929, but his family confirms that he actually left Ireland in 1930; the correct date is noted in parenthesis.

Kirby re-presented similar material in various books published over a thirty-two-year period. Where similar content is found in more than one text reproduced in this book, the repetitions have been deleted, and editorial deletions are indicated in square brackets, as follows: [...]. Occasionally this book includes material drawn from two previously published essays, as in the case, for example, of Kirby's writing on local folklorist Seán Ó Conaill. The substantive previously published source is 'Seán Ó Conaill: King of the Storytellers' in *Skelligs Sunset*, but some additional material is added from 'Some Poets and a Storyteller', published in *Skelligside*.

I warmly acknowledge the innumerable insights and unstinting support of Anne Coffey, Pat Coffey, Tim Kirby, Declan Kirby, Paddy Bushe, Antony Farrell, Seán Ó Leidhin, Máirín Nic Eoin, and Dan McCrohan. The Lilliput Press

Editorial Note

team was meticulous and professional, and especial credit and thanks are due to Bridget Farrell and Ruth Hallinan. Tim O'Neill's detailed map of Michael Kirby's territory is an invaluable addition to the book. I am grateful to Fionán O'Connell for the reproductions of Michael Kirby's paintings.

Mary Shine Thompson

INDEXES

GENERAL

This index excludes personal names and placenames of Iveragh, South Kerry.

Acheron, 292
Aladdin, 198
'An Díbirtheach ó Éirinn', 71
'An Spailpín Fánach' [Donncha Rua Mac Conmara], 125
Anglo-American Cable Company, 55
Annals of Loch Léin, The [recte *The Annals of Inisfallen*], 4
Annals of the Four Masters, The, 4
Ansonia Clock Company, 67
Argentina, 72
Atlantic, xiii, 8, 20, 28, 29, 32, 36, 48, 52, 55, 136, 145, 181, 182, 183, 191, 205, 210, 215, 231, 244, 249, 252, 256, 265, 266, 267, 268, 269, 271, 276
South Atlantic, 252
Australia, 72
Azores, 261, 267

ball seirce, 284, 287
'Bán Chnoic Éireann Ó', 71
Bangor, 12
Beara, 91, 128, 255, 292
Bible, 65, 98
Blarney, 160
Bluebeard's Castle, xiv, 274
Board of Public Works, 194
Boyne, 160
Boats and ships
  Buccaneer, 47
  Cardigan Castle, 206
  Cleopatra, 205
  Colonia, 48
  Dunraven Castle, 205
  George Ward, 48
  Glassy Gander, 141
  Great Eastern, 48
  Helga, 205
  Hercules, 24, 209–12
  Isaac Walton, 205
  John W. MacKay, 48
  Labore et Honore, 206
  Lady of the Isles, 48
  Lord Kelvin, 48
  Lusitania, 217
  Marie Louise MacKay, 48
  Menthaur, 38–41
  Nielsen Hauge, 29, 36–41
  Princess Alexandria, 206
  Princess Maria Jose, 206
  QE2, 181
  S.S. America, 181
  S.S. Andrea Doria, 181
  S.S. Bremen, 181
  S.S. Dresden, 181, 182, 186, 208, 276
  S.S. Europa, 181
  S.S. Jane Black, 175, 176
  S.S. Queen Mary, 181
  S.S. Rex, 181
  S.S. Saint Louis, 192
  Sea Thrift, 203
  Tar Pot, 204
  Tenby Castle, 205
  Thomas Booth, 205
  Titanic, 54
Brest, 116, 203
Britain, 193
British Empire, 32, 94, 205
Bronze Age, 139, 140
Buenos Aires, 72

Canada, 53, 72, 261
  Albany, 177
  Canadian Pacific Rail Road, 188
  Gulf of Saint Laurence, 177
  Halifax, Nova Scotia, 54

Index

Labrador, 136–7
Montreal, 177
Newfoundland, 54, 99, 136
Nova Scotia, 54, 99, 136
Quebec, 177
Saint John's, 118
Saint Laurence River, 177
Toronto, 7
Vernon, British Columbia, 53, 54
[Cape] Horn, 267
Cashel, 125, 160, 284
Cavan, 187
Christian Brothers, 72
Circuit of Ireland Motor Rally, 83
Clare, 34, 184, 217
Coiscéim, xvii
Concarnau, 116
Cnoc Áine, 331
Cnocán Calvair, 325
Cobh, 177, 180, 208
Congested Districts' Board, 106
Conradh na Gaeilge, 281
Cork, 112, 217, 292
Corrane, 160
Croke Park, 79
Cuba, 192

Dáil Éireann, 47
Danes, 17, 302
Department of Culture, Heritage and the Gaeltacht, 334
Dingle Bay, 280
Direct United States Cable Co. Ltd, 53
Doon, 284
Dublin, xv, 86, 110, 161, 292
Dundalk, 184

Eden, 94
EEC, 94
Erin, 71, 160, 170

Faeroes, 261
Falkland Islands, 267
Fanning Island, 47
Fastnet Rock, 182

Gaeltacht, 57, 334
Georgia Chain Gang, 180
Germany, 6, 7, 44, 192
Great Famine, 34, 40, 123, 133, 144, 175–9, 196, 212, 219, 220, 240, 242, 293
Great War, 22, 60, 217, see World Wars
Grim Reaper, 83, 88, 100

Hades, 233, 310
Halifax, Nova Scotia, 54
Hamburg, 183
    Hamburg American Line, 181, 192, 208
Hens
    Rhode Island Red hens, 59, 105, 235
    Sicily Buí, 105
    Black Minorca, 105
Hong Kong, 207
Hull, 205

Iceland, 136, 261
India, 72
    Indian corn, 40
    Mumbai, 206
Ireland, i, xvii, xxi, 5, 10, 18, 23, 25, 32, 36, 51, 55, 76, 79, 116, 140, 152, 160, 164, 166, 171, 180, 187, 189, 192, 193, 205, 210, 218, 219, 249, 281, 283, 304, 334, see Irish Republic
Ireland on Sunday, iv
Irish Land Commission, 105
Irish Republic, 94

Jesuits, 101

Index

Kanturk, 160
Killarney, 31, 160, 293

Land's End, 261
Lilliput Press, The, xii, 335
Limerick, 123, 124, 175
Lios Tuathail, 326
Listowel, xvi, 326
London, 46, 52, 54, 78, 212

MacCarthy Cup, 79
Maigh Nuad, 329, see Maynooth
Malaysia, 72
Marseilles, 206
Maynooth, 185, 329
Mexico, 5
    Gulf of Mexico, 242, 266
Merryweather of London, 46
Milford Haven, 205
Mons, 44, 51
Mumhan, 332, see Munster
Munster, 30, 40, 193, 219, 220, 283,
    see Mumhan
    Munster Fusiliers, 44, 51
Music
    'After the Ball Was Over', 111
    'An Buachaill Caol Dubh', 110
    'An Spailpín Fánach', 125
    'Apple Blossom Time', 184
    'Bean ag Baint Duileasc', 107
    'Boney's Retreat', 107
    'Eochaill', 170
    'Garden of Daisies', 107
    'Haste to the Wedding', 107
    'Lucky Jim', 111
    'Raca Breá Mo Chinn', 147
    'Red Sails in the Sunset', 194
    'Siúil, A Rún', 111
    'The Connerys', 137
    'The Holy Ground', 207–8
    'The Leaving of Liverpool',
        207–8
    'The Sailor's Hornpipe', 110
    'The Shamrock Shore', 110
    'You Broke my Cups and
        Saucers', 107

National University, 139
Nazareth, 196
Nemesis, 215
New Zealand, 72

Ordnance Survey, 280

Pacific Ocean, 47, 144, 255
    Canadian Pacific Rail Road, 188
Paradise, 8, 88, 101, 121, 122, 292
Paris, 53
Penzance, 52
Placenames Database of Ireland, 334
Pharisees, 113
Polynesian Islands, 255

Redcoats, 31, 106
Redemptorist Order, 74
Revenue Commissioners, 33, 39, 126
Rhodesia, 101
Rockall, 261, 267
Roinn Bhéaloideas na hÉireann, 281
Rome, 15, 175
Royal Irish Constabulary, 126, 218

Saint Patrick's College
    Drumcondra, xii
Saint Malo, 116, 203
Salvation Army, 190
Scillies [Scilly Isles], 267
Scotland, 81
    Aberdeen, 205
    Hebrides, 267
    Scottish border, 53
    Scottish Borders, 51
    Scottish contractors 46
    Scottish kilt, 69
Séadna, 167
Sherwood Foresters, 51

Index

Ships, see Boats and ships
Simon Community, 94
Sinn Féin, 52
Sneem, 160
Spain, 160
Stone Age, 15, 52, 58
Swansea, 205

Táin Bó Cuailnge, 281
Teampall an Ghleanntáin, 326–7
Tierra del Fuego, 267
'Tim of the Sparks', 167
Tipperary, 123, 186
Tír na nÓg, 79, 257
Tralee, 106, 123, 152
    Tralee Hospital, 84, 87
Trinity College, Dublin, 105, 176
Tyrol, 166, 189

Uncle Tom's Cabin, 99
USA, 67, 80, 181, 183, 185, 187, 192, 255, see United States of America
United States of America, xiii, xv, xvii, 46, 52, 72, 166, 187–93
    Boston, 166, 175, 178, 187
    Brooklyn Bridge, New York, 78
    Connecticut, 67, 144, 180
    Grand Central Station, New York, 190
    Hartford, Connecticut, 166, 188
    Hudson River, 74
    Key West, 52
    Long Island Sound, 255
    Louisville, Kentucky, 178
    Maine, 191, 242
    Miami, 52, 54
    New England, 187, 209
    New Haven, Connecticut, 67, 166, 187, 188, 190, 191, 255
    New Jersey, 175
    New York, 53, 54, 55, 74, 166, 187, 190, 191, 242
    Pine Head, Maine, 242
    Prince Edward County, 178
    Prohibition Act, 191
    Shelby County, Kentucky, 178
    San Francisco, 191
    Tennessee, 178
    Sullivan County, Tennessee, 178
    US Department of Immigration, 180
    Vicksburg, Mississippi State, 178
    Virginia, 178
University College Cork, xii, xvii
University College Dublin, xii, 279, 281

Van Diemen's Land, 136
Vikings, 17
Voyage of the Damned, 192

World Wars, 126, see Great War
    World War One, 55
    World War Two, 193, 253, 272
Wall Street Crash, 180, 188
Western Union Telegraph Company, 55, 281
Westminster, 78

Youghal, 170

LOCAL PLACENAMES

This index contains placenames in the South Kerry area mentioned in Skelligs Haul. Other placenames are in the general index.

Abha an Churraigh, 24
Abhainn an Gharraí, 286
An Charraig Shuncáilte, 28
An Chráiteach, 27
An Coireán, 23, see Waterville
An Cromán, 21
An Drom, 26
An Fhaill Dhearg, 23
An Lúb, 108
An Mheadar, 27
An Phriaracht, 25, see Ballinskelligs Abbey
An Rinn Chaol, 29
An Seanduine, 22
An Stráice Caol, 26
An tSeanbhean, 22
Aonach, 27, see Ceann an Aonaigh
Athghort, 29

Baile an Sceilg / Baile 'n Sceilg, 134, 326, 327, see Ballinskelligs
Ballinskelligs, i, iv, xiii, xv, xvi, 3, 6, 7, 12, 13, 18, 22, 24, 29, 32, 33, 48, 49, 51, 52, 53, 55, 57, 76, 77, 79, 82, 101, 105, 106, 108, 112, 117, 123, 124, 134, 147, 152, 157, 163, 164, 165, 166, 168, 170, 171, 172, 175, 177, 178, 192, 194, 196, 205, 209, 210, 217, 228, 261, 281, 282, 283, 288, 289, 290, 305
Ballinskelligs Abbey, 25, 33
Ballinskelligs Bay, 24, 31, 42, 48, 53, 91, 225, 227, 266, 273, 278, 282, 289
Ballinskelligs Cable Station, 32, 46–55
Ballinskelligs Harbour, 25, 245
Ballinskelligs National School, 32, 60, 61–73
Ballinskelligs Strand, 24, 244
Ballinskelligs West, 228, 298
Banba, 291
Banc Bán, 25
Bay Rock, 229, 235
Béal Átha an Inne, 23
Béal Inse, 279
Bealach, 229, see Horse Island Sound
Bealach an Oileáin, 26
Bealach na nÉamh, 30
Bealach Scarbh, 22
Bean an Uaill, 4, see Wailing Woman
Beara, 91, 128, 255, 292
Bearna Dhearg, 24
Bearna na gCorp, 25, 220
Blind Man's Cave, 3, 275
Blue Man's Cave, 14, 17
Bog of the Hummocks, 104
Boig a' Chaisleáin, 244
Boilg Anders, 39, 281
Boilg Thomáis, 28
Bolus, 147, 175, 210, 213–17, 218, 271, 272, 274, 278, 317, 318
Bolus Head, 2, 28, 43, 224, 227, 230, 264, 289
Bolus Headland, 26, 44, 249, 258
Boolakeel, 47, 163, 218, 229, 242
Boolakeel Strand, 27, see Tráigh Fraisce
Bosca an Pheidhléara, 28, 281
Brácathrach, 196
Bréitse, 25
Builg an Phriósúin, 29
Bun na Féithe, 39, 40

343

Index

Caherdaniel, 111, 281, 289, 290
Cahersiveen, 32, 51, 67, 72, 105, 147, 166, 167, 175, 177, 193, 289
Caladh an Bháid, 29
Canuig, 106, 165, 309
Canuig Mountain, 230, 304
Carraig, 229, 234, 245
Carraig an Eascú, 220, 223, 242
Carraig an Phollóig, 26, 142
Carraig an Scealaí, 229, see Scéalaí Rock
Carraig an Staighre, 27
Carraig Dhaingean na nGabhar, 28
Carraig Éanna, 23, 281
Carraig na bhFiach, 27
Carraig Oisín, 23, 281
Cave of Elinore, 229, 281, see Cuas Elinore
Cave of Paddy Bhuí, 29
Cave of the Rock Doves, 142
Cave of the Silver, 212
Ceann an Aonaigh, 27, 231, 281
Ceann Bólais, 318, see Bolus Head
Ceann Dubh, 30
Ceann Garbh, 29
Ceann Muice, 22, see Hog's Head
Céim, 26
Christ's Saddle, 3, 5, 17
Cill Rialaig, 27, 278, 279, 282, see Kilreelig
Clais an Locháin, 26
Clais na nÉamh, 21, 32
Clais Rua, 26
Cloch an Chófra, 24
Cloigeann an Chrainn, 27, 143
Cnocán na mBuachaillí, 24, 25
Coinigéar-Conneigire, 25
Cois an Oileáin, 25
Coom, xvi, 38, 106, 107, 108, 139, 290, 303
Corcacha an Mhuirígh, 23, see Muiríoch
Corrane, 160
Cormorants' Cave, 229
Cráiteach, 27, 234

Creatlach, 27
Cuaisín an Ghrin, 26
Cuas an Airgid, 24, 212
Cuas an Bháid, 22
Cuas an Chopair, 21
Cuas an Daimh, 28
Cuas an Fháin, 29
Cuas an Ghabhair, 22
Cuas an Iallait, 27
Cuas an Mhadra Uisce, 24, 211
Cuas an Mhaoláin, 28
Cuas an tSeaga, 28
Cuas an tSéideacháin, 26
Cuas an tSleabháin, 24
Cuas an tSolais, 21, 32
Cuas an tSrutháin, 29
Cuas an Tuairín, 36
Cuas Beag na Muice, 22
Cuas Elinore, 281
Cuas Mór, 22, 26
Cuas na Cáige, 24
Cuas na Gaoithe, 27
Cuas na gColúr, 27
Cuas na Leacach, 26
Cuas na Léime, 27, 278
Cuas na Móna, 27, 229
Cuas na nDrisleoga, 21
Currach na nDamh, 149
Cusbae / Cusbao, 25

Deenish Island, 22, 91
Derrynane, 31, 82, 289, 290
Devil's Cliff, 28
Dingeacha na Scairbhe, 38
Dromore, 105
Duchealla / Dúchealla, 28, 224, 272, 274, 318
Dubh Inis, 225, 308
Dún Géagáin, 24, see Dungeagan
Dúna, 29
Dungeagan, 47, 124, see Dún Géagáin

Eel Rock, 223
Emlagh, 23

Index

Faha, 29, see Faich
Faich, 29, see Faha
Faill an Deamhain, 28, see Devil's Cliff
Faill an Reithe, 28, 213
Faill an Rois, 24
Fermoyle Castle, 82

Gamhnach / Gownach Rock, 27, 229
Gleann Orcáin, 30, 81, see Glen of Prior
Glen of Prior, 81, see Gleann Orcáin
Gob an Dá Chaol, 122, 149

Hector's Point, 24, 211, see Pointe Hector
Hog's Head, 22, 91, 235, see Ceann Muice
Horse Island, 17, 25, 26, 35, 39, 111, 115–18, see Oileán na gCapall
Horse Island Sound, 199, 229, 234, see Bealach an Oileáin

Ibraceuse, 12
Imleach, 23, see Emlagh
Imleach Draighneach, 23
Imleach Mór, 23
Imleach na Muc, 23
Inny Strand, 23, 39, see Tráigh na hAoine
Iveragh, xiii, xiv, xv, xvi, 30, 31, 32, 45, 57, 105, 170, 225, 272, 289, 292, see South Iveragh; see also Uíbh Ráthach

Keel Strand, 29, see Trá na Cille
Kells, 32
Kerry Reeks, 229
Kilreelig, 229, 304, see Cill Rialaig
Kinard, 163, 303
   Kinard East, 76
   Kinard West, 293

Láimh Cláir, 28
Leac a' Phriosúin, 281

Leac an Chinn, 250
Leac an Loiscreáin, 281
Leac an tSaighne, 26
Leac na bhFachán, 26
Leac na mBan, 29
Leac na mBeathach, 27, 28
Licín Rua, 28
Loch an Duilisc, 243, see Lough of the Dulse
Lochán na nDonnán, 26
Lohar, 160
Lomán / Loman Rock, 8, 30
Loop of Rinneen, 22, 210
Loop of the Flagstones, 227
Lough of the Dulse, 221, see Loch an Duilisc
Lúb an Rinnín, 22, 210, see Loop of Rinneen
Lúb na Leacach, 227

MacCarthy Castle, 229
Magairle na Muice, 22
Mainistir Mhichíl, 25, 283, see Ballinskelligs Abbey
Maothroisc, 29, 261, see Moyrisk
Marcach na Bearna Deirge, 24
Mill a' Ghóilín, 24
Monks' Rock, 4
Moyrisk, 29, 261, see Maothroisc
Muiríoch, 23

Na Deanncacha, 21, see Scariff Wedges
Na Fiacla, 26
Na Fir Ghorma, 23, see The Blue Boys / The Blue Men
Na Glaibhinní, 22
Na hUmaracha, 28
Na Mná, 2, 15, see The Women, Washerwoman
Needle's Eye, 4, 17

Oileán Dairbhre, 279, see Valentia
Oileán na bhFaoileán, 44, 272, 274
Oileán na bhFionn, 319

Index

Oileán na gCánóg, 30
Oileán na gCapall, 25, see Horse Island
Old Pound, 25, see Seanphóna

Páirc an Tobair, 26
Páircín, 26
Pointe an Fhionnaidh, 26
Pointe Buí, 26
Pointe Hector, 24
Pointe na mBiorraí, 22, 210
Poll a' Chait, 128, 132, 133
Poll Pipín, 28
Pollack Rock, 142, see Carraig an Phollóig
Portmagee, 32, 82, 133, 175, 289, 290
Prior, 12, 30, 76, 82, 159, 293, see An Phriaracht
Priory, 12, 13, 17, 18, 25, 144, see An Phriaracht
Puffin Island, 30, 261, 263, 267, 268
Púicín an Tobac, 29
Púicín na gCeann, 25

Reeks of Kerry / Kerry Reeks, 225, 229
Reen, 22, 26, 32, 289, see Rinn
Reenard, 22
Reenroe, 22
Réidh na gCúl, 149
Rinn an Chaisleáin, 29
Rinn Dubh, 39, 221, 223, 234, 237, 238, 239, 240, 241, 242, 243
Rinn Rua, 24
Rinneen, 22, 23
Rinneen Point, 22

Saint Finan's Bay, 26, 28, 29, 36, 170, 171, 261
Saint Finan's Glen, 30, 36, 175, 290
Saint Michael's Abbey, 12, 33, 144, 220
Saint Michael's Shrine, 6, 7
Saint Michael's Well, 131
Scairbh Thiar, 279

Scariff Island, 18, 21, 22, 30–2, 91, 225, 235, 279, 309
Scariff Island Wedges, 38, see Na Deanncacha / Dingeacha na Scairbhe
Scariff Wedges, 21
Scéalaí Rock, 27, 233, 278
Sceilg, 279, 300, 326–7, 331, 332, see Skellig
Sceilg Mhichíl, 2, 179, 302–3, see Skellig Michael
Scoth na hEaglaise, 27
Seanphóna, 25, see Old Pound
Skellig / Skelligs, i, xiv, 2, 4, 5, 11, 12, 14, 18, 122, 158, 262, 263, 267, 268, 279, 303–5
Skellig Michael, xiii, xiv, xviii, 2, 4, 5, 12, 13–18, 19, 25, 261, 267, 268, 301, 309, see Sceilg Mhichíl
Great Skellig, 2, 3, 4, 5, 6, 7, 8, 81, 220, 230, 269, 274, see Sceilg Mhichíl
Little Skellig, xix, 8, 12, 20, 216, 258
Skellig Rock, 45, 92
Small Skellig, 21, 260
South Iveragh, 21, 30, 40, 70, 147, 152, 153, 175, 181
South Kerry, 36, 83, 126, 194, 203, 267, 283, 286

Teach Uí Dhuinn, 279
The Blue Boys / The Blue Men, 23
The Stream of the Old Church, 76
The Women, 2, see Na Mná
Tooreen, 29, 36, see Tuairín
Trá Leagaígh, 29
Trá na Cille, 29
Trá na Spáinneach, 23
Tráigh Fraisce, 242–4, 334, see Boolakeel Strand
Tráigh an Ghleanntáin, 24
Tráigh na hAoine, 23

Index

Tráigh na Sasanach, 23
Tuairín, 36, see Tooreen

Uíbh Ráthach, xii, xiii, xxii, 303, 331, 329

Valentia, 26, 31, 32, 47, 48, 52, 55, 136, 137, 175, 279

Wailing Woman, 4
Washerwoman, 15, see Na Mná
Water Dog's Cave, 211, 212, see Cuas an Mhadra Uisce
Waterville, xv, xvi, 23, 32, 47, 52 55, 289

PERSONAL NAMES

Acheron, 292
Adam, 4
Adams, Tommy, 34, 35
Alexander, [T.J.], 60
Armstrong girls, 51
Armstrong, Mr [-], 47
Armstrong, Herbert, 53, 54, 55
Armstrong, John Garnet, 53, 54
Aunt Nell, [Ellie O'Sullivan, née Cremin], 120

Bacchus, 111, 132
Ballantyne, [R.M.]
  Coral Island, 125
Barry, Patrick, 251
Bennett, [James Gordon], 52
Bernhardt, Mr [-], 188, 189
Blathmac Sgellice, 4
Blenheim, Mr [-], 47
Blowick, 12
Bodhaire, 117, 118
Breault, Frederick, 189, 190
Broderick, Mr [P.B.], 47
Browne, Paddy, 183–6
Bushe, Paddy, xv, xxii, 334
  Duanaire Mhaidhcí, xv, 307

Cable O'Learys, 49
Casanova, 209
Caesar, 126, 149
Chaplin, Charlie, 169
Christ, 15, 17, 85, 101, 103, 122, 294, 323, 325
Cobley, Mr [G.H.], 47, 53, 54
Coffey, Anne, xii, xvii, 334
Coffey, Pat, xii, xiii, xvii, 334
Coleridge, [Samuel Taylor], 84
  'The Rime of the Ancient Mariner', 72, 84
Collins, Andrew, 101
Columbus, 320
Connell, Eileen, 124

Connor, Paddy, 71
Cornwall, Inez, 51
Cowper, William, 204
[Cremin], Aindí Fada, 119–22
Cremin, Mary Fitzgerald [author's grandmother], 79, 119–22
Cromwell / Cromail, Oliver, 17, 18, 30, 31, 33, 278, 332
Cúchulainn, 279, 281
Cullen, Bill, iv
Cupid, 157, 207
Curran, Connie, 71
Curran, Michael, 203–4, 224
Curran, Patas, 141, 143
Cuthbert, Mr [-], 49

Dale, [F.H.], 60
Dan the Pedlar, 130–3
Darwin, [Charles], 95
de Maio, John, 189
Defoe, [Daniel]
  Robinson Crusoe, 125
Delargy, James / Seamus, 5, 12, 279–83
Denny, Richard, 23
Diarmuid, 279
Don, 279
Drum, Mr [-], 47

Éanna, 23, 281
Edmond, A.M., 176
Einstein, [Albert], 95
Eros, 207
Evans, Mark, iii
Eve, 4

Fahy, Parson, 52
Faircloud, Mr [-], 47
Farrell, Antony, 334
Farrell, Bridget, 335
Feiritéir, Piaras, 31
Fenton, Annie, 111

349

Index

Fenton, Jamesie, 165, 166
Fenton, Mary, *aka* Mary Kirby, [author's grandmother], 159, 166
Fenton, Maurice, 110
Fenton, Miss [Bridie], 6, 7
Fenton, Tom, 106
Fentons of Coom, 38, 107
Finch, Francis Miles, 178
Fionn, 279, 281
Fitzgerald, David [of Horse Island], 116
Fitzgerald, David, 182
Fitzgerald, Jack, 6, 8, see Fitzgerald, John
Fitzgerald, Jim, 3, 5, 8, 9, 43
Fitzgerald, John, 216, see Fitzgerald, Jack
Fitzgerald, John [son of David Fitzgerald, above, and Julia Kirby], 35, 111
Fitzgerald family, 25, 105, 204
Flann Macallach, 4
Foil, Mr [-], 47

Galileo, 185
Galvin, 'Pardner', 141
Galvin, Dermot, 159
  'The Spirit', 159
  'The Fairy Horse', 159
Galvin, Johnny Morty, 196,
Géagán, 24
Goggin, W., 47
Golden, Mr [T.F.], 47
Gráinne, 279
Gurney, Dorothy Frances, 93

Hallinan, Ruth, 335
Hamlet, 88
Hardy, Thomas, i
Haren, Paddy, 33, 34, 35
Harms, John, 32
Hartnett, Michael, *aka* Micheál Ó hAirtnéide, 326, 328
  'An Práta' / 'The Potato', 328
Harty, Mr [J.J.], 47

Harty, John, *aka* Seana Sheán, 281
Harty, Margaret, 53
Higgs, [H.A.], 47
Hoare, Mary, 212
Hydra, 89

Irr, 4

Jamesie Stock, 127–33

Kate, 114–15
'Kate the Souper', 175–6
Keating, Paddy, 34, 108, see Ó Céitinn, Paddy
Keating, Mr [G.F.], 47
Kelly, Eamon, ii
Kelly, Jimmy, 85–6
Kennelly, Brendan, ii
Kirby, Declan [author's son], 334
Kirby, Ellen, *aka* Ellen O'Connell / Ellen Kirby O'Connell [author's grand-aunt], 177, 178
Kirby, Ellen, *aka* Eileen / Ellen O'Rahilly [author's great-grandmother], 289–90, 296–7
Kirby, Jerry [author's great-grandfather], 289, 296–7
Kirby, Jerry [author's grand-uncle], 177, 178
Kirby, John [author's brother], 199
Kirby, John [author's father], *aka* Seán Ua Ciarmhaic, xiv, xxi, 13, 21, 30, 38, 48, 59, 103, 104, 105, 116, 120, 134, 150, 153, 154, 159, 182, 192, 196, 197, 212, 218–24, 226–37, 242, 243, 244–5, 249–51, 254, 261, 280, 289, 294–8, 307
Kirby, John [author's grand-uncle], 177, 178
Kirby, Julia [author's aunt Mrs David Fitzgerald], 115, 117–18

Index

Kirby, Mary [author's sister], aka Mary Reardon, 171, 181, 187, 188, 190, 191
Kirby, Mary, née Cremin, [author's mother], 30, 57, 59, 96, 104, 105, 107, 111, 119, 120, 122, 123, 124, 141, 145, 148, 153, 155, 159, 170, 180, 192, 193, 226, 229, 235, 296
Kirby, Mary, née Fenton [author's grandmother], 159, 166
Kirby, Michael [author], aka Kirby, Maidhcí / Micheál, aka Micheál Ua Ciarmhaic, passim
  Barra Taoide, 301, 312
  Cliathán na Sceilge, xiii, xvi
  Íochtar Trá, 303, 307, 309, 316, 319, 320, 323, 325, 326, 327, 328, 330, 332
  Skelligs Sunset, i, xii, 61, 83, 88, 93, 99, 106, 133, 139, 213, 278, 294, 305, 309, 310, 312, 321, 323, 334
  Skelligside, 2, 30, 57, 61, 73, 79, 103, 115, 119, 122, 141, 145, 147, 150, 153, 157, 161, 163, 164, 168, 172, 175, 209, 217, 278, 283, 302, 307, 310, 315, 317, 334
Kirby, Nancy O'Connell, 179
Kirby, Paddy [author's brother], 110, 141–4
Kirby, Peggy, née O'Sullivan / Sullivan, 84, 90, 92, 194
Kirby, Sheila, aka Sheila Kelly [author's sister], 58, 187–8, 242
Kirby, Tim [author's son], 334
Kirby, Timothy [author's brother], 180
Kirby, Timothy [author's grandfather], aka Tadhg na nGadhar, 82, 159, 296

Kirbys / Kirby family, 193, 330
Knox, Harry, 32
Lawlor, Paddy, 110
Lehane, [D.], 60
Lily Marlene, 209
Locke, John, 270
Lloyd, [G.H.], 47
Lloyd, Natalie, 51

Mac an tSíthigh, Seán, ii
Mac Coluim, Fionán, 281
Mac Mathúna, Liam, xii
Mac Neasa, Conor, 281
MacCarthy, Denis Florence, 93
MacKay, [William], 52
Madden, Aodhan, iii
Main girls, 51
Main, [David Patrick], 47
Mannanan, 197, 265
Marcach na Bearna Deirge, 24
Marks, Samuel, 189
Marquis of Lansdowne, 105
Masefield, John, 199
Mataí na Leathchoise / Mataí Peg-Leg, 203, 204
Matthew, evangelist, 99
Maxfield, Howard, 179
McCarthy, Donal, 34–5
McCarthy, Justine, ii
McCarthy, Margaret, 106, 108
McCrohan, [probably Eugene], 48
McGready, John, 32–3, 37–9
McMichael, Kathleen, 51
McMichael, Mr [-], 47
Merriman, Brian, 278
  Cúirt an Mheán Oíche, 278
Mickey, 135–6
Mickey Bawn, 155–6
Milesius, 4, 23, 279
Mo Ruth, 279
Moore, Mr [-], 47
Moran, Mike, 182, 183, 187
Moran, Seán Jeremiah, 163
Morgan-Witts, Max, 192

Index

Morpheus, 101
Murphy, [-], 38

Nash, Mr [-], 47
Neptune, 197, 202
Newman, John Henry, 97
Niamh Chinn Óir, 23
Nic Eoin, Máirín, 334

Ó Céitinn, Paddy, 33
Ó Conaill, Seán, xii, xvii, 27, 278–83, 334
    Leabhar Sheáin Uí Chonaill, 279
Ó Dochartaigh, Brian, 310
Ó Duilearga, Seamus, xii, see Delargy, James / Seamus
Ó Fiannachta, Padraig, 329
Ó hAirtnéide, Micheál, 326, 328, see Hartnett, Michael
Ó hÓgáin, Dáithí, xii, 330
Ó Leidhin, Seán, 334
Ó Siochrú, Micheál, 316
Ó Snodaigh, Pádraig, xvii
Ó Súilleabháin, Eoghan Rua, 283–9
    'Seo Leo a Thoil', 284–6
Ó Súilleabháin, Tomás Rua, xvi, 30, 279, 289
    'Amhrán na Leabhar', xvi, 289–92
Ó Súilleabháin, Seán Brúnach, 167
O'Connell, Mr [Mortimer], 47
O'Connell, Daniel [emancipator], 292
O'Connell, Daniel [son of Ellen Kirby O'Connell], 177
O'Connell, Fionán, 335
O'Connell, John [son of Ellen Kirby O'Connell], 177
O'Connell, Mary [daughter of Ellen Kirby O'Connell], 177
O'Connell, Maurice 'Hunting Cap', 212
O'Connell, Michael Geoffrey, 177–8
O'Connell, Mortimer, 54
O'Connell, Nelly, *aka* Eileen Connell, 124
O'Connell Kirby, Ellen, 177, 178
O'Connell, Pat, 150
O'Connell, Tadhg Phats, 119–22
O'Connell, Thomas, 163
O'Connell family [Derrynane], 31
O'Connell family [Kinard West], 293
O'Connor, Frank, ii
O'Connor, Aidan, ii
O'Leary, Brigid, 106
O'Leary, Denis, 49, 106
O'Leary, Seamus, 69–70
O'Leary family, 70, 106,
O'Mahony, Mary, 105
O'Neill, Tim, 335
O'Rahilly, Dermot Rua, 289–91
O'Rahilly, Ellen / Eileen, 289, 290, see Kirby, Ellen
O'Riordan, Colm, 101
O'Riordan, John, 292
O'Shea, Diarmuid, 288
    'An Scur', 288–9
O'Shea, Dr [Naoise], 83
O'Shea, John Peter / O'Shea, John, 9
O'Sullivan, Andy Gow, 123
O'Sullivan, Daniel / Dónall, 30
O'Sullivan, Dermot, 292–4
    'The Pleasant Prince', 293–4
O'Sullivan, Francis, *aka* an Bráthair Rua, 30–1, 310
O'Sullivan, Mary, 47
O'Sullivan, Paud Jack, 3
O'Sullivan, Peggy, 193, see Kirby, Peggy
O'Toole, Joe, iii
Oisín, 23

Paddy Tom, 127–33
Paul, 77–9
Pipín, 28
Poseidon, 19

Index

Queen Elizabeth I, 17, 23, 176
Queen Maeve, 281
Queen Victoria, 170

Ratton, [D.C.], 47
Reardon, Paddy, 187–9, 191
Rickard, Mr [-], 47
Roche, Nano / Nora, 7, 110
Rodgers, John, 185
Roosevelt, F.D., 193
    New Deal, 193
Rushe, Des, iii

Saint Augustine, 4, 12
Saint Bernard, 50
Saint Brigid, 60
Saint Finan, 4
Saint Francis, 14, 30, 31
Saint George, 251
Saint John, 31
Saint Malachy, 12
Saint Patrick, 7
Saint Peter, 43, 122
Sargent, Epes, 198
Satan, 61
Scott, Walter, 81
    'The Stag Hunt', 81
Séamus Fada, 44
Seamus Jack, 117
Seán [O'Shea], *aka* John O'Shea, 136–7, see O'Shea, John Peter / O'Shea, John
Seekins, William George, 47, 54
Shakespeare, William, 217
    Macbeth, 71
    Hamlet, 88
    Yorick, 88–9
Shanahan, Cornelius, 58
Shea, John, 223
Shea, Margaret, 47
Shea, Mike, 142
Sheehan, Ronan, iv
Shine Thompson, Mary, xv, xxii, 335
Shirley, James, 100

Sigerson, Francis, 212, 288
Solomon, 99, 323
Spencer, Mr [-], 47
Stevenson, R.L., 95
    Treasure Island, 125
Stone, Beattie, 51
Sugrue, Mr [-] [operator], 47
Sugrue, Michael [Dungeagan], 47
Sugrue, Michael P. / Mike [Ballinskelligs West], 228–36
Sugrue, Tomáisín, 123, 295
[Sullivan], Con [Tadhg Eoin], 139
[Sullivan], Florrie, 139
[Sullivan], Jack, 139
Sullivan, Jerome, 47
Sullivan, Tom, 67–8
Sullivans, 'Ceann Eiche' or 'Horse Head', 30

Tadhg na nGadhar, 82, see Kirby, Timothy
Tamas, Christian, xii
    Riul năvalnic, xii
Tennyson, Alfred, 204
Thomas, Gordon, 192
Thompson, Mr [-], 47
Tom 'the bull', 154, 156
Topping, Mr [-], 47, 50
Topsy, 99
Twells, H., 319, 333
Twomey, Bob, 32

Ua Ciarmhaic, Micheál, see Kirby, Michael [author]
Ua Ciarmhaic, Seán, 134, see Kirby, John
Uí Chiarmhaic clan, 115
Urquhart, Jane, i

Vanderbilt, [A.G.], 217
Virgin Mary, 84, 103, 122, 219, 288
Verne, Jules
    Twenty Thousand Leagues Under the Sea, 72

Index

Walsh, Ned, 107
Waterstone, Mr [-], 47
Watson, [G.L.], 47
Welply, [W.H.], 60
Westbrook, [E.H.], 47, 54
Westbrook, Florrie, 51
Whelan, Mrs [-], 187

Widget, Tom, iv
William [-], 185
Wordsworth, William, i, 280
   'The Old Cumberland Beggar', 280
Wyndham, Ursula, iv